A Charlton Standard Catalogue

COLLECTABLES

Fourth Edition

By

Pat Murray

Publisher

W. K. Cross

The Charlton Press

Toronto, Ontario • Palm Harbor, Florida

Library and Archives of Canada has catalogued this publication as follows:

Murray, Pat.
    Wade Collectables : a Charlton standard catalogue

Biennial.
4th ed. -
Continues: Charlton standard catalogue of Wade.
ISSN 1719-7252
ISBN 978-0-88968-274-0 (4th edition)

    1. Figurines--England--Catalogs--Periodicals. 2. George Wade and
Son--Catalogs--Periodicals. 3. Miniature pottery--England--Catalogs--Periodicals.
I. Title

NK8473.5.W33M8   738.8'2   C2006-902711-0

Printed in Canada in the Province of Quebec

The Charlton Press

Editorial Office
P.O. Box 820, Station Willowdale B, North York, Ontario M2K 2R1
Telephone: (416) 488-1418 Fax: (416) 488-4656
Telephone: (800) 442-6042 Fax: (800) 442-1542
www.charltonpress.com e-mail: chpress@charlotnpress.com

EDITORIAL

Editor	Jean Dale
Assistant editor	W. T. Cross
Graphic technician	Davina Rowan

ACKNOWLEDGEMENTS

The Charlton Press wishes to thank those who have assisted with the fourth edition of the *Charlton Standard Catalogue of Wade Collectables*.

Special Thanks

Special thanks to Messrs. Jeremy and George Wade for inviting us to visit their home and allowing us take photographs of models in their collection, and our thanks to BettyAnn and Monroe Robbins who invited us to their home to take photographs of their collection, and to Ed and Bev Rucker for their work on money boxes.

I am grateful to Dr. John Wright and Ms. Eileen Moore (Wade Ireland) for detailed information on the Wade Irish Porcelain Song Figures and the Pixie and Toad.

Contributors to the Fourth Edition

The Publisher and the Author would like to thank the following individuals and companies who graciously supplied photographs or information or allowed us access to their collections for photographic purposes.

Helen Barker; Lloyd Barnes; Bob and Gail Barnhart; Norma Beatle; John Beatty; Alice Bedlington; Ben Bendee; Sara Bernotas; Paul Birdsall; Sarah Blackwell; Nellie Bligh; Elizabeth Bowden; Lyn and Ian Bowman; Sue Braithwaite; Linda Bray; Margaret Brebner; Peter Brooks; Lisa Burlington; Hilary Gibbs, Mary Carter, Cadbury World; Lorenzo Cerri, Lizzi Chambers, Tetley GB; Elizabeth and John Clark; Gail Clarke; Mark Colclough; Sue Cooper; Father David Cox; Mr. and Mrs. A. Dalal; Joyce and David Devilbiss; Pam Donne; Terence Dove; Steve and Heather Dubbleu; Dolores, June and Trevor Edlin; Sandy Elphick; Denis Esdale; Catherine Evans; Janet and Mike Evans "Yesterdays"; Elizabeth Everill; Adran Evers; Robert and Maurice Fenton; Tom Fish; Ken Freemantle; Nancy Fronczac; Jean-Pierre Gauthier; Bill Gilson; Kerrie and Stewart Glenard; May Graham; Bobbie Greatstuff; Teresa Green; Dennis Haebich; Dan Hammeredden; Betty and Dennis Hannigan; David Hawkes; Janet Ellen Hayden; Jean and Rachel Higham; Brenda J. Hochreiter; John Homefish; Sue Horbury; Karen and Jobie Hudgins; Tom and Gail Hughes; Marion Hunt; Norman Ingram, Ivy Rose Antiques; Jolene and Richard Jackson; Rachel Janie; Linda Janis; The Jaques Family; Paul Jennie; Lynda Jessup; Peg and Roger Johnson; Dennis and Connie Johnston; Justerini and Brookes, J&B Whisky: Gary Kear; R.J. Kent; Donna Kinder; W. Kirk; Esther Kramer; Deborah LaFemme; Ruth Lambusta; John Lawless; Diane LeBlanc; Dave Lee; John Lejeune; Lindsay Lynton; James Lyttle; James MacCaig; Sue McLeod; Neil MacDonald; Mr. MacGregor; Jeff Mackey; Mr. McEwen; Andy McPherson; Mary Marquez Marshall; Chris Martin; Mark Maye; Erwin Meelosches; Ms. Eileen Moore; Ed and Kathy Morgan; Brian and Judi Morris; Rose and Chad Muniz; Helen and Bob Murfet; Daniel Murray; Murray Sons & Co Ltd; Molly and Pete Newman; Tom Nicholls; Roy Nunn; Patty O'Meara; Roger Owen; Nick Padgett; Mrs. H. Palmer; Fay Palmer, British Tea Council; Phyllis Palvio; Margaret Parsons; Roberta A. Patton; Michael Pole; JoAnn Postlewaite; Magaret and Graeme Remihana; BettyAnn and Monroe Robbins; Eileen Moore, Wade Ireland; Janet and Brian Robinson; Rosemarie Rodiebee; Margaret of 'Rosetiques'; Ed, Beverly, Quenton; Tabor and Victoria Rucker; Charley and Judy Sayre; Diane Self; Philip Sharp; Katie Shaw; Robert Sheba; Judy Shoper; Mr. and Mrs. A. Simmonds; Nadine Skinner; Carol Smith; Marcia, Marco and Saxon Stoof, Stuff-N-Nonsence; Annabel and Keith Sutherland; Dawn Sutton; Thelma and Jeff Swinhoe, T & A Collectables; Simon Templeman; Michelle Tenty; Bob Thomas; Charlotte Thompkins; Val Tolfrey; Jason Tool; Shirley Tumelty; Peter Vincent, Wade Ceramics, Wade PDM; Mrs. Naseem Wahlah; Eve Widda; Joyce Walker, Wellbid Auctions; Naseem Wahlah; Mary Wilkins; Sue Williams; Annie and Steve Windsor; John Wright; Sandy and Bob Wright; Diane Wye; Mary and Steve Yager; Kelly York.

A Special Note to Collectors

We welcome and appreciate any comments or suggestions in regard to *Wade Collectables* (A Charlton Standard Catalogue). If any errors or omissions come to your attention, please do not hesitate to write to us, or if you would like to participate in pricing or supply previously unavailable data or information, please contact Jean Dale at (416) 488-1418, or e-mail us at chpress@charltonpress.com.

CONTENTS

HOW TO USE THIS CATALOGUE

THE PURPOSE

This publication has been designed to serve two specific purposes. Its first purpose is to furnish the collector with accurate and detailed listings that provide the essential information needed to build a rewarding collection. Its second function is to provide collectors and dealers with current market prices.

STYLES AND VERSIONS

STYLES: A change in style occurs when a major element of the design is altered or modified as a result of a deliberate mould change. An example of this is Betty Style One and Betty Style Two.

VERSIONS: Versions are modifications in a minor style element of the piece, such as Grace, Version One, long stemmed flowers and Grace, Version Two, short stemmed flowers.

VARIATIONS: A variation indicates a change in the colour or pattern in the design.

THE LISTINGS

A Word on Pricing

On the pages that follow Wade models are listed, illustrated, described and priced.

The measurements of the models are given in millimeters. Most items are measured according to their height. For relatively flat objects—ashtrays, dishes and some plaques—the measurement listed is the diameter of a round item, the side of a square or the longest length of a rectangle or oval. For a few items, such as boxes, some candlesticks, some plaques and posy bowls; both height and width are provided.

Although the publisher has made every attempt to obtain and photograph all models listed, several pieces, naturally, have not come into the publisher's possession.

A Word on Order

This catalogue is run in alphabetical order for the major categories. Within the major categorues the listings also run alphabetically. There are places within the major categories that we have reverted to date order for ease of listing, but these departures are few.

A word on Pricing

The Purpose of this catalogue is to give readers the most accurate up-to-date retail prices for Wade models in the United States, Canada and the United Kingdom.

However, one must remember that these prices are indications only and that the actual selling price may be higher or lower by the time the final transaction agreement is reached.

To accomplish this The Charlton Press continues to access an international pricing panel of Wade experts who submit prices based on dealer and collector retail price activity, as well as current auction results in U.S., Canadian and U.K. markets. These market figures are carefully averaged to reflect accurate valuations for the Wade models listed herein in each of these three markets.

A necessary word of caution. No pricing catalogue can be, or should be, a fixed price list. This catalogue should be considered as a guide only, one that shows the most current retail prices based on market demand within a particular region.

A Word on Condition

The prices published herein are for items in mint condition. Collectors are cautioned that a repaired or restored piece may be worth as little as 50 percent of the value of the same model in mint condition. Those collectors interested strictly in investment potential must avoid damaged items.

All relevant information must be known about an item in order to make a proper valuation. When comparing auction prices to catalogue prices, collectors and dealers should remember two important points. First, to compare "apples and apples," be sure that auction prices include a buyer's premium, if one is due. Prices realized for models in auction catalogues may not include this additional cost. Secondly, if an item is restored or repaired, it may not be noted in the listing, and as a result, the price will not be reflective of that same piece in mint condition.

Technical Information

On the pages that follow Wade models are listed, illustrated, described and priced. The items are categorized by type, for example CATS and DOGS. The models are then listed within a table, for example: Alsatian, Cat, seated, Jack Russell, Scottie and Spaniel. The colourway of the model is next in the table, then the size, then the price in three currencies. The measurements of the models are given in millimeters. Most of the items are measured according to their height. For relatively flat objects —bowls, dishes and plates— the measurement listed is the diameter of a round item.

INTRODUCTION

History

The Wade Heath Royal Victoria Pottery (formerly Wade and Co.) was originally founded by a furniture maker, John Wade who had followed his father (also named John) into the furniture trade. In the mid-1800s however, the younger John Wade began to see that there was more profit to be made in pottery production, an already well-established art in the Staffordshire towns where the essential ingredients of clay and felspar were found in the soil of the surrounding countryside. Thus, John Wade turned his interest and his talent to this trade.

In 1867 John joined in partnership with James and Henry Colclough and they began trading under the names of "Wade and Colclough." Later the name was changed to "John Wade & Co." The pottery was known as the "Toy Works." John's nephew William Wade also worked for Wade & Colclough and John, who had no children of his own, took William under his wing and taught him the pottery business. Their main production at that time was teapots and their accompaniments - teapot stands, sugar bowls and water and milk jugs, etc. As these early items were intended for domestic use they were produced in a dark heavy earthenware china rather than the whiter and lighter porcelain the English Wade Potteries are now famous for.

It was some twenty years later, in 1887, that John Wade broke with the Colcloughs and left to form his own pottery, with his nephew William and William's brother, Albert J Wade. The pottery was renamed "Wade & Co." and used the trademarks of an impressed "WADES" and also an ink stamped "W and Co B." The "B" stood for Burslem and it was added to distinguish the W & Co. mark from another pottery, "Whittaker & Co" of Hanley, Staffordshire, which used the same "W & Co" trademark.

John and his nephews expanded their "Toy Works" pottery and purchased the "High Street Works" pottery which was situated next door to the "Toy Works." In 1888, William and Albert formed "J & W. Wade & Co" which specialised in the manufacture of tiles for fireplace surrounds, floors and walls. In 1891 the "J & W Wade & Co" pottery was christened the "Flaxman Tile Works."

William Wade retired from the pottery business and in 1913 went to live in California where he died in a freak car accident when returning from the funeral of A.J. Wades brother-in-law Francis Stoker in 1914. Francis, with William Wade's help and advice, had intended to start a pottery in Los Angeles, California.

In 1927 Albert J. Wade, who had, on the death of his uncle John and his brother William, inherited the "Wade & Co" and the "Flaxman Tile Work" potteries, formed a new company with a friend George Heath and changed the name of "Wade & Co" to "Wade Heath & Co." The main items produced by this partnership were domestic and decorative products.

The "Flaxman Tile Works," which was still owned and operated by Albert J. Wade, carried on its business of producing tiles and fireplace surrounds until, with the ever growing popularity of gas fires in Britain, ceramic fireplace surrounds and tiles were no longer a viable product and the "Flaxman Tile works" finally ceased trading in 1970.

In 1933 Albert Wade died, and his nephew George Albert Wade, later to become Sir George Wade and founder of the "George Wade & Son" Pottery now famous for its "Whimsies,"

became Chairman of the "A.J. Wade Ltd. Flaxman Tile Works" and "Wade Heath & Co Ltd." with George Heath as managing director.

In 1938 the "Wade Heath & Co Ltd." pottery was moved to a new location at the "Royal Victoria Pottery" in Westport Road, Burslem. With the death of Sir George Wade at the age of 94 in 1986, and the early death of his son George Anthony Wade from leukaemia a year later in 1987, the Wade Potteries were taken over by "Beauford Engineering PLC." The Wade Potteries were renamed "Wade Ceramics Ltd." The former "Wade Heath/Royal Victoria Pottery" is still in production today under it's new name of "Wade Ceramics."

1947 saw the acquisition of a Pottery in Northern Ireland, which in 1950 was named "Wade (Ulster) Ltd." The pottery concentrated on the production of industrial wares such as electrical insulators for telephone poles.

In 1953, "Wade (Ulster) Ltd." was asked to fill an order for "Coronation Tankards" which the "Wade Heath" and "George Wade" potteries could not fill due to Government restrictions. With the success of their tankards with their distinctive "Irish" glaze, the Ulster pottery branched out into new fields of Giftware and Domestic Tableware production.

In 1966 the Pottery was renamed "Wade Ireland Ltd." and continued giftware production until 1986, when they reverted back to Industrial Wares and Tableware production.

"Wade Ireland" was taken over by "Beauford Engineering PLC" upon the death of George Anthony Wade and was renamed "Seagoe Ceramics" in 1990. Seagoe continued to manufacture domestic tablewares until 1992 when its production reverted back to industrial ceramics.

The Production Process

The earthenware and Irish porcelain items in this book are made from a hard, solid china, sturdy enough to stand up to regular domestic use. They are produced from a mixture of ball clay, used for its plasticity, china clay, which gives the item a white body and plasticity, and china stone, used as a bonding agent.

Wade's porcelain, or bone china, items differ from earthenware in that they are of a lighter weight, thinner and are translucent. For these models a mixture of china clay, china stone and animal bone, which gives strength and transparency to the pieces, is used.

These materials are mixed in large vats of water, producing a thick sludge or "slip." The slip is passed into a filter to extract most of the water, leaving large flat "bats" of porcelain clay, approximately two feet square and three inches thick. The clay bats are dried and then ground into dust ready for the forming process. Paraffin is added to the dust to assist in bonding and as a lubricant to remove the formed pieces from the steel moulds. Once pressed into the required shape, the clay articles are allowed to dry, then all the press marks are removed by sponging and "fretting," the scraping off of surplus clay with a sharp blade.

One or more ceramics colours is applied to the model, which is then sprayed with a clear glaze that, when fired, allows the colours underneath to show through. This process is known as underglaze decoration. On-glaze decoration —which included enamelling, gilding and transfer printing—can also be done after the article has been glazed and fired.

Insuring Your Collection

As with any other of your valuables, making certain your models are protected is very important. It is paramount that you display or store any porcelain items in a secure place, preferably one safely away from traffic in the home.

Your models are most likely covered under your basic homeowner's policy. There are generally three kinds of such policies—standard, broad and comprehensive. Each has its own specific deductible and terms.

Under a general policy your models are considered part of the contents and are covered for all the perils covered under the contractual terms of your policy (fire, theft, water damage and so on). However, since some models are extremely delicate, breakage is treated differently by most insurance companies.

There is usually an extra premium attached to insure models against accidental breakage by carelessness of the owner. This is sometimes referred to as a "fine arts" rider. You are advised to contact your insurance proffessional to get all the answers.

In order to help protect yourself, it is critical that you take inventory of your models and have colour photographs taken of all your pieces. This is the surest method of clearly establishing, for the police and your insurance company, any items lost or destroyed. It is also the easiest way to establish their replacement value.

Backstamps

Most of the ink stamps used are black, although some Wade Heath and Wade marks are red, grey, green, brown or orange. The earliest ink stamps found in this book, which were used in the early 1930s, have a lion included in the stamp, along with "Wade England" or "Wadeheath England."

From the mid 1930s, the lion was omitted from the backstamp and often the design name - such as Flaxman Ware or Orcadia Ware - was included. Toward the end of the 1930s the name *Wadeheath* was split into two to make *Wade Heath*; by the end of World War II, the *Heath* was dropped, leaving a *Wade* backstamp.

Beginning in the mid 1950s, Ware Ireland also used ink stamps to mark its models.

Transfer-printed backstamps were introduced in 1953, and from that date onwards, they were used by both the English Wade potteries. Wade Ireland did use transfer prints, but they are not as common as ink stamps or their impressed and embossed backstamps.

THE WADE POTTERIES, c.1887-2006

1. WITHOUT WADE NAME

A. EMBOSSED
a) "Made in England"

B. IMPRESSED
a) "Made in England" (c.1930), with or without registration mark

C. INK STAMPS
Black:
a) "England" (c.1938)
b) "Made In England" (c.1938-c.1942)

c) "Made in England" with letter A, B or J added (c.1939-1945)

2. "WADES"

A. EMBOSSED
a) Registered "Diamond" (c.1867-1887)

B. IMPRESSED
a) "Wades" (c.1887-1890)

C. INK STAMPS
Black:

a) "W & Co B" with or without design name (c.1887-1900)
b) "Wades England" (c.1900-1927)

Orange:

a) "Wades England" with lion (c.1927-1933)

b) "Wades Orcadia Ware" with lion (c.1933)

3. "WADEHEATH" (one word)

A. INK STAMPS
Black:

a) "Flaxman Ware Hand Made Pottery by Wadeheath England" (c.1935-1937) with or without design name

b) "Wadeheath by permission Walt Disney England" (c.1935-1940)

c) "Wadeheath England" with letter A, B or J added (c.1939-1945)

d) "Wadeheath England" with lion (c.1934-1937)

e) "Wadeheath Orcadia Ware British Made" (c.1934-1935)

f) "Wadeheath Ware by permission Walt Disney Mickey Mouse Ltd. Made in England" (c.1935)

g) "Wadeheath Ware England" (c.1934-1937)

h) "Wadeheath Ware made in England manufactured by permission Walt Disney Mickey Mouse LTD" (c.1935)

Orange:

a) "Wadeheath England" with lion (c.1933-1934)

b) "Wadeheath Orcadia Ware" (c.1933-1934)

4. "WADE HEATH" (two words)

A. INK STAMPS
Black:

a) "England" (c.1937-1940)

b) "Flaxman Wade Heath England" (c.1937-1939) with or without design name added

c) "Wade Heath England" (rounded W 1937-1940)

d) "Wade Heath England" (rounded W) with letter A, B or J added (c.1939-1945)

e) "Wade Heath England" (straight W c.1945)

f) "Wade Heath England J" (straight W c.1942-c.1945)

Green:

a) "Wade Heath England" (rounded W 1937-1940)

b) "Wade Heath England" (rounded W) with letter A, B or J added (c.1939-1945)

c) "Wade Heath England" (straight W c.1945)

d) "Wade Heath England J" (straight W c.1942-c.1945)

5. "WADE"

A. INK STAMPS
Black:

a) Circular "Royal Victoria Pottery Wade England" (c.1952-c.1965)
b) "Wade Bramble England" (c.1950-1953)
c) "Wade England Flaxman" (c.1945-c.1948)
d) "Wade England" (crossed W c.1948-1953)

Green:

a) "Wade England" (crossed W c.1948-1953) (with or without design name)
b) "Wade England" with letter A, B or J added (crossed W c.1942-c.1945)

B. TRANSFER PRINTED
Black:
a) "Wade" between two lines (with or without design name)
b) "Wade" (c.1990-1993) (with or without design/designer name)

c) "Wade England" (with or without design/designer name)

d) "Wade Staffordshire England" (c.1982-1986) (with or without design name)
e) "Genuine Wade Porcelain" (c.1982)
f) "Wade Potteries PLC" (c.1989) (with or without design name)
g) "Designed Exclusively for Boots by Wade Ceramics" (c.1990-1991) (with or without design/designer name)
h) "Wade England" with two lines (c.1990-present) (with or without design name)

i) "Wade Made in England" (1991) (with or without design name)

Gold:
a) Circular "Royal Victoria Pottery Staffordshire Wade England" (c.1960-1970)

b) Semi circular "Wade made in England Hand Painted" (c.1953-c.1962) (with or without design name)
c) "Wade made in England Hand Painted" (c.1955-c.1952) (with or without design name)

Green:
a) "Wade England" (c.1961)

Red:
a) "Wade England" (c.1953-c.1962)
b) Semi Circular "Royal Victoria Pottery Staffordshire Wade England" (c.1980-c.1988)

Silver:
a) Semi Circular "Wade made in England Hand Painted" (c.1953)

WADE IRELAND, c.1952-1991

A. EMBOSSED

a) "Irish Porcelain (curved over shamrock) Made in Ireland by Wade Co. Armagh" in straight lines (c.1952-c.1989)
b) "Made in Ireland Porcelain - Wade - eire tire a dheanta" (c.1971-c.1989) (no "Irish")
c) "Made in Ireland by Wade" in straight line (c.1970)

d) "Wade Porcelain Made In Ireland" (c.1970)
e) "Irish Porcelain (curved over large shamrock and crown)
f) Wade Ireland" in straight line (c.1975-1987)

Circular:

a) "Celtic Porcelain by Wade Ireland" in Irish Knot wreath (c.1965)

b) "Irish Porcelain (centre shamrock) made in Ireland" (with potter's initial included) (c.1952-c.1989)
c) "Irish Porcelain (curved over shamrock) Wade Ireland" in straight line (c.1975-1987)
d) "Irish Porcelain Wade Made in Ireland" with shamrock and crown in the centre (c.1982-c.1986)
f) "Made in Ireland Irish Porcelain (central small shamrock and crown) Wade eire tira dheanta" (c.1971-1976)

Curved:

a) "Irish Porcelain" over straight "Made in Ireland" (c.1975-1987)

Oval:

a) "Shamrock Pottery Made in Ireland" (c.1956-1989)

b) "Irish Porcelain (over a small shamrock) Made in Ireland" in Irish Knot wreath (with or without designers name added under the wreath) (c.1962)

B. IMPRESSED

a) Hand written "(number of ounces) W.G. White London" with impressed "Wade Porcelain Co. Armagh" (on Caviar Pots)

b) "Irish Porcelain (curved over large shamrock) Made in Ireland" in straight line (c.1955-c.1979)
c) "Irish Porcelain (slanted over shamrock) Wade Co Armagh" in straight line (c.1955)
d) "Irish Porcelain (curved over shamrock) Made in Ireland" (with potters initial included) (c.1952-c.1989)

e) "Irish Porcelain (curved over large shamrock and crown) Wade Ireland" in straight line (c.1982-1987)

f) "Irish Porcelain (curved over shamrock with or without potters initial in shamrock) Made in England" (c.1980-c.1989)

g) "Made in Ireland by Wade"

Circular:

a) "Irish Porcelain (curved over shamrock) Made in Ireland by Wade Co. Armagh" in straight lines (c.1950-c.1989)

b) "Irish Porcelain (shamrock in centre) made in Ireland" (potters initial included) (c.1955-1969)

C. INK STAMPS

Black:

a) "Irish Porcelain (centre Shamrock) Made in Ireland" (c.1960-c.1989)

Green:

a) Circular "Seagoe Ceramics Wade '91 Ireland" (1991)

D. TRANSFER PRINTED

Black:
a) "Irish Porcelain (slanted over shamrock) Wade Co Armagh" in straight line (c.1955)

b) "Irish Porcelain (curved over shamrock) Wade County Armagh" in straight line (c.1960-c.1989)

c) "Wade Ireland" (c.1970)

d) "Irish Porcelain (centre shamrock and crown) Wade Made in Ireland" (c1985-1990)

e) "Irish Porcelain (centre shamrock and crown) Wade Ireland" (c1985-1990)

Black Circular:
a) "Celtic Porcelain made in Ireland by Wade Co. Armagh" (1965)

b) "Made in Ireland Porcelain Wade eire tir A dheanta" (c.1978-c.1982)

Blue Semi Circular:
a) "Made In Ireland Wade Classic Linen eire tir A dheanta"

Green Circular:
a) "Made in Ireland Porcelain Wade eire tir A dheanta" (1983-1986)

Green Oval:
a) "Shamrock Pottery made in Ireland" (c.1956-1961)

MODELLERS

The following modellers have worked for Wade. We have listed below some of the different models that they designed.

HARPER, WILLIAM K., 1954-1962

Bard of Armagh
Irish Emigrant
Little Crooked Paddy
Little Mickey Mulligan
Molly Malone
Phil the Fluter
Star of County Down
Widda Caffertyt

HOLMES, KEN, 1975 to the present

Dunbar Cake Decorators,
    wedding cake topper
The Great Priory of England and Wales
Knight Templer
Imperial Tobacco, St. Bruno Key Ring
J. W. Thornton, delivery van money boxes
Lyons Tetley Tea Brew Gaffer items
Lyons Tetley Tea delivery van money boxes
My Fair Ladies
Sophisticated Ladies

LANG, FAUST, 1939

Brown Bear
Budgerigar on Branch
Budgerigars
Chamois Kid
Ermine
Grebe
Highland Stag
Horse
Capuchin on Tree
Panther
Parrot
Weasel

MASLANKOWSKI, ALAN, 1975

The Cheetah and Gazelle
The Connoisseur's Collection
University Treasures, Razorback Pigs
The World of Survival series

MELLOR, FREDERICK, 1979

Peter Thompson, The Thistle and the Rose
Historical Chess Set

RAYMOND PIPER

Felicity
Herself
Himself

SZEILOR, JOHN, late 1940s-early 1950s

Siamese Kittens
Begging Puppy

VAN HALLEN, JESSIE, 1930-1939

Lady figures
Flowers

FURTHER READING

Pre-War and More Wades, 1st Edition 1991 by Pat Murray
The Charlton Standard Catalogue of Wade Volume One General Issues, 2nd Edition 1996;
    3rd edition, 1999 by Pat Murray
The Charlton Standard Catalogue of Wade Volume Two Decorative Ware, 3rd edition 1996,
    by Pat Murray
The Charlton Standard Catalogue of Wade Volume Three Tableware, 2nd edition, 1998, by
    Pat Murray
The Charlton Standard Catalogue of Wade Volume Four Liquor Containers, 2nd edition 1996,
    3rd edition 1999, by Pat Murray
The Charlton Standard Catalogue of Wade Whimsical collectables, 2nd, 3rd, 4th, 5th, 6th 7th
    and 8th editions, 1996-2007, by Pat Murray
The Wade Collectors Handbook, 1997, by Robert Prescott-Walker
The Wade Dynasty, 1996 by Dave Lee
The World of Wade, 1988, by Ian Warner with Mike Posgay
The World of Wade book 2, 1994, by Ian Warner and Mike Posgay
The World of Wade Price Trends, 1996, by Ian Warner and Mike Posgay
Whimsical Wades, 1st edition, 1986 by Pat Murray

CLUBS AND NEWSLETTERS

The Official International Wade Collector's Club

Founded in 1994, The Official International Wade Collector's Club provides an information service on all aspects of the company's products past and present. A club magazine, Wade's World,. is published four times a year with information on new products and current events that will keep the collector up-to-date on the happenings in the world of Wade. Upon joining the club, each new member will receive a free gift and invitations to special events and exclusive offers.

To join the Wade Collectors Club contact the club directly at:

The Official International Wade Collector's Club
Wade Ceramics Limited
Royal Victoria Pottery
Westport Road,
Burslem, Stoke-on-Trent
Staffordshire ST6 4AG
England
Email: club@wade.co.uk
www.wade.co.uk

ANIMALS

Wade animal models created from the early 1930s to 1939 and from the late 1940s up to the early 1950s are slip cast (hollow) and have a circular casting hole in the base. Beginning in the early 1950s, Wade started producing solid models.

The glazes used from the 1930s to the early 1950s are in delicate pastel and natural colours and are very different from the darker colours used from the late 1950s. Many of the models that were first produced in the early 1930s proved to be popular and were reissued in the late 1940s and early 1950s.

BACKSTAMPS

Handwritten Backstamps

Handwritten backstamps were used to mark small models that had no room for an ink stamp from 1930 to 1939.

Black Handwritten, 1930-1939

Ink Stamps

Ink stamps were used from 1935 to 1953. The size of the mark has no relevance to the date; large ink stamps were used on models with large bases, small ink stamps on small bases. Many of the smaller models are unmarked.

Green Ink Stamp, 1940s-1953

Brown Ink Stamp, Early 1940s-1953

Transfer Prints

Beginning in 1953 transfer prints were used.

Transfer Print, 1953-Late 1950s

Transfer Print, 1976-1982

CELLULOSE MODELS, c.1930-1939

CATS and DOGS

The Spaniel Puppy is found in Flaxman ware and high gloss glazes. The Jack Russell terrier has also been found in Flaxman glazes. For high gloss models see pages 10-19 and for Flaxman ware models see pages 39-45.

Alsatian, large size

Jack Russell Terrier

Cat, seated

Spaniel Puppy

Backstamp:
  A. Black handwritten "Wade Made in England"; black ink stamp of a leaping deer
  B. Black handwritten "Wade," stamped "Made in England" [name of model]
  C. Ink stamp "Wade England"

Name	Colourways	Size	U.S. $	Can. $	U.K. £
Alsatian	Mottled browns; red tongue	Small/115	125.00	150.00	65.00
Alsatian	Mottled yellow/black; pink tongue	Small/115	550.00	675.00	275.00
Alsatian	Black/tan; red tongue	Large/255	300.00	350.00	150.00
Alsatian	Dark brown all over	Large/255	550.00	675.00	275.00
Cat, Seated	Black; white on chest; yellow eyes; pink nose and mouth	Large/255	375.00	450.00	185.00
Jack Russell	White; brown markings; pink tongue	95	150.00	185.00	75.00
Scottie	Black	120	200.00	250.00	100.00
Spaniel Puppy	Brown/black	85	160.00	200.00	80.00

Note: For an illustration of the Scottie in high gloss see page 17.

HIGH GLOSS MODELS, c.1930-2000

BEARS

Bear Cub with Honey Pot, c.1935-c.1939

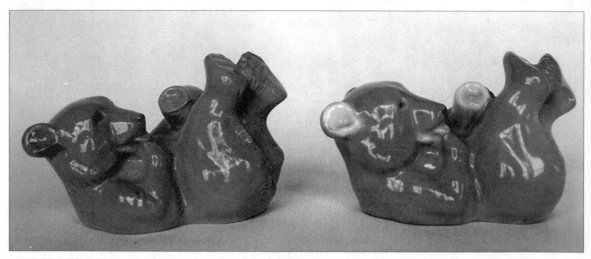

Bear Cub

Backstamp: Black handwritten "Wade England"

Name	Colourways	Size	U.S. $	Can. $	U.K. £
Bear Cub	Beige; white ears; white honey	50	450.00	525.00	225.00
Bear Cub	Brown; white ears; yellow honey	50	450.00	525.00	225.00
Bear Cub	Beige all over	50	450.00	525.00	225.00
Bear Cub	White; pink ears; brown feet; yellow honey	50	450.00	525.00	225.00

Brown Bear, 1939

The "Brown Bear" was modelled by Faust Lang.

Backstamp: Blue handwritten "Wade England 1939 Brown Bear" and the incised signature of Faust Lang

Name	Colourways	Size	U.S. $	Can. $	U.K. £
Brown Bear	Beige; green/blue/grey rocky base	245	2,000.00	2,250.00	1,000.00

Polar Bear, 1939

The "Polar Bear" was modelled by Faust Lang.

Backstamp: Blue handwritten "Wade England 1939 Polar Bear" and the incised signature of Faust Lang

Name	Colourways	Size	U.S. $	Can. $	U.K. £
Polar Bear	White; pink ears/mouth; turquoise blue and beige base	195 x 290	2,250.00	2,500.00	1,150.00
Polar Bear	White; pink ears/mouth; turquoise blue and white base	195 x 290	2,250.00	2,500.00	1,150.00

CALVES, c.1930-c.1948

First issued in the early 1930s, these models were reissued in the late 1940s and early 1950s. The reissues can be identified by the backstamp. The original price was 2/6d each.

Calf, eyes closed; Calf, eyes open

Calf, standing

Backstamp: **A.** Handwritten "Wade England"
B. Black ink stamp "Wade England"
C. Black ink stamp "Made in England"

Name	Colourways	Size	U.S. $	Can. $	U.K. £
Calf, standing	White/brown patches	65	250.00	300.00	125.00
Calf, mooing, eyes closed	White/brown patches; pink ears; no mouth line	45	250.00	300.00	125.00
Calf, mooing, eyes open	White/brown patches; brown ears; black mouth	45	250.00	300.00	125.00

CATS

ABC Cats, c.1930–c.1955

The "ABC Cats" are identified by letters used by Wade in the sales catalogues. Only six cats are illustrated in the publication, but a seventh cat, which is looking at a dish, has been reported. Originally issued circa 1930, these cats were so popular they were reissued during the late 1940s, and again from 1953 to circa 1955. The price for these models in the 1950s was 1/6d each. Care must be taken when purchasing an unmarked cat, as many Japanese and German cats have been produced in very similar poses as the "ABC Cats." Whenever possible, compare such models with marked models first.

    Cat A — Sitting cat with paws on ball, bow on left of neck
    Cat B — Cat lying on its back, ball held in its front paws
    Cat C — Sitting cat looking down at ball
    Cat D — Sitting cat with paws on ball, bow on right of neck
    Cat E — Drinking from dish of milk
    Cat F — Cat on back with ball to mouth

Backstamp: **A.** Black handwritten "Wade Made in England"
               B. Brown ink stamp "Wade England"
               C. Black transfer "Wade England"

Name	Colourways	Size	U.S. $	Can. $	U.K. £
Cat A	White/ginger cat; blue ribbon; yellow ball	38	175.00	200.00	85.00
Cat A	White/grey cat; blue ribbon, ball	38	175.00	200.00	85.00
Cat A	White/grey cat; blue ribbon; yellow ball	38	175.00	200.00	85.00
Cat A	White/grey cat; yellow ribbon; blue ball	25	175.00	200.00	85.00
Cat A	White/grey cat; green bow; pink ball	38	175.00	200.00	85.00
Cat B	White/ginger cat; blue ribbon; yellow ball	27	175.00	200.00	85.00
Cat B	White/grey cat; blue ribbon; ball	30	175.00	200.00	85.00
Cat B	White/grey cat; yellow ribbon; blue ball	25	175.00	200.00	85.00
Cat C	White/ginger cat; blue ribbon; yellow ball	40	175.00	200.00	85.00
Cat C	White/grey cat; blue ribbon, ball	40	175.00	200.00	85.00
Cat C	White/grey cat; blue ribbon; green ball	35	175.00	200.00	85.00
Cat D	White/grey cat; blue ribbon, ball	40	175.00	200.00	85.00
Cat D	White/grey cat; blue ribbon; green bal	40	175.00	200.00	85.00
Cat D	White/grey cat; blue ribbon; red ball	40	175.00	200.00	85.00
Cat E	White/grey cat; blue ribbon, dish	22	175.00	200.00	85.00
Cat E	White/grey; cat yellow ribbon; grey dish	25	175.00	200.00	85.00
Cat E	Grey cat; blue bow; dark blue dish	25	175.00	200.00	85.00
Cat E	Grey cat; yellow bow; light blue dish	25	175.00	200.00	85.00
Cat F	White/grey cat; blue ribbon, ball	25	175.00	200.00	85.00

Siamese Kittens, c.1948–c1953

Only four models of Siamese Kittens have been found to date. The same models can be found marked 'Szeiler' or 'Studio Szeiler'. Joseph Szeiler worked for Wade before establishing his own Studio Szeiler pottery. Sir George and Anthony Wade loaned Szeiler some of Wade's discontinued moulds to help him get started in his business with the stipulation that the models were clearly marked Szeiler. Unfortunately, as with all early ink stamps the backstamps wear away over time. Szeiler models are found in different colourways to the Wade models.

Kitten, sitting, paw raised

Kitten, standing

Kitten, sleeping

Backstamp: **A.** Black ink stamp "Wade England"
B. Black transfer stamp "Wade England"

Name	Colourways	Size	U.S. $	Can. $	U.K. £
Kitten, seated, paw down	Off white; grey markings; blue/black eyes	60	250.00	300.00	125.00
Kitten, seated, paw raised	Off white; grey markings; blue/black eyes	60	250.00	300.00	125.00
Kitten, standing	Off white; grey markings; blue/black eyes	45	250.00	300.00	125.00
Kitten, sleeping	Off white; grey markings	35	250.00	300.00	125.00

Towser The Mouser, 2000

Towser was a female Tortoiseshell cat kept at the Glenturret Distilleries in Crief, Scotland, she died in 1999, and is entered in the *Guinness Book of Records* as a Champion Mouser with a recorded catch of 28,899 mice. Her successor is a female white and ginger cat named 'Amber'. The lettering around the base of the model reads "Towser World Mousing Champion, Glenturret Distillery, Crief, Scotland. 28,899 Mice." Towser was modelled by Simon Millard of Wade and was available from the Distillery shop for £24.00.

Backstamp: Printed "Exclusively Designed for Glenturret Distillery, Crief, Scotalnd Wade"

Name	Colourways	Size	U.S. $	Can. $	U.K. £
Towser	Beige, black and white; pink nose; black lettering around the base	110.00	80.00	95.00	40.00

CAMELS

Baby Bactrian Camel, 1939

This model of a baby Bactrian camel with two humps was taken from wood carvings produced by Faust Lang. Because the legs are so long and delicate it is hard to find a model in perfect condition and therefore considered extremely rare.

Backstamp: Hand written "Wade" on one foot and "Made in England" on another

Name	Colourways	Size	U.S. $	Can. $	U.K. £
Baby Bactrian Camel	Light/dark brown	200	2,500.00	3,000.00	1,250.00

DOGS

Airedale, c.1935-1939

This very fine high gloss model of an Airedale dog is just one of a series of large sized dog models produced by the Wade pottery between 1935 and 1939.

Backstamp: Ink stamp "Wade Made in England" with handwritten "Airedale" on feet

Name	Colourways	Size	U.S. $	Can. $	U.K. £
Airedale	Tan brown; black markings	180 x 200	800.00	900.00	400.00

Alsatian, c.1935-1939

Backstamp: Blue handwritten "Wade England"; model name

Name	Colourways	Size	U.S. $	Can. $	U.K. £
Alsatian, small	Dark grey and black; pink tongue	115	250.00	300.00	125.00

Borzoi, c.1935-1939

*Photograph not available
at press time*

Backstamp: Unknown

Name	Colourways	Size	U.S. $	Can. $	U.K. £
Borzoi	White; black patches	300	800.00	900.00	400.00

Bulldog "H.M.S. Winnie", c.1948

The sitting bulldog wears a sailor cap with "H.M.S. Winnie" on the hat band.

*Photograph not available
at press time*

Backstamp: Black ink stamp "Wade Made in England"

Name	Colourways	Size	U.S. $	Can. $	U.K. £
Bulldog "H.M.S. Winnie"	Beige; grey muzzle; white/blue sailor cap	100	Extremely Rare		

Bulldog, Seated c.mid 1930s

This bulldog is similar to the "H.M.S. Winnie" model, but does not have the sailor cap.

Backstamp **A:** Hand written black ink "Wade Made in England Bulldog"
B: Handwritten in black ink "Wade England Bulldog"

Name	Colourways	Size	U.S. $	Can. $	U.K. £
Bulldog	Cream	115	800.00	900.00	400.00
Bulldog	White; grey ears; black patch	115	800.00	900.00	400.00

Note: The author would welcome images of the Borzoi and Bulldog "H.M.S. Winnie".

CHAMPIONSHIP DOGS SET, 1975–1981

Championship Dogs is a set of five dogs, all standing on green, oval bases. When produced, a bright orange label that reads "Wade England" was affixed to the base; some models still have them. These models are solid porcelain. The original price was £2.65 per model.

Backstamp: Raised "Wade England"

Name	Colourways	Size	U.S. $	Can. $	U.K. £
Afghan Hound	Beige/white; light brown face, paws	85 x 90	90.00	100.00	45.00
Cocker Spaniel	Beige/off white; black patches	80 x 90	125.00	150.00	60.00
Collie	Honey/dark brown	85 x 85	125.00	150.00	60.00
English Setter	Beige/off white; black patches	80 x 90	125.00	150.00	60.00
Old English Sheepdog	Grey and white	85 x 90	125.00	150.00	60.00

Dachshunds, c.1930

In these models of a dachshund sits begging with its head turned slightly to the front, its tail curled around its front leg. The original price was 2/6d.

Dachshund

Dachshund Mustard Pot Posy Bowl

Backstamp: **A.** Black handwritten "Wade Made in England"
B. Black handwritten "Wade England"
C. Black handwritten "England"

Name	Colourways	Size	U.S. $	Can. $	U.K. £
Dachshund	Red-brown; white chest	80	175.00	225.00	90.00
Dachshund	Beige all over	80	175.00	225.00	90.00
Dachshund	Dark brown all over	80	175.00	225.00	90.00
Dachshund	Beige; white flash on chest	80	175.00	225.00	90.00
Dachshund	Dark/light brown	80	175.00	225.00	90.00

Dachshund Derivatives

Dachshund Posy Bowls, c.1940

Sir George Wade's policy of creating new items by combining unsold stock from the George Wade Pottery and the Wade Heath Pottery produced many unusual and delightful "Stick-em-on-somethings." Unsold models were mounted on a new base with bramble-ware mustard pots or basket-weave egg cups to form posy bowls. The multicoloured posy bowls usually have a moulded porcelain flower added to the bowl. Posy bowls in one colour with the added flower are rarely seen. All the posy bowls were produced in the Wade Heath Pottery.

Backstamp: Green-brown ink stamp "Wade England"

Name	Colourways	Size	U.S. $	Can. $	U.K. £
Mustard Pot	Dark brown dog; multicoloured bowl, flower	90	200.00	250.00	100.00
Mustard Pot	Matt green	90	150.00	200.00	85.00
Mustard Pot	Matt cream	90	150.00	200.00	85.00
Mustard Pot	Pale orange	90	150.00	200.00	85.00
Egg Cup	Matt green	90	150.00	200.00	85.00

Dalmatian, c.1935-1939

Backstamp: **A.** Blue handwritten "Wade England" [name of model]
B. Hand written "Wade England" on sole of feet

Name	Colourways	Size	U.S. $	Can. $	U.K. £
Dalmatian	White; black markings	220	800.00	950.00	400.00

English Setters, c.1930-c.1955

Backstamp: **A.** Black handwritten "Wade Made in England"
B. Black transfer "Wade England"

Name	Colourways	Size	U.S. $	Can. $	U.K. £
English Setter	White; black patches	57	300.00	350.00	150.00
English Setter	White; orange patches	57	300.00	350.00	150.00
English Setter	White; orange patches	50	135.00	150.00	70.00
English Setter	White; black patches	50	135.00	150.00	70.00

Irish Setter c.1930-1939

The author would welcome any photographs of the large Wade Irish Setter.

Photograph not available
at press time

Backstamp: Unknown

Name	Colourways	Size	U.S. $	Can. $	U.K. £
Irish Setter	Red-brown	150	800.00	950.00	400.00

Playful Pup

This model is the Cellulose 'Spaniel Puppy' reissued in a high gloss glaze and named "Playful Pup".

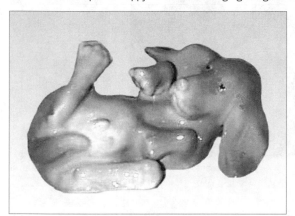 

Backstamp: Blue hand written "Wade England Playful Pup"

Name	Colourways	Size	U.S. $	Can. $	U.K. £
Playful Pup	Black and white	85	800.00	900.00	400.00
Playful Pup	Light brown	85	800.00	900.00	400.00

Puppies, c.1948–c.1953

Only three models of the puppies have been reported to date. The same models can be found marked 'Szeiler' or 'Studio Szeiler'. Joseph Szeiler worked for Wade before establishing his own 'Studio Szeiler' pottery. Sir George and Anthony Wade loaned Szeiler some of Wade's discontinued moulds to help him get started in his business with the stipulation that the models were clearly backstamped Szeiler. Unfortunately, as with all early ink stamps the backstamp wears away over time. Szeiler models are found in different colourways to the Wade models.

Puppy, begging

Puppy, seated

Puppy with slippers

Backstamp: **A.** Black hand painted "Wade"
B. Black transfer "Wade England"

Name	Colourways	Size	U.S. $	Can. $	U.K. £
Puppy, begging	White; beige ears; blue/black eyes; blue collar	60	400.00	450.00	200.00
Puppy, seated	White; beige ears; blue/black eyes; blue collar	50	400.00	450.00	200.00
Puppy with slipper	White; beige ears, patch; black/blue eyes; blue slipper	45	500.00	475.00	250.00

Scottie, 1935-1939

This very fine high gloss model of a Scottie dog is just one of a series of large sized dog models produced by the Wade pottery between 1935 and 1939. It has also been reported in a Cellulose glaze (see page 3).

Backstamp: Ink stamp "Wade Made in England" with hand written "Scottie" on feet

Name	Colourways	Size	U.S. $	Can. $	U.K. £
Scottie	Black	110 x 155	700.00	800.00	350.00

Spaniel, 1935-1939

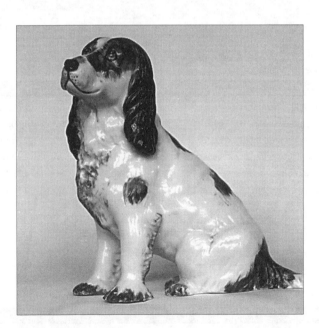

Backstamp: Black handwritten "Wade Made in England," red ink stamp of a leaping deer

Name	Colourways	Size	U.S. $	Can. $	U.K. £
Spaniel, seated	White; black markings, nose	135	800.00	950.00	400.00
Spaniel, seated	White; brown markings; black nose	135	800.00	950.00	400.00

Spaniel, Seated on Round Base, 1945-1953

Photograph not available
at press time

Backstamp: Unmarked

Name	Colourways	Size	U.S. $	Can. $	U.K. £
Spaniel, seated on base	Honey/grey body; blue-grey ears; green base	75	50.00	60.00	25.00

Terriers, Begging, c.1935-c.1948

Terrier, begging

Terrier Egg Cup Posy Bowl

Backstamp: **A.** Black handwritten "Wade Made in England"
B. Black ink stamp "Wade England"

Name	Colourways	Size	U.S. $	Can. $	U.K. £
Terrier, begging	White; one black eye, ear	80	175.00	200.00	90.00
Terrier, begging	White; light brown ear, eye, collar	80	175.00	200.00	90.00
Terrier, begging	White; two black ears; grey collar	80	175.00	200.00	90.00
Terrier, begging	White; two black ears; brown collar	80	175.00	200.00	90.00
Terrier, begging	White; grey ears and patches	80	175.00	200.00	90.00
Terrier, begging	Light tan all over; dark brown collar	80	175.00	200.00	90.00

Terrier, Begging Derivatives

Terrier Posy Bowls, c.1948–1953

These derivatives were made from the "Terriers, begging,"

Backstamp: Green-brown ink stamp "Wade England"

Name	Colourways	Size	U.S. $	Can. $	U.K. £
Egg Cup	White dog; black ears; multicoloured bowl	82	160.00	185.00	85.00
Egg Cup	White dog; brown ears; multicoloured bowl	82	160.00	185.00	85.00
Mustard Pot	Green all over - reglazed	82	160.00	185.00	85.00

Terrier, Standing, 1935-c.1940

 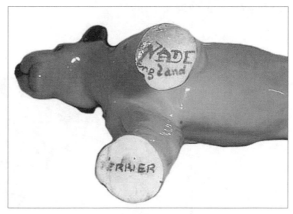

Terrier, standing

Backstamp: Ink stamp "Wade England" "Terrier"

Name	Colourways	Size	U.S. $	Can. $	U.K. £
Terrier, standing	White; brown/black markings	180	800.00	950.00	400.00

West Highland Terrier, c.1948

*Photograph not available
at press time*

Backstamp: Unknown

Name	Colourways	Size	U.S. $	Can. $	U.K. £
West Highland Terrier	White; blue spots	50	800.00	950.00	400.00

DONKEY

Donkey Foal, c.1938-c.1953

Backstamp: **A.** Black handwritten "Wade England"
B. Black transfer "Wade Ireland"

Name	Colourways	Size	U.S. $	Can. $	U.K. £
Donkey Foal	Grey all over	48 x 40	300.00	350.00	150.00
Donkey Foal	Light grey; black mane	48 x 40	300.00	350.00	150.00
Donkey Foal	Beige; black mane, tail tip	50 x 45	300.00	350.00	150.00

ELEPHANT, c.1930, c.1950

The issues of the 1930s and 1950s can be identified by their backstamps. The original price of this model was 2/6d.

Backstamp: **A.** Black handwritten "Wade England," 1930s
B. Black transfer "Wade England," 1950s

Name	Colourways	Size	U.S. $	Can. $	U.K. £
Elephant	Pale grey; black eyes	50	400.00	450.00	200.00

ERMINE, 1939

The "Ermine" is a weasel in its winter coat of white. Designed by Faust Lang, this mould was also used to produced the "Weasel" (see page 38).

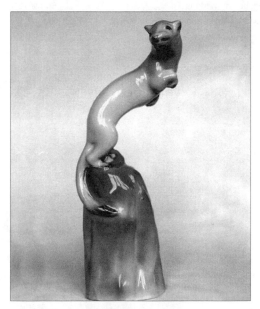

Backstamp: Blue handwritten "Wade England 1939 Ermine"

Name	Colourways	Size	U.S. $	Can. $	U.K. £
Ermine	White; pink ears; black tail tip; blue-grey base	220 x 95	1,500.00	1,750.00	750.00

FAWNS, c.1938

These fawn models can be found in a variety of browns and greys. Most of the miniature models have no backstamps.

Fawn, facing right

Fawn, facing left

Backstamp: Black handwritten "Wade"

Name	Colourways	Size	U.S. $	Can. $	U.K. £
Fawn, facing right	Beige; light brown markings	Miniature/39	375.00	425.00	200.00
Fawn, facing right	Beige; dark brown markings	Miniature/30	375.00	425.00	200.00
Fawn, facing right	Blue all over	Miniature/30	375.00	425.00	200.00
Fawn, facing right	White; grey markings	Miniature/30	375.00	425.00	200.00
Fawn, facing right	Off white; dark brown markings	Small/61	375.00	425.00	200.00
Fawn, facing right	Off white; grey/light brown markings	Small/61	375.00	425.00	200.00
Fawn, facing right	White; light brown markings	Small/61	375.00	425.00	200.00
Fawn, facing left	Off white; light brown markings	Small/61	400.00	425.00	200.00
Fawn, facing left	Off white; grey/light brown markings	Small/61	400.00	425.00	200.00

Fawn Derivatives

Ashtray

The Fawn ashtrays have been found in three sizes.

Backstamp: Blue Ink stamp "Wade England"

Name	Colourways	Height	U.S. $	Can. $	U.K. £
Ashtray, Fawn facing right	Brown/white fawn; beige S-shaped ashtray	45	325.00	375.00	175.00
Ashtray, Fawn facing right	Brown/white fawn; green S-shaped ashtray	52	325.00	375.00	175.00
Ashtray, Fawn facing right	Brown/white fawn; yellow S-shaped astray	75	325.00	375.00	175.00

GIRAFFE, 1938

This small giraffe model has very thin and delicate legs therefore it is very hard to find in perfect condition and is considered extremely rare.

Backstamp: Black handwritten "Wade" on front foot and "England" on back foot

Name	Colourways	Size	U.S. $	Can. $	U.K. £
Giraffe	Cream; beige markings	77		Extremely Rare	

GOATS

Chamois Kid, 1939

The "Chamois Kid" was modelled by Faust Lang.

Backstamp: Blue handwritten "Wade England 1939 Chamois Kid" and the incised signature of Faust Lang

Name	Colourways	Size	U.S. $	Can. $	U.K. £
Chamois Kid	Honey/beige; green/blue rocky base	125	800.00	900.00	400.00

Mother Goat and Kid, c.1930-c.1950

This set was first issued in the 1930s and was so popular that it was reissued in the 1940s and in the 1950s. The issues of the 1930s, 1940s and 1950s can be identified by their backstamps.

Mother Goat

Kid

Backstamp: **A.** Black handwritten "Wade England"
  B. Black ink stamp "Made in England"
  C. Black transfer "Wade England"

Name	Colourways	Size	U.S. $	Can. $	U.K. £
Mother Goat	Beige; creamy brown markings	55	300.00	350.00	150.00
Mother Goat	Off white; orange-brown markings	55	300.00	350.00	150.00
Kid	Beige; creamy brown markings	45	350.00	375.00	175.00
Kid	Off white; fawn markings	40	300.00	350.00	150.00

Kid Derivatives

Ashtray, c.early 1950s

This ashtray is one of Sir George Wade's famous "Stick-em-on-somethings." The S-shaped art deco ashtray has also been found with the Comic Rabbit (Little Laughing Bunny), and the Mini Bunnies mounted on the back rim. Sylvac produced a similar ashtray with small animals attached, including "Kissing Bunnies." The ashtray has an impressed registered Sylvac design number on the base which is different to that of Wade.

Backstamp: **A.** Ink stamp "England 27631"
  B. Ink stamp "Made in England Rgd #27631

Name	Colourways	Size	U.S. $	Can. $	U.K. £
Kid Ashtray	White/beige kid; beige ashtray	102	250.00	300.00	125.00
Kid Ashtray	White/brown kid; honey tray	55 x 80	250.00	300.00	125.00

Mountain Goat In Winter Coat, c.1939–c.1953

Although this model had previously been given the name Ibex Ram further research has identified it as a male Mountain Goat in it's thick winter coat. At other times mountain goats have a brown coat.

Backstamp: **A.** Black handwritten "Wade Made in England," c.1939
B. Black ink stamp "Wade Made in England," c.1948-1953

Name	Colourways	Size	U.S. $	Can. $	U.K. £
Mountain Goat	Cream/beige; dark grey horns; blue/grey rock base	80 x 65	1,100.00	1,250.00	550.00
Mountain Goat	White; grey horns; green/beige rock base	80 x 65	1,100.00	1,250.00	550.00

HIPPOPOTAMUS, c.1930

Backstamp: Black handwritten "Wade England"

Name	Colourways	Size	U.S. $	Can. $	U.K. £
Hippopotamus	Light grey; brown eyes	50 x 90	500.00	575.00	250.00

HORSES

Foals, 1930-1950

Sylvac produced a model of the medium foal with head down which is virtually identical to the Wade foal and in the same colourways, the only difference, if it still exists, is the backstamp.

Foal, head back   Foal, head down

Backstamp: **A.** Black handwritten "Wade England"
B. Black transfer "Wade England"

Name	Colourways	Size	U.S. $	Can. $	U.K. £
Foal, head back	Beige; grey mane	Large/65	250.00	300.00	125.00
Foal, head back	White; grey mane	Medium/55	250.00	300.00	125.00
Foal, head back	Beige, grey mane	Small/40	250.00	300.00	125.00
Foal, head down	Beige; grey mane, tail, hooves	Medium/55	250.00	300.00	125.00
Foal, head down	White; grey mane, tail, hooves	Medium/55	250.00	300.00	125.00
Foal, head down	White; beige mane, tail, hooves	Small/40	250.00	300.00	125.00
Foal, head down	White; grey mane, tail, hooves	Small/40	250.00	300.00	125.00

Foals, c.1948-1953

The foals can be found in two different styles. The legs on these models are so thin that it is difficult to find a perfect example.

Foal, rear leg forward

Foal, rear legs parallel

Backstamp: Black ink stamp "Wade England"

Name	Colourways	Size	U.S. $	Can. $	U.K. £
Foal, rear leg forward	Light brown; black mane, tail; brown hooves	Large/120	400.00	450.00	200.00
Foal, rear leg forward	White; blue mane, spots, tail, hooves	Large/120	400.00	450.00	200.00
Foal, rear leg forward	White; ginger mane, spots, tail, hooves	Large/120	400.00	450.00	200.00
Foal, rear leg forward	Light brown; white mane, tail; brown hooves	Small/108	400.00	450.00	200.00
Foal, rear leg forward	Dark brown; black mane, tail, hooves	Small/108	400.00	450.00	200.00
Foal, rear legs parallel	Dark brown; black mane, tail, hooves	Small/102	400.00	450.00	200.00
Foal, rear legs parallel	Light brown; black mane, tail, hooves	Small/102	400.00	450.00	200.00
Foal, rear legs parallel	White; blue mane, tail, spots, hooves	Small/102	400.00	450.00	200.00

Horse, 1939

This is a Faust Lang model.

Brown Colourway

White Colourway

Backstamp: Blue handwritten "Wade England 1939 Horse" and the incised signature of Faust Lang

Name	Colourways	Size	U.S. $	Can. $	U.K. £
Horse	Brown; brown mane, tail; dark brown hooves; blue/green base	215	2,000.00	2,250.00	1,000.00
Horse	Brown; white socks; blue/green base	215	2,000.00	2,250.00	1,000.00
Horse	White; light brown shading in mane, tail and hooves, blue/green base	215	2,000.00	2,250.00	1,000.00

LIONS

Lion Cubs, 1939

These are Faust Lang models.

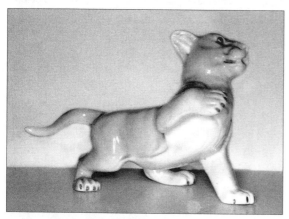

Lion Cub, Paw Raised

Lion Cub, Crouching

Backstamp: Blue handwritten "Wade England 1939"

Name	Colourways	Size	U.S. $	Can. $	U.K. £
Lion Cub, paw raised	Brown; white tail tip	135	2,250.00	2,500.00	1,200.00
Lion Cub, crouching	Brown; white tail tip	135	2,250.00	2,500.00	1,200.00

MONKEYS

Capuchin on Tree, 1939

This is a Faust Lang model.

Backstamp: Blue handwritten "Wade England 1939 Capuchin"

Name	Colourways	Size	U.S. $	Can. $	U.K. £
Capuchin	Pastel grey; pastel blue tree trunk, blue/brown base	248	2,250.00	2,500.00	1,200.00

Seated Monkeys, c.1930s

The seated monkey, his hand on his cheek, resembles a young "Capuchin" monkey and is finely detailed. He is one of two small monkeys produced by Wade in the 1930s.

Backstamp: Handwritten "Wade Made in England"

Name	Colourways	Size	U.S. $	Can. $	U.K. £
Monkey, seated hand on face	Light brown; creamy white markings	70	400.00	450.00	200.00
Monkey, seated hand on face	Light brown; black and cream markings	70	400.00	450.00	200.00
Monkey, seated hand on face	Red-brown; cream markings	70	400.00	450.00	200.00
Monkey, seated arms by side	Light brown	35	200.00	225.00	100.00

OTTER, 1939

Backstamp: Blue ink stamp "Wade England"

Name	Colourways	Size	U.S. $	Can. $	U.K. £
Otter	Brown; light brown paws	102 x 275	1,500.00	1,700.00	750.00

PANDAS

Baby, c.1939

These small pandas are believed to have been produced at the same time as the popular "Panda" nursery ware sets.

Backstamp: **A.** Black handwritten "Baby Panda 2 Wade Made in England"
B. Black hand written "Wade England"

Name	Colourways	Size	U.S. $	Can. $	U.K. £
Panda, sitting	Black; white markings	50	400.00	450.00	200.00
Panda, walking	Black: white markings	40	400.00	450.00	200.00

Panda, Waving, c.1939

This model of a waving panda found in three sizes was produced at the same time as the "Panda" nursery ware sets, and is seen in Wadeheath advertising along with the nursery dishes. The Panda Waving is also found in blue and green Flaxman ware glazes see page 46. An impressed shape number 338 can be seen on the large size Pandas.

Large and Small Waving Pandas

Backstamp: Green ink stamp "Wade Heath England"

Name	Colourways	Size	U.S. $	Can. $	U.K. £
Panda, waving	Black and white	Large/200	1,100.00	1,250.00	550.00
Panda, waving	Black and white	Medium/165	800.00	950.00	400.00
Panda, waving	Black and white	Small/153	600.00	700.00	300.00

PANTHER, 1939

The "Panther" was modelled by Faust Lang.

Backstamp: Blue handwritten "Wade England 1939 Panther" and the incised signature of Faust Lang

Name	Colourways	Size	U.S. $	Can. $	U.K. £
Panther	Light brown; blue eyes; green tree trunk base	215	1,500.00	1,750.00	750.00
Panther	Red brown; green tree trunk base	215	1,500.00	1,750.00	750.00

RABBITS

Bunnies, c.1930-c.1955

This series was first produced in the early 1930s, and due to its popularity, it was reissued in the late 1940s and again in the early 1950s. The reissued figures show very slight variations in colour and sizes.

The original price for the "Miniature Bunny" was 6d, the small "Double Bunnies" was 9d, the medium "Double Bunnies" sold for 1/-, and the large "Double Bunnies" cost 3/-.

Miniature, Double and Large Bunnies

Backstamp: **A.** Black handwritten "Wade Made in England"
B. Black ink stamp "Made in England"
C. Brown ink stamp "Wade England"
D. Black transfer "Wade England"

Name	Colourways	Size	U.S. $	Can. $	U.K. £
Bunny	White; light brown patches	Miniature/23	175.00	200.00	90.00
Bunny	Brown; white patches	Miniature/23	175.00	200.00	90.00
Bunny	White; light grey patches	Miniature/23	175.00	200.00	90.00
Double Bunnies	White; grey patches	Small/21	175.00	200.00	90.00
Double Bunnies	Brown; white patches	Small/21	175.00	200.00	90.00
Double Bunnies	White; pale grey patches	Small/21	175.00	200.00	90.00
Double Bunnies	White; grey patches	Medium/32	200.00	225.00	100.00
Double Bunnies	White; grey patches	Large/45	250.00	300.00	125.00
Double Bunnies	White; grey patches, ears	Large/45	250.00	300.00	125.00
Double Bunnies	White; grey patches; pink ears	Large/45	250.00	300.00	125.00
Double Bunnies	White; dark grey tail	Large/45	250.00	300.00	125.00

Bunnies Derivatives

Ashtrays

These small ashtrays have the miniature bunny attached to the back rim.

Mini Bunny S-shaped Ashtray

Mini Bunny Round Shaped Ashtray

Backstamp: Ink stamp "Wade Made in England"

Name	Colourways	Size	U.S. $	Can. $	U.K. £
S-shaped Ashtray	White/grey bunny; cream ashtray	45 x 80	150.00	175.00	75.00
Round Ashtray	White/grey bunny; cream ashtray	40	150.00	175.00	75.00

SHEEP

Lambs, 1930-c.1955

This set comprises three running lambs with long tails. The first two styles are very similar, but one lamb has its legs apart and the other has its legs closer together. Due to their delicate legs and tails, these models are easily damaged. Their original price was 2/6d each.

Lamb, Tail out (left) Lamb, Tail in (right)

Backstamp:
A. Black handwritten "Wade Made in England"
B. Black handwritten "Wade England"
C. Black handwritten "Wade"
D. Black ink stamp "Wade England"
E. Black transfer print "Wade England" Name

Name	Colourways	Size	U.S. $	Can. $	U.K. £
Lamb, tail out, legs apart	Dark brown; black/brown markings cream hooves	53	300.00	350.00	150.00
Lamb, tail out, legs apart	Off white; grey markings and hooves	53	300.00	350.00	150.00
Lamb, tail out, legs apart	Beige; cream markings and hooves	53	300.00	350.00	150.00
Lamb, tail out, legs apart	Brown; cream markings; dark brown hooves	53	300.00	350.00	150.00
Lamb, tail in, legs together	Beige; cream markings and hooves	53	500.00	575.00	250.00
Lamb, tail in, legs apart	Off white; grey markings and hooves	53	300.00	350.00	150.00
Lamb, tail in, legs apart	Beige; cream markings and hooves	53	300.00	350.00	150.00
Lamb, tail in, legs apart	Brown; cream markings; dark brown hooves	53	300.00	350.00	150.00

SQUIRRELS, c.1930-c.1955

Both versions were first produced in the 1930s, the smaller model being reissued in the 1940s and 1950s, and the larger squirrel reissued in the 1940s. The original price for the "Squirrel, seated" was 1/-. The "Squirrel, lying" was recoloured and produced as a posy bowl.

Squirrel, Sitting

Squirrel, Lying

Backstamp: **A.** Black handwritten "Wade England"
B. Brown ink stamp "Wade England"
C. Black ink stamp "Wade England"
D. Black transfer "Wade England"

Name	Colourways	Size	U.S. $	Can. $	U.K. £
Squirrel, lying	Light grey all over	65	300.00	350.00	150.00
Squirrel, lying	Red-brown; black eyes; white back of tail; brown acorn	65	300.00	350.00	150.00
Squirrel, lying	Light tan all over; back of tail white; green acorn leaf	65	300.00	350.00	150.00
Squirrel, lying	Beige; black eyes; white back of tail; green acorn	65	300.00	350.00	150.00
Squirrel, seated	Dark grey; brown nut	40	150.00	175.00	75.00
Squirrel, seated	Red-brown all over	40	150.00	175.00	75.00
Squirrel, seated	Light brown; dark brown acorn	40	150.00	175.00	75.00
Squirrel, seated	Light grey; white markings, brown claws	40	150.00	175.00	75.00

Squirrel Derivative

Posy Bowl, c.1948–1953

The multicoloured "Squirrel Bramble Ware Posy Bowl" was made from the model "Squirrel, lying" and had a moulded porcelain flower attached to the posy bowl. All posy bowls were produced in the Wade Heath Pottery.

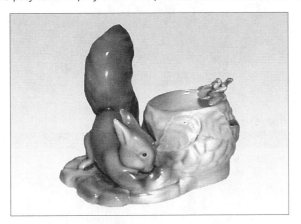

Backstamp: Green-brown ink stamp "Wade England"

Name	Colourways	Size	U.S. $	Can. $	U.K. £
Posy Bowl	Red-brown squirrel; green/pink/yellow flower	70 x 97	150.00	175.00	75.00

STAG, 1939

The "Stag" was modelled by Faust Lang with a 'full rack of antlers'. The antlers were so delicate they were packaged separately in the box with the Stag. Over time many were lost and broken. The model illustrated does not have the original antlers.

Backstamp: Blue handwritten "Wade England 1939 Highland Stag" and the incised signature of Faust Lang

Name	Colourways	Size	U.S. $	Can. $	U.K. £
Stag	Beige; blue/green rocky base	245	2,000.00	2,250.00	1,000.00

Note: A stag with the original full rack of antlers would be worth considerably more than the price quoted above.

TORTOISE, c.1930

Backstamp: Black handwritten "Wade England"

Name	Colourways	Size	U.S. $	Can. $	U.K. £
Tortoise	Beige; blue grey patches on shell	55	700.00	800.00	350.00
Tortoise	Fawn	55	700.00	800.00	350.00

WEASEL, 1939

The "Weasel" was modelled by Faust Lang. This mould was later used to make the model "Ermine" (see page 21 for an illustration).

Photograph not available
at press time

Backstamp: Blue handwritten "Wade Weasel designed in 1939 by Faust Lang"

Name	Colourways	Size	U.S. $	Can. $	U.K. £
Weasel	Fawn; black eyes; blue/green rock base	220	2,000.00	2,250.00	1,000.00

FLAXMAN WARE MODELS, 1935-c.1940

The following models were made in the Wade Heath Pottery in Flaxman Ware matt glazes.

DOGS, 1935-1939

Alsatians, 1935-1939

The models of a resting Alsatian were produced with and without glass eyes.

Backstamp: **A.** Black ink stamp "Flaxman Ware Hand Made Pottery by Wadeheath England"
B. Black ink stamp "Flaxman Wade Heath England"
C. Impressed "British"

Name	Colourways	Size	U.S. $	Can. $	U.K. £
Alsatian, glass eyes	Green; black/yellow glass eyes	120	300.00	350.00	150.00
Alsatian, glass eyes	Beige; black/yellow glass eyes	120	300.00	350.00	150.00
Alsatian	Pale orange	120	250.00	275.00	125.00
Alsatian	Orange	120	250.00	275.00	125.00
Alsatian	Beige	120	250.00	275.00	125.00
Alsatian	Green	120	250.00	275.00	125.00
Alsatian	Blue	120	250.00	275.00	125.00

Fox Terrier, c.1935-1937
Shape No. 528

This standing "Fox Terrier" with a smiling face has glass eyes. The shape number 528 is impressed on the stomach. Sylvac produced a similar model named 'Terrier Dog' which has an impressed shape number 1121.

Backstamp: Black ink stamp "Flaxman Ware Hand Made Pottery by Wadeheath England" with impressed number "528" (1935-1937)

Name	Colourways	Size	U.S. $	Can. $	U.K. £
Fox Terrier	Beige; black/yellow glass eyes	120	200.00	225.00	100.00
Fox Terrier	Blue; black/yellow glass eyes	120	200.00	225.00	100.00

Greyhound, 1940s

Backstamp: **A.** Ink stamp "Flaxman Ware Hand made pottery by Wadeheath England"
B. Ink stamp "Flaxman Wade Heath England"

Name	Colourways	Size	U.S. $	Can. $	U.K. £
Greyhound, leaping	Light grey	190		Rare	
Greyhound, leaping	Orange	190		Rare	

Jack Russell Terrier
Shape No. 334

The terrier is sitting with his mouth open and his tongue out as though panting. For similar model with impressed shape number 334 on the base see Cellulose animals (page 3).

Backstamp: Ink stamp "Wadeheath England"

Name	Colourways	Size	U.S. $	Can. $	U.K. £
Jack Russell Terrier	Green	101	200.00	225.00	100.00
Jack Russell Terrier	Orange	101	200.00	225.00	100.00
Jack Russell Terrier	Blue	101	200.00	225.00	100.00

Long-Haired Dachshund, 1937-1939

Backstamp: Black ink stamp "Wadeheath Ware England"

Name	Colourways	Size	U.S. $	Can. $	U.K. £
Long-Haired Dachshund	Orange	95	250.00	300.00	125.00
Long-Haired Dachshund	Blue	95	250.00	300.00	125.00
Long-Haired Dachshund	Pale green	80	250.00	300.00	125.00

Mongrel Puppy

Backstamp: Ink stamp "Flaxman Wade England"

Name	Colourways	Size	U.S. $	Can. $	U.K. £
Mongrel Puppy	Green	110	200.00	225.00	100.00

Playful Pup / Spaniel Puppy

This model of a Spaniel Puppy is also found in cellulose named Spaniel, and in high gloss glazes named Playful Pup. For cellulose and high gloss models see pages 3 and 15 respectively.

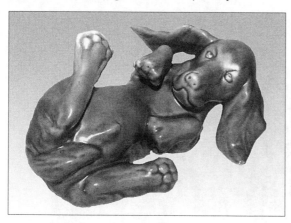

Backstamp: Ink stamped "Flaxman Ware Hand Made Pottery by Wadeheath England"

Name	Colourways	Size	U.S. $	Can. $	U.K. £
Playful Pup	Blue	85	800.00	900.00	400.00

Puppy in a Basket, 1937-1939

Backstamp: Black ink stamp "Flaxman Wade Heath England"

Name	Colourways	Size	U.S. $	Can. $	U.K. £
Puppy in a Basket	Orange	155	300.00	350.00	150.00
Puppy in a Basket	Green	155	300.00	350.00	150.00

Scottie, Crouching, 1937-1939, Shape No. 527

This crouching Scottie has an elongated body and glass eyes. Sylvac produced a similar model to the crouching Scottie named 'Comic Scottie Dog' which has an impressed shape number 1123.

Backstamp: Impressed "Made in England 527"

Name	Colourways	Size	U.S. $	Can. $	U.K. £
Scottie, crouching	Green	110 x 185	300.00	350.00	150.00

Scottie, Seated, Shape No. 327

Backstamp: **A.** Embossed "327" in a square
B. Black ink stamp "Flaxman Wade Heath England", impressed "327"

Name	Colourways	Size	U.S. $	Can. $	U.K. £
Scottie, seated	Brown	140	200.00	225.00	100.00
Scottie, seated	Light brown	140	200.00	225.00	100.00
Scottie, seated	Orange	140	200.00	225.00	100.00
Scottie, seated	Light blue	140	200.00	225.00	100.00
Scottie, seated	Light green	140	200.00	225.00	100.00
Scottie, seated	Dark blue	140	200.00	225.00	100.00

Scottie, Walking

Backstamp: Unknown

Name	Colourways	Size	U.S. $	Can. $	U.K. £
Scottie, walking	Unknown	115		Rare	

Terrier, Seated, 1935-1937, Shape No. 520

The Terrier, with one ear up, and the other down, has glass eyes. The shape number is impressed on the base of the black models. Sylvac produced a similar model which was named 'Monty the Mongrel' and has an impressed shape number 1118.

Terrier, seated

Terrier, seated (black)

Backstamp: **A.** Black ink stamp "Flaxman Ware Hand Made Pottery By Wadeheath England"
B. Impressed "Made in England 520"

Name	Colourways	Size	U.S. $	Can. $	U.K. £
Terrier, seated	Beige; dark brown glass eyes	160	200.00	225.00	100.00
Terrier, seated	Black; black glass eyes	160	200.00	225.00	100.00
Terrier, seated	Blue; dark brown glass eyes	165	200.00	225.00	100.00
Terrier, seated	Green	165	200.00	225.00	100.00

Terrier, Standing, 1935-1937

Only an illustration in an advertisement has been seen, but the Flaxman Ware Terrier, standing is very similar in style to the high gloss Terrier, standing.

Photograph not available
at press time

Backstamp: Unknown

Name	Colourways	Size	U.S. $	Can. $	U.K. £
Terrier, standing	Brown	125	300.00	350.00	150.00
Terrier, standing	White; glass eyes	160	350.00	400.00	175.00

PANDA, c.1939

Waving, Shape No. 338

These large Flaxman ware Pandas are believed to have been produced at the same time as the high gloss Pandas (see page 31).

Backstamp: **A.** Ink stamp "Flaxman Wade Heath England'
B. Impressed shape number "338"

Name	Colourways	Size	U.S. $	Can. $	U.K. £
Panda, waving	Blue	200	800.00	900.00	400.00
Panda, waving	Green	200	800.00	900.00	400.00

RABBITS

Rabbit, Crouching, 1935-c.1940, Shape No. 337

Backstamp: Black ink stamp "Flaxman Wadeheath England," impressed "337"

Name	Colourways	Size	U.S. $	Can. $	U.K. £
Rabbit, crouching	Orange-brown; dark brown eyes	110 x 145	200.00	225.00	100.00

Rabbit, Seated, Shape No. 305

The popular seated rabbits have been found in six sizes. A number of models have been found with the shape number 305 impressed on the bases. Unmarked Wade seated rabbits are very hard to separate from unmarked Sylvac rabbits, but on close inspection you will see that the lined pattern of the fur on the Wade rabbit runs downwards only and is sparse. The pattern on the fur of the Sylvac rabbits is lined and speckled and much more profuse. There is also a slight difference in the tails: the Wade rabbits have humps on the top and bottom of the tail; the Sylvac tail is squared. On smaller models and worn moulds the difference in the tail is very hard to detect.

Rabbits, seated

Backstamp:
    A. Black ink stamped "Flaxman Ware Hand Painted Pottery by Wadeheath England"
    B. Black ink stamped "Flaxman Wadeheath England"
    C. Black ink stamped "Made in England"
    D. Black ink stamped "Flaxman Wadeheath England" with Impressed "305"
        These models can also be found with no backstamp

Name	Colourways	Size	U.S. $	Can. $	U.K. £
Rabbit, seated	Light brown	Miniature/75 x 60	150.00	175.00	75.00
Rabbit, seated	Light green	Miniature/75 x 60	150.00	175.00	75.00
Rabbit, seated	Orange	Miniature/75 x 60	150.00	175.00	75.00
Rabbit, seated	Brown	Small/105 x 88	150.00	175.00	75.00
Rabbit, seated	Light brown	Small/105 x 88	150.00	175.00	75.00
Rabbit, seated	Light green	Small/105 x 88	150.00	175.00	75.00
Rabbit, seated	Orange	Small/105 x 88	150.00	175.00	75.00
Rabbit, seated	Yellow	Small/105 x 88	150.00	175.00	75.00
Rabbit, seated	Brown	Medium/135 x 115	175.00	200.00	90.00
Rabbit, seated	Light brown	Medium/135 x 115	175.00	200.00	90.00
Rabbit, seated	Green	Medium/135 x 115	175.00	200.00	90.00
Rabbit, seated	Orange	Medium/135 x 115	175.00	200.00	90.00
Rabbit, seated	Turquoise	Medium/135 x 115	175.00	200.00	90.00
Rabbit, seated	Brown	Large/152 x 130	175.00	200.00	90.00
Rabbit, seated	Light green	Large/152 x 130	175.00	200.00	90.00
Rabbit, seated	Orange	Large/152 x 130	175.00	200.00	90.00
Rabbit, seated	Blue	Large/165 x 135	175.00	200.00	90.00
Rabbit, seated	Brown	Extra Large/190 x 160	200.00	225.00	100.00
Rabbit, seated	Light green	Extra Large/190 x 160	200.00	225.00	100.00
Rabbit, seated	Orange	Extra Large/190 x 160	200.00	225.00	100.00

Rabbit, seated Derivatives

Matchbox Holder, 1937–1939

Sylvac produced a similar model to the Rabbit Matchbox Holder. The matchbox holders on the Sylvac models are upright and almost touch the rabbit's ears. The Sylvac model has an impressed shape number 1064.

Backstamp: Black ink stamp "Wadeheath Ware England"

Name	Colourways	Size	U.S. $	Can. $	U.K. £
Matchbox Holder	Light green	105 x 85	250.00	285.00	125.00

SQUIRRELS
Shape No. 325

Backstamp: **A.** Impressed "Made in England 325"
           B. Black ink stamp "Flaxman Ware Hand Made Pottery by Wadeheath England" impressed "325" (1935-1937)

Name	Colourways	Size	U.S. $	Can. $	U.K. £
Squirrel feeding	Light green	165 x 135	200.00	225.00	100.00
Squirrel feeding	Light blue	165 x 135	200.00	225.00	100.00
Squirrel feeding	Light brown	165 x 135	200.00	225.00	100.00
Squirrel feeding	Off white; brown painted eyes	165 x 135	200.00	225.00	100.00
Squirrel with Glass Eyes	Blue	180 x 150	300.00	350.00	150.00
Squirrel with Glass Eyes	Light green	145 x 155	300.00	350.00	150.00

BISCUIT PORCELAIN MODELS, 1976-1991

Cheetah and Gazelle, 1991

Only six copies of the beautifully sculptured "Cheetah and Gazelle" are known to have been produced. This figure of a cheetah chasing a Grant's gazelle was modelled by Alan Maslankowski and made of biscuit porcelain. Each model was sold with a signed and numbered limited edition certificate. The original price direct from the Wade Pottery was £1,200.

Cheetah and Gazelle, front view

Cheetah and Gazelle, back view

Backstamp: The model is unmarked, but a gold-coloured metal plaque on the front of the wooden base is inscribed "Survival" with the model number

Name	Colourways	Size	U.S. $	Can. $	U.K. £
Cheetah and Gazelle	Orange/yellow/black cheetah; orange/white/black gazelle	240 x 200		Extremely Rare	

Razorback Pig, 1981

This model, produced in biscuit porcelain, depicts a North American wild pig called a razorback. It was designed by Alan Maslankowski, who modelled Wade's *Survival Animals* series. A limited edition of 500 models was produced for the University of Arkansas, whose football team mascot is a razorback pig. These models are extremely rare. The rarely seen red brown model was a trial colourway and only a few models are known. On the base of the model can be seen an embossed letter 'A' for Arkansas

Backstamp: Black ink stamp "Wade England"

Name	Colourways	Size	U.S. $	Can. $	U.K. £
Razorback	Dark grey	130	750.00	1,000.00	500.00
Razorback	Red brown	130		Rare	

Note: For the Wildlife Animals made by Wade Ireland see page 357.

THE WORLD OF SURVIVAL SERIES, 1976–1982

British Anglia Television's *World of Survival* film series has won world-wide acclaim. Naturalists and film makers have praised these documentaries featuring many endangered species. George Wade and Son Ltd. collaborated with Anglia Television to produce two sets of six models. The figures are perfect in every detail. They are slip cast and open cast (standing on their feet, not on a base). Produced in a biscuit porcelain, they are matt and rough to the touch and completely unlike any other Wade models. Due to their expensive retail prices, necessitated by high production costs, only a limited number of models were released. Their original prices started from £45 to £65.

Set 1

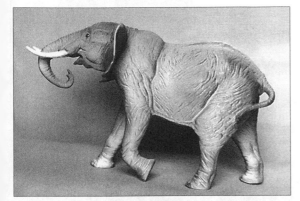
African Elephant

American Bison

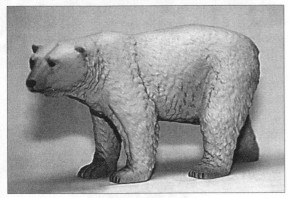
Polar Bear

Tiger

Backstamp: **A.** Black transfer print "World of Survival Series by Wade of England Copyright Survival Anglia Limited 1976 All rights reserved"

B. White transfer print on brown label "World of Survival Series by Wade of England Copyright Survival Anglia Limited 1976 All rights reserved"

Name	Colourways	Size	U.S. $	Can. $	U.K. £
African Elephant	Grey; white tusks	160 x 260	700.00	800.00	350.00
African Lion	Biscuit brown; dark brown mane	110 x 200	700.00	800.00	350.00
American Bison	Dark brown body; charcoal-grey mane	120 x 190	700.00	800.00	350.00
Black Rhinoceros	Light grey; white horns	110 x 240	700.00	800.00	350.00
Polar Bear	White; black eyes, nose	110 x 210	700.00	800.00	350.00
Tiger	Orange, yellow, white and black	95 x 190	700.00	800.00	350.00

Set 2

African Cape Buffalo

American Brown Bear

Amercian Cougar

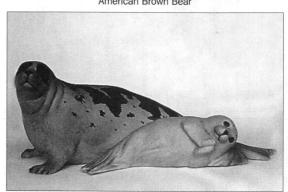

Harp Seal and Pup

Hippopotamus

Mountain Gorilla

Backstamp: Black transfer print "World of Survival Series, by Wade of England. Copyright Survival Anglia Limited. 1976 All rights reserved"

Name	Colourways	Size	U.S. $	Can. $	U.K. £
African Cape Buffalo	Dark brown; grey/white horns	170 x 240	800.00	900.00	400.00
American Brown Bear	Dark brown; black nose	105 x 145	800.00	900.00	400.00
American Cougar	Beige; dark grey muzzle	150 x 225	800.00	900.00	400.00
Harp Seal and Pup	Off white; light grey/black markings	85 x 220	800.00	900.00	400.00
Hippopotamus	Chocolate brown/pink; pink mouth	105 x 220	800.00	900.00	400.00
Mountain Gorilla	Black body; silver grey mane; copper head	150 x 150	800.00	900.00	400.00

BIRDS

Wade bird models created from the early 1930s to 1939 and from the late 1940s up to the early 1950s are slip cast. Beginning in the early 1950s, Wade started producing solid models.

The glazes used from the 1930s to the early 1950s are in delicate pastel and natural colours and are very different from the darker colours used from the late 1950s. Many of the models that were first produced in the early 1930s proved to be popular and were reissued in the late 1940s and early 1950s.

BACKSTAMPS

These bird models were produced in both the Wade Heath and the George Wade potteries, which accounts for the various backstamps used in the same time spans.

Handwritten Backstamps

Handwritten marks are found on models produced from the early 1930s to the 1940s.

Black handwritten, early 1930s-1940s

Blue handwritten, 1939-1940s

Blue handwritten, 1939-1940s

Ink Stamps

Ink stamps were used from the late 1940s to 1953.

The size of the mark has no relevance to the date; large ink stamps were used on models with large bases, small ink stamps on small bases. Many of the smaller models are unmarked

Black, brown or green ink stamp,
late 1940s-1953

Transfer Prints

Transfer prints have been used from 1953 to the present.

Transfer print, 1978-1982

HIGH GLOSS MODELS, c.1930-c.1955

BIRDS

Bluebirds, c.1930s

These novelty bluebird models with floral bases, one on a nest, the other on a stump, were produced as a pair during the mid to late 1930s, and are believed to have been modelled by Jessie Van Hallen who worked for Wadeheath from 1930-1940. Jessie Van Hallen is well known to Wade collectors for her lady figurines, and she also modelled the Wade flowers, some of which have the same mottled moss and floral bases that are seen on the bluebird models.

Bluebird on Floral Nest

Bluebird on Floral Stump

Backstamp: **A.** Black handwritten "Wade 9 England No 123" sometimes found with the letter L added (possibly the painter's identifying initial

B. Black handwritten "Wade 9 England No 124" sometimes found with the letter L added (possibly the painter's identifying initial

Name	Colourways	Size	U.S. $	Can. $	U.K. £
Bluebird on nest	Blue/white/yellow bird; mottled brown maroon/yellow/pink/blue flowers	50 x 76	500.00	575.00	250.00
Bluebird on stump	Blue/white/yellow bird; mottled brown maroon/yellow/pink/blue flowers	90	500.00	575.00	250.00

Budgerigars, 1939-c.1955

The Budgerigars were originally modelled by Faust Lang in wood, after which Wade cast them in porcelain. They can be found with handwrittem dates on the bases 1939, 1940 or 1941.

Budgerigar, Style One

Budgerigar, Style Two

Budgerigars

Backstamp: **A.** Blue handwritten "Wade England," date, name of model
B. Green-brown ink stamp "Wade England"
C. Black ink stamp "Wade England"
D. "Wade England 1940"

Name	Colourways	Size	U.S. $	Can. $	U.K. £
Budgerigar, Style One	Pale blue, yellow bird; fawn branch; pale blue/green mottled base	190	700.00	800.00	350.00
Budgerigar, Style One	Yellow, dark green bird; dark brown stump; brown/green mottled base	190	700.00	800.00	350.00
Budgerigar, Style One	Yellow, green bird; dark brown stump; brown/green mottled base	190	700.00	800.00	350.00
Budgerigar, Style Two	Pale green and black bird; light brown tree branch; dark blue flower; brown/green mottled base	175	700.00	800.00	350.00
Budgerigar, Style Two	Pale blue /grey; yellow head; light green tree branch; pink flower; brown/green base	175	700.00	800.00	350.00
Budgerigars	Yellow/blue/green bird; all green bird; fawn branch; pale blue/grey/green mottled base	195	900.00	1,100.00	450.00
Budgerigars	Yellow bird with green tail; all green bird; fawn branch; pale blue/grey/green mottled base	195	900.00	1,100.00	450.00

Chick, c.1940-1953

The "Chick" in the light and dark blue colourway is a reissue of the earlier models.

Backstamp: **A.** Brown handwritten "Wade Made in England"
B. Brown ink stamp "Wade England"

Name	Colourways	Size	U.S. $	Can. $	U.K. £
Chick	Pastel blue/grey; pink beak	55	400.00	450.00	200.00
Chick	Light/dark grey; yellow eyes; pink beak	55	400.00	450.00	200.00
Chick	Light/dark blue; black eyes; grey beak	55	400.00	450.00	200.00

Cockatoo, 1939-1955

This is a Faust Lang model. The original issue price for the "Cockatoo" was 5/9d.

Backstamp: **A.** Blue handwritten "Wade England," date, name of model
B. Green-brown ink stamp "Wade England"
C. Black ink stamp "Wade England"

Name	Colourways	Size	U.S. $	Can. $	U.K. £
Cockatoo	White; bright yellow crest; beige-pink eyes, beak	160	1,000.00	1,150.00	500.00
Cockatoo	White; bright pink crest, beak, wing tips; yellow feet	160	1,000.00	1,150.00	500.00
Cockatoo	White; bright pink crest, beak; grey wing tips; yellow feet	160	1,000.00	1,150.00	500.00
Cockatoo	Grey; pale pink crest, beak; beige feet	160	1,000.00	1,150.00	500.00

Cockerel, c.1940

Cockerel

Cockerel Posy Bowl

Backstamp: Black handwritten "Wade Made in England"

Name	Colourways	Size	U.S. $	Can. $	U.K. £
Cockerel	Off white; pink comb, eyes, beak, legs; pale green base	90	300.00	350.00	150.00

Cockerel Derivatives

Cockerel Posy Bowls, c.1940

A single Cockerel model was mounted on a base with a bramble ware mustard pot to make a posy bowl.

Backstamp: Green-brown ink stamp Wade England

Name	Colourways	Size	U.S. $	Can. $	U.K. £
Mustard Pot Posy Bowl	Brown; pink comb, beak; multicoloured and posy	95	200.00	225.00	100.00
Mustard Pot Posy Bowl	Creamy beige/orange all over	95	175.00	200.00	90.00

Drake and Daddy, c.1938-1953

The original price of this model was 2/6d.

Backstamp: **A.** Black handwritten "Wade England"
B. Brown ink stamp "Wade England"

Name	Colourways	Size	U.S. $	Can. $	U.K. £
Drake and Daddy	Daddy: white/brown; blue head; pink beak, feet; Drake: white; grey wings; pink beak, feet	90	275.00	325.00	135.00
Drake and Daddy	Daddy: blue head; beige/white body; grey wings; yellow beak/feet; Drake: white; grey wings; yellow beak, feet	90	275.00	325.00	135.00

Ducks and Drakes, c.1932-1953

It is possible to make pairs of these ducks as the models were produced as female ducks with straight tail feathers and male drakes with curled tail feathers. Although the original Wade name for this series of models is unknown perhaps a good choice would be Ducks and Drakes.

Some of the Duck models can be found marked "Szeiler". Joseph Szeiler worked for the Wade Potteries as a caster in the early 1950s. Sir George and Anthony Wade loaned Joseph Szeiler discontinued Wade moulds to help him start his own 'Studio Szeiler' pottery. The moulds were loaned with the stipulation that all models be clearly marked Szeiler. Unfortunately, as with all early ink stamps some of the backstamps over time wore away. Most Szeiler models are brighter colours than the George Wade models.

Japanese copies of the Wade Ducks in an all over one-colour blue glaze have been found, although unmarked they have a different base than the Wade models as seen in the illustrations.

Drake, head forward, curled tail feathers

Duck, head back, straight tail feathers

Drake, pecking, made in Japan   Drake, pecking, made by Wade

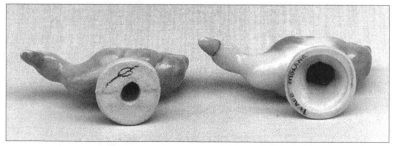

Drake pecking, base
(made in Japan)

Drake pecking, base
(made by Wade)

Drake, head forward; Drake, pecking

Duck, head back; Duck. preening

Backstamp: **A.** Black handwritten "Wade Made in England"
B. Black handwritten "Wade England"
C. Brown ink stamp "Wade England"
D. Black transfer "Wade England"

Ducks and Drakes

Name	Colourways	Size	U.S. $	Can. $	U.K. £
Head forward	Beige/white; blue-grey head; dark grey wings; pink beak, feet	Large/90	275.00	325.00	150.00
Head forward	Beige/white; grey head; grey wings; pink beak, feet	Small/75	275.00	325.00	150.00
Head forward	White/beige; grey head; grey wings; pink beak, feet	Small/75	275.00	325.00	150.00
Head forward	Beige/white; blue head; grey wings; yellow beak, feet	Small/75	275.00	325.00	150.00
Head forward	White; blue/green head, wings; yellow beak, feet	Small/70	275.00	325.00	150.00
Preening	Beige/white; blue/grey head; dark blue wings; pink beak, feet	Large/85	275.00	325.00	150.00
Preening	White /beige; grey head, wings; pink beak, feet	Medium/80	275.00	325.00	150.00
Preening	White/grey; grey blue head; blue/green wings; yellow beak, feet	Medium/80	275.00	325.00	150.00
Preening	White; blue/green head, wings; yellow beak, feet	Small/70	275.00	325.00	150.00
Preening	White; light grey head, wings, base; yellow beak, feet	Small/70	275.00	325.00	150.00
Head back	White; grey head, wings; pink beak, feet; grey base	74	250.00	300.00	125.00
Head back	Beige/white; grey head; blue wings; yellow beak, feet	74	250.00	300.00	125.00
Head back	White; blue/green head, wings; yellow beak, feet	74	250.00	300.00	125.00
Pecking	White /light grey body, head; blue wings; pink feet, beak	44	250.00	300.00	125.00
Pecking	Dark grey /white body, head; blue/black wings; pink beak, feet	44	250.00	300.00	125.00
Pecking	White; light grey head; deep blue wings, base; yellow beak	44	250.00	300.00	125.00
Pecking	White/beige; grey blue head; blue wings; yellow beak, feet	44	250.00	300.00	125.00
Pecking	White; blue/green head, wings; yellow beak, feet	44	250.00	300.00	125.00

Ducks and Drakes Derivatives

Posy Bowls, c.1948-1953

The multicoloured posy bowls have a moulded porcelain flower attached to the rim of the bowl. One-colour posy bowls are rarely found with the added flower decoration.

Drake, pecking, posy bowl

Duck, preening, posy bowl

Backstamp: Green-brown ink stamp "Wade England"

Ducks and Drakes

Name	Colourways	Size	U.S. $	Can. $	U.K. £
Head forward	Multicoloured	80	200.00	225.00	100.00
Preening	Multicoloured	85	200.00	225.00	100.00
Preening	Dark blue	85	150.00	175.00	75.00
Preening	Light green	85	150.00	175.00	75.00
Preening	Pale yellow	85	150.00	175.00	75.00
Pecking	Multicoloured	55	200.00	225.00	100.00
Pecking	Dark blue	55	150.00	175.00	75.00
Pecking	Pale blue	55	150.00	175.00	75.00

Ducks, Open Wings, 1935-1953

All three ducks have open wings. The "Duck, preening" has turned its head over its back, beak open, as though preening a wing. The "Duck, head forward" has its head tilted, beak closed. The "Duck, head up" has its head up and its beak closed.

Duck, head forward

Duck, head up

Open Wings Duck
Backstamp

Backstamp: **A.** Black handwritten "Wade England"
             B. Black transfer "Wade England"

Name	Colourways	Size	U.S. $	Can. $	U.K. £
Duck, preening	White; light brown head, wings; pink feet	35	250.00	300.00	125.00
Duck, preening	White; blue-grey head, wings; black beak; pink feet	35	250.00	300.00	125.00
Duck, head forward	White; blue-grey head, wings; black beak; pink feet	45	250.00	300.00	125.00
Duck, head up	White body; blue-grey head, wings; black beak; pale pink feet	45	250.00	300.00	125.00

Flicker, c.late 1930s

The "Flicker," a North American bird of the Woodpecker family, has been documented as modelled by Jessie Van Hallen; therefore it is possible that a few other birds were also modelled by Jessie during her ten years with Wade Heath.

Flicker, blue colourway

Flicker, yellow colourway

Backstamp: Blue handwritten "Wade England Flicker"

Name	Colourways	Size	U.S. $	Can. $	U.K. £
Flicker	White; yellow beak; blue head/back/tail; yellow tree	115	450.00	500.00	225.00
Flicker	White; grey beak; dull yellow tail/wing tips; pink tree	115	500.00	575.00	250.00

Goldfinches, 1946-1953

The original price of these models was 6/6d each.

Goldfinch, wings closed

Goldfinch, wings open

Backstamp:
A. Green-brown ink stamp "Wade England"
B. Black ink stamp "Wade England"
C. Black ink stamp "Wade Made in England"
D. Black ink stamp "England"

Name	Colourways	Size	U.S. $	Can. $	U.K. £
Goldfinch, wings closed	Yellow, black, brown and green	100	675.00	750.00	350.00
Goldfinch, wings open	Yellow, black, brown and green	100	675.00	750.00	350.00

Grebe, 1939

This is a Faust Lang model.

Backstamp: **A.** Blue handwritten "Wade England," date, name of model
  B. Blue handwritten "Wade England," name of model

Name	Colourways	Size	U.S. $	Can. $	U.K. £
Grebe	White, grey, dark grey, yellow, blue and green	235	1,300.00	1,500.00	650.00
Grebe	White, light grey, brown, yellow and blue	235	1,300.00	1,500.00	650.00

Heron, 1946-1953

Backstamp: Green-brown ink stamp "Wade England"

Name	Colourways	Size	U.S. $	Can. $	U.K. £
Heron	Dark blue, grey, pink, orange, brown and green	190	850.00	1,000.00	425.00
Heron	Pale blue, green, pink and orange	190	850.00	1,000.00	425.00

Indian Runner Ducks, c.1932-1953

These three Indian Runner or Peking-type ducks were first produced in the early 1930s and reissued in the late 1940s to 1953. They have long thin bodies; the mother is looking down at her two ducklings, one with its head up the other with the head down. The original selling price was 9d for a set of three.

Duckling, head up; Duckling, head down

Backstamp: **A.** Black handwritten "Wade England"
B. Black transfer print "Wade England"

Name	Colourways	Size	U.S. $	Can. $	U.K. £
Mother Duck	Blue/grey/white; light brown head; yellow beak, feet	95	400.00	450.00	200.00
Duckling, head down	White; yellow beak, feet; pale blue base	53	250.00	300.00	125.00
Duckling, head up	White; yellow beak, feet; pale blue base	55	250.00	300.00	125.00

Owl, 1940

Backstamp: Black handwritten "Wade Made in England," date and name of model

Name	Colourways	Size	U.S. $	Can. $	U.K. £
Owl	Brown/white; black markings; pale blue log	146	1,000.00	1,250.00	500.00

Parrot on Stump, 1939

This is a Faust Lang model.

Backstamp: Blue handwritten "Wade England," date and name of model

Name	Colourways	Size	U.S. $	Can. $	U.K. £
Parrot on Stump	Peach beak and chest; green head and stump; blue back and wings	267	1,500.00	1,750.00	750.00
Parrot on Stump	Grey beak, back and wings; pink and peach head; peach chest; green stump	267	1,500.00	1,750.00	750.00

Pelican, 1946-1953

The original price of this model was 6/6d.

Backstamp: **A.** Blue handwritten "Wade England," date and name of model
B. Green-brown ink stamp "Wade England"
C. Black ink stamp "Wade England"
D. Handwritten "Pelican Wade England 1939"

Name	Colourways	Size	U.S. $	Can. $	U.K. £
Pelican	White; bright yellow beak; pale green feather tips; brown/orange feet; black claws	170	800.00	900.00	420.00
Pelican	White; yellow beak; brown feet; black claws	170	800.00	900.00	420.00
Pelican	Pearl white with green feathering; yellow/black eyes and feet	170	800.00	900.00	420.00

Penguin

Backstamp: Handwritten "Wade England"

Name	Colourways	Size	U.S. $	Can. $	U.K. £
Penguin	Grey-blue and white; beige feet	65 x 40	750.00	850.00	375.00

Rose Breasted Grosbeak, c.1939

Backstamp: Blue hand written "Wade England Rose Breasted Grosbeak"

Name	Colourways	Size	U.S. $	Can. $	U.K. £
Rose Breasted Grosbeak	Blue; yellow beak; red breast; green; pink floral base	115 x 115	750.00	850.00	375.00

Sapsucker, 1939

This model named "Sapsucker" is from the same mould as Woodpecker, Style Two. The Sapsucker is a native North American bird.

Backstamp: Blue hand written "Wade England Sapsucker"

Name	Colourways	Size	U.S. $	Can. $	U.K. £
Sapsucker	Black and white; red patch on head and throat; blue green trunk	184	1,000.00	1,150.00	500.00

Seagull On Rock, c.1948-1953

This rarely found model was produced in the late 1940s and reissued in 1953. The original price of the reissue was 3/-.

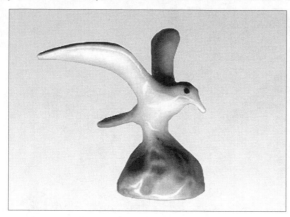 

Backstamp: **A.** Black ink stamp "Wade Made in England"
B. Black transfer "Wade England," 1953

Name	Colourways	Size	U.S. $	Can. $	U.K. £
Seagull	White; grey head; blue rock	40	450.00	500.00	225.00
Seagull	Grey and white; pale blue rock	40	450.00	500.00	225.00

Toucan, 1946-1953

The original issue price for the "Toucan" was 10/-.

*Photograph not available
at press time*

Backstamp: **A.** Green-brown ink stamp "Wade England"
B. Black ink stamp "Wade England"

Name	Colourways	Size	U.S. $	Can. $	U.K. £
Toucan	White; dark grey head and wings; orange beak; brown stum	175	1,000.00	1,150.00	500.00
Toucan	White; light grey head and wings; orange beak; beige stamp	175	1,000.00	1,150.00	500.00

Woodpecker, 1939-1953

The original issue price for the "Woodpecker" was 10/-.

| Woodpecker, Type One 1939 Issue | Woodpecker, Type Two c.1939 Issue | Woodpecker, Type Three First Version, 1940 Issue | Woodpecker, Type Three Second Version, 1946-1953 |

Backstamp:
- **A.** Blue ink hand written "Wade England Woodpecker"
- **B.** Blue hand written "Wade England 1940 Woodpecker"
- **C.** Green brown ink stamp "Wade England"
- **D:** Black ink stamp "Wade England"

Type One: Long branch curving upward; Woodpecker's head tilts forward its beak almost touching the branch (1939)

Name	Colourways	Size	U.S. $	Can. $	U.K. £
Woodpecker	White body; blue head, wings and tail; orange beak, feet; green tree trunk	155	700.00	825.00	350.00
Woodpecker	white body; red head, green wings and tail; grey beak/feet; mottled orange tree trunk	155	700.00	825.00	350.00

Type Two: Short branch; Woodpecker upright, head tilted down, slightly left (c.1939)

Name	Colourways	Size	U.S. $	Can. $	U.K. £
Woodpecker	Black and white striped wings and tail; maroon patch on head and chest; black beak; grey feet; jade green tree trunk	184	700.00	825.00	350.00

Type Three, First Version: Short branch; Woodpecker upright, head looking left (1940)

Name	Colourways	Size	U.S. $	Can. $	U.K. £
Woodpecker	White body; bright blue head, wings and tail; brown/orange beak; green tree trunk	184	700.00	825.00	350.00

Type Three, Second Version: Short branch; Woodpecker upright, head looking left (1946-1953)

Name	Colourways	Size	U.S. $	Can. $	U.K. £
Woodpecker	White body; maroon patch on head and stripe on chest; mottled green/orange wings and tail; mottled orange and green tree trunk	184	700.00	825.00	300.00

BISCUIT PORCELAIN MODELS, 1976-1982

THE CONNOISSEURS COLLECTION, 1978-1982

This series of 12 British birds was made in the same biscuit porcelain as that used for the *World of Survival* animals. The models are all slip cast and produced in their natural colours and settings. Their original retail prices ranged from £20 to £45. Set 1 was issued without plinths while Set 2 was issued with circular polished wooden plinths.

Set 1 Without Plinths

Goldcrest

Nuthatch

Robin

Wren

Backstamp: Black transfer "The Connoisseurs Collection by Wade of England," model name and number

Name	Colourways	Size	U.S. $	Can. $	U.K. £
Bullfinch	Black head; brown body; pink breast; yellow caterpillar	185	500.00	575.00	250.00
Coaltit	Black/grey bird; green holly; red berries	145	500.00	575.00	250.00
Goldcrest	Yellow stripe on head; off-white body; brown branch	135	500.00	575.00	250.00
Nuthatch	Grey/white bird; yellow/brown log	125	500.00	575.00	250.00
Robin	Brown body; red breast; orange mushrooms	125	500.00	575.00	250.00
Wren	Brown bird; grey stones	115	500.00	575.00	250.00

Set 2 - With Plinths

Three of the illustrations are shown without their base due to adhesive failure over time.

Bearded Tit

Kingfisher

Woodpecker (on plinth)

Dipper

Yellow Wagtail

Backstamp: Stamped on metal disk set in base "The Connoisseurs Collection by Wade of England," model name and number

Name	Colourways	Size	U.S. $	Can. $	U.K. £
Bearded Tit	Reddish brown; grey head	165	550.00	600.00	275.00
Dipper	Light brown/pale brown bird; grey pebbles	140	550.00	600.00	275.00
Kingfisher	Blue/grey/white/orange; grey stump	180	550.00	600.00	275.00
Redstart	Grey/black/reddish brown	180	550.00	600.00	275.00
Woodpecker	Red/white/black/yellow; brown/yellow stump	165	550.00	600.00	275.00
Yellow Wagtail	Pale yellow/grey/black; grey/brown pebbles	115	550.00	600.00	275.00

Ruddy Duck, 1976

The "Ruddy Duck" is a slip-cast model produced in a bisque porcelain and was commissioned by Sir Peter Scott of the Slimbridge Wildfowl Trust. Issued in a limited edition of 3,500 the original price was £1.75. The base, or nest, the duck sits in is embossed Wade England, the duck itself is unmarked

Backstamp: Embossed "Wade England"

Name	Colourways	Size	U.S. $	Can. $	U.K. £
Ruddy Duck	Red-brown body; black head, wings; blue bill, black base	35	500.00	575.00	250.00
Ruddy Duck	Red-brown body; black head, wings; blue bill, grey base	35	500.00	575.00	250.00

CHARACTER, TOBY JUGS and DECANTERS

Toby jugs are named after an 18th-century drinking character named Toby Philpot. The first toby jug was produced in the early 18th century by the Ralph Wood Pottery of Burslem, Staffordshire. It was modelled after Toby Philpot sitting on a barrel with a glass of ale in his hand, and carries his name. The Wadeheath Pottery produced few character and toby jugs. Toby jugs represent the full figure of a person; character jugs depict only the head and shoulders.

BACKSTAMPS

Ink Stamps

Jugs and tankards produced from the late 1940s to the early 1950s are stamped with some variation of "Wade Heath England" or "Wade England."

Reddish brown ink stamp, c.1948-c.1955

Transfer Prints

From 1953 to the present, most jugs and tankards, except for Ulster Ware, were given transfer-printed backstamps.

Transfer print, 1953--c.1968

Commissioned pieces issued from the mid 1950s included the name Wade Regicor in the backstamp:

Trasnfer print, c.1953-c.1958

CHARACTER JUGS, c.1948-1968

Coachman, c.1948

A horse whip forms the handle of this jug.

Backstamp: Black ink stamp "Wade England"

Name	Colourways	Size	U.S. $	Can. $	U.K. £
Coachman	Green	Miniature/80	70.00	75.00	35.00

Fisherman, c.1948-c.1953

A fish forms the handle of this jug.

Backstamp: **A.** Grey ink stamp "Wade England"
B. Red transfer print "Wade England"

Name	Colourways	Size	U.S. $	Can. $	U.K. £
Fisherman	Beige/pink	Miniature/75	70.00	75.00	35.00
Fisherman	Dark green	Miniature/75	70.00	75.00	35.00
Fisherman	Light green	Miniature/75	70.00	75.00	35.00

George Wimpey PLC

This caricature character jug was commissioned by George Wimpey PLC. George Wimpey are well known house builders in the UK. No other information has been found to date.

Wimpey Green Colourway

Wimpey Orange Hat Colourway

Backstamp: Embossed "George Wimpey PLC Wade" with 'W' Wimpey logo.

Name	Colourways	Size	U.S. $	Can. $	U.K. £
George Wimpey	Green	95 x 120	90.00	100.00	45.00
George Wimpey	Orange hat and handle; pink face; white collar; red tie	95 x 120	110.00	125.00	55.00

Indian Chief, c.1958-c.1962

The "Indian Chief" wears a feathered bonnet.

*Photograph not available
at press time*

Backstamp: Red transfer print "Wade England"

Name	Colourways	Size	U.S. $	Can. $	U.K. £
Indian Chief	White/brown war bonnet; brown shoulders	Unknown	Possibly not put into production		

Jim, 1968

This character jug was modelled as the head and shoulders of a smiling man and based on the well-loved British radio and television comedian Jimmy Edwards, famous for his handlebar moustache.

Backstamp: Black ink stamp "Wade Regicor, Hand painted in Staffordshire England" with "Toby Jim Jug" impressed on the back of the collar

Name	Colourways	Size	U.S. $	Can. $	U.K. £
Jim	Black hat; brown moustache; green coat	Large/110	180.00	200.00	95.00

R.C.M.P., c.1958-c.1962

This jug depicts the head and shoulders of an R.C.M.P. offier in uniform with a wide brimmed hat

*Photograph not available
at press time*

Backstamp: Red transfer print "Wade England"

Name	Colourways	Size	U.S. $	Can. $	U.K. £
R.C.M.P.	Brown hat; red jacket	Unknown	Possibly not put into production		

McCallum

These character jugs are in the form of a bearded Scotsman wearing a Glengarry, with the ribbons forming the handle. They were first issued by Wade in the early 1950s, then reissued in collaboration with Regicor in the late 1950s.

A Melbourne, Australia company produced the McCallum jugs in a darker amber glaze, their version has an incised 'Elischer' backstamp. The same jug has also been seen with only an incised shape number 219, and has also been found unmarked. The Elischer version is much lighter in weight because the porcelain is much thinner. Some examples are smaller than the Wade models. The detailing on the Australian version is not as pronounced as the Wade model. The two jugs are shown below, the Wade jug is on the left, the difference in the detail can easily be seen when the two are side by side.

Large, Medium and Small McCallum Jugs

Wade McCallum on left, Australian McCallum on right

Backstamp: **A.** "Wade Regicor, London, England"
B. Ink stamp "Wade England"
C. Ink stamp "Wade made in England Hand Painted"

Name	Colourways	Size	U.S. $	Can. $	U.K. £
McCallum	Honey	Miniature/70	125.00	150.00	60.00
McCallum	Amber	Miniature/70	150.00	175.00	75.00
McCallum	Honey	Small/115	140.00	160.00	70.00
McCallum	Amber	Small/115	170.00	200.00	85.00
McCallum	Honey	Large/160	200.00	225.00	100.00
McCallum	Amber	Large/160	230.00	260.00	115.00
McCallum	Coloured pink face	Large/160	150.00	175.00	75.00

Pipe Maker, c.1948-c.1953

This miniature character jug has a clay pipe forming the handle.

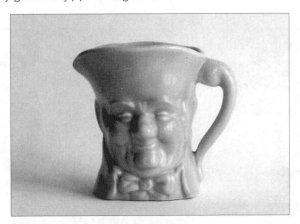

Backstamp: Black ink stamp "Wade England"

Name	Colourways	Size	U.S. $	Can. $	U.K. £
Pipe Maker	Light green	Miniature/75	70.00	75.00	35.00

Sailor, c.1948

This miniature character jug depicts the head of an 18th-century sailor. A plaited rope forms the handle.

Backstamp: Black ink stamp "Wade England"

Name	Colourways	Size	U.S. $	Can. $	U.K. £
Sailor	Green	Miniature/75	70.00	75.00	35.00
Sailor	Honey	Miniature/75	70.00	75.00	35.00
Sailor	Pink	Miniature/75	70.00	75.00	35.00
Sailor	Green and black patterned hat; honey face; brown handle	Miniature/75	100.00	115.00	50.00

TOBY JUGS, c.1948-c.1955

Charrington

"Charrington"

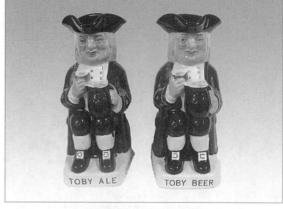

"Toby Ale" and "Toby Beer"

Backstamp: "Wade Regicor, London England, Hand Painted

Name	Colourways	Size	U.S. $	Can. $	U.K. £
Charrington	Maroon trousers; dark green coat; lettering "Charrington"	180	350.00	400.00	170.00
Toby Ale	Maroon trousers; dark green coat; lettering "Toby Ale"	180	350.00	400.00	170.00
Toby Beer	Maroon trousers; dark green coat; black lettering "Toby Beer"	180	350.00	400.00	170.00

Highway Man, c.1948-c.1955

There were 1,000 "Highway Man" toby jugs issued.

Backstamp: **A.** Brown ink stamp "Wade England" inside an ornate crown
B. Black ink stamp "Wade England Highway Man"

Name	Colourways	Size	U.S. $	Can. $	U.K. £
Highway Man	Copper lustre	150	175.00	200.00	90.00
Highway Man	Gold lustre	150	175.00	200.00	90.00
Highway Man	Black coat	150	275.00	300.00	135.00
Highway Man	Red coat	150	275.00	300.00	135.00

Pirate, c.1948-c.1955

There were 750 "Pirate" toby jugs produced.

Backstamp: **A.** Brown ink stamp "Wade England" inside an ornate crown, with the model name
B. Black ink stamp "Wade England Pirate"

Name	Colourways	Size	U.S. $	Can. $	U.K. £
Pirate	Copper lustre	150	175.00	200.00	90.00
Pirate	Gold lustre	150	175.00	200.00	90.00
Pirate	Black/yellow hat; green/yellow coat; purple trousers	150	275.00	300.00	135.00
Pirate	Black hat; green coat; blue trousers	150	275.00	300.00	135.00

Toby Philpot, c.1953-c.1958

The miniature toby depicts a seated Toby Philpot holding a pint of ale. It has a straight handle. The small and large Toby Philpots are sitting with a glass of ale in one hand and a jug in the other.

Photograph not available
at press time

Backstamp: **A.** Red transfer print "Wade England"
B. Black transfer print "Wade Rigicor, Hand painted in Staffordshire, England"

Name	Colourways	Size	U.S. $	Can. $	U.K. £
Toby Philpot	Green coat; black hat, trousers, shoes	Miniature/75	75.00	85.00	40.00
Toby Philpot	Black hat, shoes; white/silver buckles; green coat; red trousers	Small/115	150.00	175.00	75.00
Toby Philpot	Black hat, shoes; white/silver buckles; green coat; red trousers	Large/180	150.00	175.00	75.00

DECANTERS, c.1938-1987

Abbot's Choice Decanter, c.1980 and 1987

This decanter was first produced c.1980 in a honey-amber glaze, with the volume of the contents listed on the label in fluid ounces. In 1987 a second bottle was issued, which was labeled in centilitres.

Backstamp: **A.** Embossed "Made Exclusively for the Abbots Choice Scotch Whisky John McEwan & Co. Ltd. Leith, Scotland"
B. Embossed "Made Exclusively for the Abbots Choice Scotch Whisky John McEwan & Co. Ltd. Leith, Scotland Liquor Bottle Scotland"

Name	Colourways	Size	U.S. $	Can. $	U.K. £
Decanter/Fluid ounces	Honey-amber	255	125.00	150.00	65.00
Decanter/Centilitres	Burnt umber	253	125.00	150.00	60.00

Asprey & Co. Ltd., London

Two whiskey flasks, one depicting a Scotsman and the other an Irishman, were commissioned in the late 1920s to late 1930s by Asprey and Co. Ltd., New Bond Street, London, England.

Each was set within a wooden tantalus, and the heads of the flasks are detachable. The Scotsman contained Scottish whisky and the Irishman, Irish whiskey (native to each country).

Many liquor companies commissioned containers from different factories in the Potteries. When a repeat order was necessary, and for whatever reason the original pottery was unable to fill it, the commissioner turned to the other potteries, Wade being one.

The moulds belonged to the commissioning company, so to move the orders between companies was simple.

Wade produced the containers in the late 1930s.

Backstamp: **A.** Irishman; Hand written black ink "Wade England for Asprey & Co. London Reg No 675852"
B. Scotsman; Hand written black ink "Wade England for Asprey & Co. London Reg No 675853"

Name	Colourways	Size	U.S. $	Can. $	U.K. £
Irishman	Dark green hat and jacket; orange headband; white pipe, shirt and handkerchief; pink waistcoat	230	475.00	525.00	240.00
Scotsman	Dark red tam; black and white check band; green-black jacket; black base	242	475.00	525.00	240.00

George Sandeman and Co. Ltd., 1958-1960

Backstamp: Embossed "Wade England," white transfer print "Wade England"

Name	Colourways	Size	U.S. $	Can. $	U.K. £
Sandeman Port	Black; ruby red glass	215	80.00	90.00	40.00
Sandeman Sherry	Black; golden yellow glass	215	80.00	90.00	40.00

CHILDREN'S SETS

Whenever a subject attracted the attention of the general public, the Wade potteries were quick to imitate it on their nursery wares with colourful transfer prints that illustrated well-known characters from a children's book, a television series or a cartoon film.

A large number of toy tea sets were produced by Wade Heath in the 1930s. Because these sets were all decorated with transfer prints, the prints could be alternated between cups, plates, jugs and sugar bowls (at the decorator's whim). The name of the character is usually included in black or red lettering.

For Disney Nursery Ware and Toy Tea Sets see pages 178 to 181 and 187 to 192 respectively.

CHILDREN'S NURSERY WARE, 1939-1957

Noddy, 1955

This set was first produced in 1955, two different backstamps have been found. It is probable that the first backstamp (A) did not have the copyright details and was changed for the second backstamp (B). The baby plate has a thick raised rim and is heavy so that it stays in place more easily.

Transfer Prints: Big Ears with Balloons   The Naughty Golliwog   Noddy and his Car
                      Noddy Would you like a Ride   Various small toys

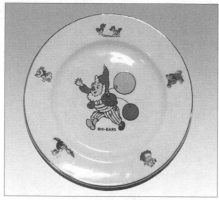

Large plate "Big Ears with Balloons"

Mug "Big Ears with Ballons"

Cup "Naughty Golliwog"

Baby plate "Noddy and his Car"

Backstamp: **A.** Circular gold printed "Royal Victoria Wade England Pottery"
              B. Black printed "Wade England Copyright 1953 by Noddy Subsidiary Rights Co. Ltd"

Name	Colourways	Size	U.S. $	Can. $	U.K. £
Baby plate	White; multicoloured print of Noddy and his car	177	60.00	70.00	30.00
Beaker, no handle	White; multicoloured print of Big Ears and Noddy	60	60.00	70.00	30.00
Beaker, with handle	White; multicoloured print of Big Ears with balloons	75	60.00	70.00	30.00
Cup/saucer	Cup — white; multicoloured print Naughty Golliwog Saucer — white; multicoloured print of Noddy	61/140	70.00	80.00	35.00
Mug	White; multicoloured print of Big Ears with balloons	82	60.00	70.00	30.00
Oatmeal bowl	White; multicoloured print of Big Ears and Noddy	152	60.00	70.00	30.00
Plate, large	White; multicoloured print of Big Ears with balloons	205	60.00	70.00	30.00
Plate, small	White; multicoloured print	152	60.00	70.00	30.00

Panda

The band on this design is wider than that found on the Pandy design.

Photograph not available
at press time

Backstamp: Green ink stamp "Wade Heath England" (round W 1937-1940)

Name	Colourways	Size	U.S. $	Can. $	U.K. £
Baby plate	White; green band; black and white panda sitting; black lettering	171	60.00	70.00	30.00
Beaker	White; green band; black and white panda	88	60.00	70.00	30.00
Cup and saucer	White; green band; black and white panda waling; black lettering	63/144	70.00	80.00	35.00
Mug	White; green band; black and white panda	82	60.00	70.00	30.00
Plate	White; green band; black and white panda sitting; black lettering	153	60.00	70.00	30.00

Pandy

There is a slight difference in the transfers on the Pandy set. The panda bear on this design is shown, when seated, with a ball and the word Pandy. The ball is between the Panda's legs.

Backstamp: Green ink stamp "Wade Heath England" (round W 1937-1940)

Name	Colourways	Size	U.S. $	Can. $	U.K. £
Baby plate	White; green band/grass; black and white sitting pandy; black lettering; black ball with green stripes	171	60.00	70.00	30.00
Beaker	White; green band; black and white panda	88	60.00	70.00	30.00
Cup and saucer	White; green band; black and white walking pandy; black lettering	63/144	70.00	80.00	35.00
Mug	White; green band; black and white panda	82	60.00	70.00	30.00
Plate	White; green band/grass; black and white sitting pandy; black lettering; black ball with green stripes	153	60.00	70.00	30.00

Quack ! Quack !, c.1949-1957

The set features a Comic Duck family.

Backstamp: Black printed "Quack - Quacks by Robert Barlow Wade England" with a multicoloured print of Dack pulling at a worm

Name	Colourways	Size	U.S. $	Can. $	U.K. £
Baby plate	White; multicoloured print of Duck family at pond	180	60.00	70.00	30.00
Cup and saucer	Cup — White; multicoloured print of Mrs. Duck and Dack (son) at picnic; Saucer —White; multicoloured print of ducklings around rim	63/144	70.00	80.00	35.00
Milk jug, ½ pint	White; multicoloured print of Mr. and Mrs. Duck holding hands	88	60.00	70.00	30.00
Mug	White; multicoloured print of Mr. and Mrs. Duck holding hands	82	60.00	70.00	30.00
Oatmeal bowl	White; multicoloured print of Mr. and Mrs. Duck talking	159	60.00	70.00	30.00
Plate, large	White; multicoloured print of Duck family at pond	205	60.00	70.00	30.00
Plate, small	White; multicoloured print of Mr. and Mrs. Duck talking	153	60.00	70.00	30.00

CHILDREN'S TOY TEA AND DINNER SETS, c.1935–1955

The toy tea and dinner items were produced in small and large sizes. The larger sizes are believed to be from the dinner sets, which would comprise of, as well as the larger cups, saucers, plates, teapot, sugar, milk jug, a platter and a vegetable tureen. A complete boxed dinner set has not yet been reported.

Berries Set

Backstamp: Black ink stamp "England" (c.1938)

Name	Colourways	Size	U.S. $	Can. $	U.K. £
Cup and saucer	White; red berries, green leaves	48	50.00	60.00	25.00
Milk jug	White; red berries; green leaves	50	50.00	60.00	25.00
Plate	White; red berries; green leaves	120	50.00	60.00	25.00
Sugar bowl	White; red berries; green leaves	35	50.00	60.00	25.00
Teapot	White; red berries; green leaves	85	70.00	80.00	35.00

Floral Set

This set has a transfer printed design of small flowers and leaves.

*Photograph of this
design not available
at press time*

Backstamp: Black ink stamp "England" (c.1938)

Name	Colourways	Size	U.S. $	Can. $	U.K. £
Cup and saucer	White; multicoloured print	46/95	50.00	60.00	25.00
Milk jug	White; multicoloured print	50	50.00	60.00	25.00
Plate	White; multicoloured print	130	50.00	60.00	25.00
Sugar bowl	White; multicoloured print	35	50.00	60.00	25.00
Teapot	White; multicoloured print	85	70.00	80.00	35.00

Muffin The Mule and Friends, c.1950

This toy tea set was produced in the early 1950s, the five characters depicted are *Muffin the Mule* and his friends *Louise the Lamb*, *Peregrine the Penguin*, *Oswald the Ostrich* and *Grace the Giraffe* all puppets from an early 1950's BBC television programme called *Children's Hour*.

Muffin and his friends were string puppets who performed on top of a grand piano while the presenter, Annette Mills, played and sang songs she had written for the programme. Ms. Mills was the sister of Sir John Mills the British actor. The dishes in this tea set do not have the characteristic orange bands that are seen on the Walt Disney toy dishes.

Transfer Prints

| Louise the Lamb | Oswald the Ostrich | Muffin the Mule |
| Peregrine the Penguin | Grace the giraffe | |

Backstamp: **A.** Ink stamp "Wade Heath England"
B. England

Name	Colourways	Size	U.S. $	Can. $	U.K. £
Cup and saucer	White; multicoloured print	48/95	50.00	60.00	25.00
Milk jug	White; multicoloured print	50	50.00	60.00	25.00
Plate, large	White; multicoloured print	127	50.00	60.00	25.00
Sugar bowl	White; multicoloured print	35	50.00	60.00	25.00
Teapot, large	White; multicoloured print	89	70.00	80.00	35.00
Teapot, small	White; multicoloured print	76	70.00	80.00	35.00

Noddy, 1955

To date only one plate in the Noddy toy tea set has been reported.

Name	Colourways	Size	U.S. $	Can. $	U.K. £
Plate, large	White; multicoloured print, Noddy and his car "Would you like a Ride"	127	50.00	60.00	25.00

Nursery Rhymes, c.1935

A variety of nursery rhyme verses are printed in black lettering on these pieces.

Transfer prints: ABC Tumble Down
Little Jumping Joan
Simple Simon Met a Pieman
Little Jack Horner

Ding Dong Bell, Pussy's in the Well
Ring a Roses
What are Little Girls Made of

Backstamp: **A.** Ink stamp "Wade Heath England"
B. Ink stamp "England"
C. Unmarked

Name	Colourways	Size	U.S. $	Can. $	U.K. £
Cup and saucer	White; multicoloured print; black lettering	46/95	50.00	60.00	25.00
Milk jug	White; multicoloured print; black lettering	50	50.00	60.00	25.00
Plate	White; multicoloured print; black lettering	130	50.00	60.00	25.00
Sugar bowl	White; multicoloured print; black lettering	35	50.00	60.00	25.00
Teapot	White; multicoloured print; black lettering	85	70.00	80.00	35.00

Pandy, 1939

As a result of the arrival of the baby panda Ming Ming at the London Zoo on Christmas Eve 1938, Wadeheath produced two sets of nursery ware with a Panda as the central design.

Pandy Set

The band on this design is wider than that found on the Pandy design. The ball is to the left of the Panda.

Backstamp: Green ink stamp "Wade Heath England" (round W 1937-1940)

Name	Colourways	Size	U.S. $	Can. $	U.K. £
Cup and saucer	White; green band, black and white panda	46/95	70.00	80.00	35.00
Milk Jug	White; green band, black and white panda face	50	60.00	70.00	30.00
Plate	White; green band; black and white panda	130	60.00	70.00	30.00
Sugar Bowl	White; green band; black and white panda face	35	60.00	70.00	30.00
Teapot	White; green band; black and white panda	88	60.00	70.00	30.00

Prudence The Cat, c.1935

Backstamp: Black ink stamp "England"

Name	Colourways	Size	U.S. $	Can. $	U.K. £
Cup and saucer	White; red, white and grey print	46/95	50.00	60.00	25.00
Milk jug	White; red, white and grey print	50	50.00	60.00	25.00
Plate	White; red, white and grey print	130	50.00	60.00	25.00
Sugar bowl	White; red, white and grey print	35	50.00	60.00	25.00
Teapot	White; red, white and grey print	85	70.00	80.00	35.00

COMMEMORATIVE WARE

The Wade potteries, primarily Wadeheath, have issued a large line of commemoratives. In 1935 Wade began its range of commemorative ware with items marking the silver jubilee of King George V and Queen Mary. Since then Wade has issued commemoratives for coronations, the silver jubilee of Queen Elizabeth, royal birthdays, royal weddings and royal births, as well as for less regal occasions.

The models are listed according to the event they commemorate, which appear here in chronological order.

BACKSTAMPS

Ink Stamps

From 1935 to 1953, the backstamps used on commemorative items were black ink stamps that included the name Wadeheath. A green ink stamped "Wade England" was introduced on some of the 1953 coronation ware.

Black ink stamp, 1937

Green ink stamp, 1953

Embossed Stamps

Also beginning in 1953, the Wade backstamp was either embossed on the model or applied on a transfer print.

Embossed, 1981

Transfer Prints

Transfer print, 1981-1990

KING GEORGE V AND QUEEN MARY SILVER JUBILEE, 1935

To celebrate the silver jubilee of George V and Queen Mary in May 1935, Wadeheath produced a set of *Jubilee Ware*. These items have transfer prints of King George V and Queen Mary on the front.

*Photograph not available
at press time*

Backstamp: Black ink stamp "Wadeheath England" with a lion

Name	Colourways	Size	U.S. $	Can. $	U.K. £
Child's Beaker	Cream; multicoloured print	75	70.00	80.00	35.00
Child's Dish	Cream; multicoloured print	165	70.00	80.00	35.00
Cup and saucer	Cream; multicoloured print	65/140	70.00	80.00	35.00
Mug	Cream; multicoloured print	Footed/135	70.00	80.00	35.00
Plate	Cream; multicoloured print	Octagonal/165	70.00	80.00	35.00

EDWARD VIII CORONATION, 1937

Wade produced a small amount of commemorative pottery for the coronation of King Edward VIII. Some of the pottery was adapted from miniature jug designs already in production at the Wade Heath Pottery. A limited supply of these jugs was produced with a multicoloured transfer print of Edward on the front and a design of flags and a scroll with the words "Long May He Reign" on the back. With the abdication of Edward, the jugs were withdrawn from sale and the transfers replaced with those of George VI and Queen Elizabeth.

The jugs are miniature and come with short- and long-loop handles and a handle of three rings. They have V-shaped moulded spouts and bright orange and blue bands around their bases and handles. The loving cup has a musical box in the base, held in place by a wooden disc, which plays "God Save the King" when lifted. The words "Long May He Reign" are printed on a gold band across the front and "Coronation King Edward VIII May 12th 1937" is on the back.

Jug, long-loop handle   Jug, short-loop handle

Loving Cup, musical

Backstamp:
- **A.** Black ink stamp "Wadeheath Ware England" and impressed "88M"
- **B.** Black ink stamp "Wadeheath Ware England" and impressed "106M"
- **C.** Black ink stamp "Wadeheath England" with a lion and impressed "113M"
- **D.** Black ink stamp "Wadeheath Ware England"

Name	Colourways	Size	U.S. $	Can. $	U.K. £
Jug, long-loop handle	Cream; orange/blue bands; multicoloured print	140	100.00	115.00	50.00
Jug, short-loop handle	Cream; orange/blue bands; multicoloured print	140	100.00	115.00	50.00
Jug, three-rings handle	Cream; orange/blue bands; multicoloured print	135	100.00	115.00	50.00
Loving Cup, musical	Cream; red/white/blue striped handles; red/blue/green print	125	400.00	450.00	200.00

KING GEORGE VI AND QUEEN ELIZABETH CORONATION, 1937

To commemorate the coronation on May 12, 1937, Wade issued several new items as well as reissuing the Edward VIII commemorative ware by replacing the original transfer prints of Edward with prints of George VI and Queen Elizabeth.

Coronation Bowls

This was a limited edition of 250 bowls. They were issued in all-over glazes of royal blue, orange and light green. A signed, limited edition of 25 bowls was issued in white with gold decoration.

White and gold decoration

Light green

Backstamp: **A.** Black ink stamp "Manufactured in England by Wadeheath and Co Ltd to Commemorate the Coronation of King George VI and Queen Elizabeth May 12th 1937. 'Long May They Reign'" and the signature of Robert R. Barlow

B. Black ink stamp "Wadeheath England" and a lion

C. Embossed "Made in England Coronation 1937"

Name	Colourways	Size	U.S. $	Can. $	U.K. £
Bowl	White and gold decoration	290	400.00	450.00	200.00
Bowl	White and silver decoration	290	400.00	450.00	200.00
Bowl	Mottled orange	290	200.00	225.00	100.00
Bowl	Light green	120	50.00	55.00	28.00
Bowl	Royal blue	120	50.00	55.00	28.00

Coronation Beaker and Plate

The beaker and plate are the same shapes as those used for the Silver Jubilee of King George V and Queen Mary. Both have a multicoloured transfer print of George VI and Queen Elizabeth.

Backstamp: "Wadeheath Ware England"

Name	Colourways	Size	U.S. $	Can. $	U.K. £
Beaker	White; multicoloured print	75	70.00	80.00	35.00
Square-cornered plate	White; multicoloured print	155	70.00	80.00	35.00

Coronation Children's Tea Set

This unusual child's tea set was from the same mould as the Wadeheath Disney children's tea set. The boxed set comprised 12 pieces—four cups, four saucers, a teapot and lid, a milk jug and a sugar bowl. The original box is blue, with a label that reads "Coronation Nursery Ware," along with portraits of the King and Queen.

Backstamp: Black transfer "Wadeheath England"

Name	Colourways	Size	U.S. $	Can. $	U.K. £
Cup and saucer	Cream; multicoloured print	48	80.00	90.00	40.00
Milk Jug	Cream; multicoloured print	49	40.00	45.00	20.00
Sugar Bowl	Cream; multicoloured print	37	40.00	45.00	20.00
Teapot	Cream; multicoloured print	83	80.00	90.00	40.00

Coronation Decorative Ware

The same three shapes used for the Edward VIII coronation jugs and loving cup were reused here, with the transfer prints changed to show King George VI and Queen Elizabeth. On the back of the jugs is a portrait of Princess Elizabeth. The "Coronation Musical Loving Cup" plays "God Save the King" and has the words "Long May They Reign'" on a gold band across the front and the initials *GR* on the back.

Jug, three-ring handle; Jug, long-loop handle

Coronation Plate

Coronation Mug

Coronation Cup and Saucer

Backstamp:
- **A.** Black ink stamp "Wadeheath England" and a lion
- **B.** Black ink stamp "Wadeheath Ware England" and an impressed "88M"
- **C.** Black ink stamp "Wadeheath England," a lion and an impressed "106M"
- **D.** Black ink stamp "Wadeheath Ware England" and an impressed "106M"
- **E.** Black ink stamp "Wadeheath England," a lion and an impressed "113M"
- **F.** Black ink stamp "Wadeheath Ware"
- **G.** Black ink stamp "Wadeheath Ware England"

Name	Colourways	Size	U.S. $	Can. $	U.K. £
Cup and saucer	White; multicoloured print	71/142	80.00	90.00	40.00
Jug, long-loop handle	Cream; orange/blue bands; multicoloured print	140	80.00	90.00	40.00
Jug, short-loop handle	Cream; orange/blue bands; multicoloured print	140	80.00	90.00	40.00
Jug, three-ring handle	Cream; orange/blue bands; multicoloured print	135	80.00	90.00	40.00
Loving Cup, musical	Cream; red/white/blue striped handles; multicoloured print	125	600.00	700.00	300.00
Milk Jug	Cream; orange spout, handle; multicoloured print	108	70.00	80.00	35.00
Mug	White; multicoloured print	72	70.00	80.00	35.00
Square-cornered plate	Cream; multicoloured print	155	70.00	80.00	35.00

KING GEORGE VI AND QUEEN ELIZABETH
ROYAL VISIT TO CANADA MAY, 1939

To date only one commemorative item produced by Wade for the Royal visit to Canada has been reported.

Backstamp: Ink stamp "Wadeheath England"

Name	Colourways	Size	U.S. $	Can. $	U.K. £
Baby plate	White; multicoloured print of King George and Queen Elizabeth and Canadian Maple leaf; black lettering	160	70.00	80.00	35.00

QUEEN ELIZABETH II CORONATION, 1953

Christmas 1952

This 1953 Coronation Christmas Dish has an unusual embossed inscription on the back rim which reads "Christmas 1952 With Compliments From Wade (Ulster) LTD Portadown." It would appear perhaps the employees of Wade Ireland were presented with a 'Coronation' dish as a Christmas gift from the pottery. The "Coronation Christmas Dish" was a scaled-down replica of the 1937 "Coronation Bowl."

Backstamp: Embossed "Wade England Coronation 1953" and "Christmas 1953 With Compliments From Wade (Ulster) LTD Portadown" embossed around the back rim

Name	Colourways	Size	U.S. $	Can. $	U.K. £
Christmas dish	Blue	120	50.00	70.00	35.00

Beakers, Cups and Saucers, 1953

Commemorative items with multicoloured transfer prints were produced by Wade England and Wade Ireland to celebrate the coronation of Queen Elizabeth II on June 2, 1953.

Backstamp: **A.** Large green ink stamp "Wade England"

Child's Beaker

Regency Cup

B. Small green ink stamp "Wade England"
C. Multicoloured transfer print "Coronation of Her Majesty Queen Elizabeth II Wade England"

Name	Colourways	Size	U.S. $	Can. $	U.K. £
Child's Beaker	White; gold rim, multicoloured print	72	70.00	80.00	35.00
Child's Tea Plate	White; gold rim, multicoloured print	170	70.00	80.00	35.00
Cup, Regency	White; gold rim; multicoloured print	67	70.00	80.00	35.00
Saucer, Regency	White; gold rim; multicoloured print	140	70.00	80.00	35.00
Cup, plain	White; gold rim; multicoloured print	72	70.00	80.00	35.00
Saucer, plain	White; gold rim; multicoloured print	140	70.00	80.00	35.00

Bowls and Dishes

The "Coronation Fruit Bowl" has a fluted body and a multicoloured transfer print of the coat of arms of Queen Elizabeth in the centre. The first "Coronation Dessert Bowl" has gold emblems around the rim and the royal coat of arms in the centre; the second has a fluted body and a portrait of Queen Elizabeth in the centre.

Backstamp: **A.** Raised "Wade England Coronation 1953"
B. Green transfer print "Wade England"
C. Small green ink stamp "Wade England"
D. Embossed "Coronation 1953" with embossed Hand and Owl (c.1950-1953)

Name	Colourways	Size	U.S. $	Can. $	U.K. £
Dish	Dark green	120	25.00	30.00	12.00
Dish	Turquoise	120	25.00	30.00	12.00
Dish	Beige	120	25.00	30.00	12.00
Dish	Dark blue	120	25.00	30.00	12.00
Dish	Honey brown	120	25.00	30.00	12.00
Dish	Light green	120	25.00	30.00	12.00
Dish	Blue	120	25.00	30.00	12.00
Dish	Green	120	25.00	30.00	12.00
Dish	Grey	120	25.00	30.00	15.00
Fruit Bowl, fluted	White; gold rim; multicoloured print	190	40.00	50.00	20.00
Dessert Bowl	White; gold band; multicoloured print	165	40.00	50.00	20.00
Dessert Bowl, fluted	White; gold band, emblems; multicoloured print	165	40.00	50.00	20.00

Jugs

The round milk jug is the same jug as that produced for the 1937 coronation of King George and Queen Elizabeth, except that the transfer print is of Queen Elizabeth II.

Photograph not available
at press time

Backstamp: Large green ink stamp "Wade England"

Name	Colourways	Size	U.S. $	Can. $	U.K. £
Milk Jug	White; gold rim; multicoloured print	108	70.00	80.00	35.00

Plates and Beer Mug

The Regency tea plate has been found with the inscription missing from the blue band around the portrait.

Regency Tea Plate

Wall Plate

Beer Mug

Orb Cup and Saucer

Regency Tea Plate "Queen Elizabeth II"

Backstamp: **A.** Large green ink stamp "Wade England"
B. Green ink stamp "Wade England"

Name	Colourways	Size	U.S. $	Can. $	U.K. £
Regency Tea Plate	White; multicoloured print; "Royal Coat of Arms"	170	40.00	45.00	20.00
Regency Tea Plate	White; multicoloured print; "Queen Elizabeth II"	170	40.00	45.00	20.00
Wall Plate	Maroon; white centre; gold edges; multicoloured print	235	80.00	90.00	40.00
Beer Mug	White; gold/red/blue bands; multicoloured print	Pint/125	70.00	80.00	35.00
Cup/saucer, orb-shaped	White; multicoloured print; "Queen Elizabeth II"	71/142	70.00	80.00	35.00

COMMISSIONED COMMEMORATIVES, 1953

Burrows and Sturgess Dish, 1953

Commissioned by Burrows and Sturgess, which produced Spa Table Waters, this dish has "Burrows and Sturgess Ltd" embossed on the top rim and "Spa Table Waters" on the lower rim. In the centre is an embossed design of a shield and laurel wreath, with the initials *ER*. Encircling the dish are embossed animals and the embossed emblems and names of some of the members of the British Empire—a lion (Great Britain), kangaroo (Australia), kiwi (New Zealand), beaver (Canada), sea lion (Newfoundland), elephant (India) and springbok (South Africa).

Backstamp: Raised "Wade England Coronation 1953" in hollow of base

Name	Colourways	Size	U.S. $	Can. $	U.K. £
Dish	Dark green	120	40.00	45.00	20.00
Dish	Turquoise	120	40.00	45.00	20.00
Dish	Mint green	120	40.00	45.00	20.00
Dish	Amber brown	120	40.00	45.00	20.00

City of Stoke-on-Trent, 1953

This round bowl with the coat of arms of the city of Stoke-on-Trent in the centre was presented as a Coronation Souvenir to the people of Stoke-on-Trent by the Lord Mayor and Lady Mayoress. The inscription on the back reads "With the Compliments of the Lord Mayor and Lady Mayoress Alderman Albert E. Bennett, J.P. and Mrs. Bennett. Coronation Year 1953-4". The bowl also has an unusual "Made in England by Wade of Burslem" backstamp.

Backstamp: Ink "Made in England by Wade of Burslem"

Name	Colourways	Size	U.S. $	Can. $	U.K. £
Bowl	Maroon outside; white inside with multicoloured print	Unknown	40.00	45.00	20.00

Reginald Corfield Ltd., 1953

The water jug is a large round-bodied jug, with a portrait of Queen Elizabeth and June 2nd 1953 on it. Produced in collaboration with Reginald Corfield Ltd., it was intended for use in public houses. (This is the same style jug as that used for Truman's Beer, page 107.)

Photograph not available
at press time

Backstamp: Black transfer print "Wade Regicor England"

Name	Colourways	Size	U.S. $	Can. $	U.K. £
Water Jug	White; multicoloured print	115	50.00	60.00	25.00

Shell Mex and British Petroleum Dish, 1953

This dish is the same as that for Burrows and Sturgess (page 105), with the words "Shell Mex and British Petroleum" on the upper rim and "North Eastern Division" on the lower rim.

Photograph not available
at press time

Backstamp: Raised "Wade England 1953"

Name	Colourways	Size	U.S. $	Can. $	U.K. £
Dish	Dark green	120	40.00	45.00	20.00
Dish	Maroon	120	40.00	45.00	20.00

Truman's - C&S Ales - Watneys, 1953

The same Dutch shape 1953 Coronation Commemorative jug as produced for Truman's Beer was also produced with C&S X-L Ales on the back, and also with a Watney's barrel on the back.

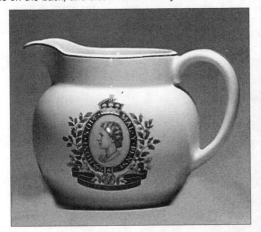

Truman's Beer Jug, Front

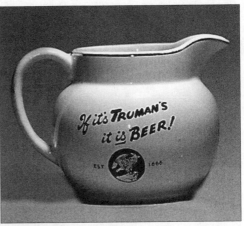

Truman's Beer Jug, Back

C&S X-L Ales Jug

Backstamp: **A.** Black transfer print "Wade Regicor England"
B. Printed "Wade Regicor London England," in laurel leaf frame, large size (1953-1962)

Name	Colourways	Size	U.S. $	Can. $	U.K. £
Jug	White; gold rim; multicoloured print; blue lettering	108	40.00	45.00	20.00
Jug C&S Ales	White; gold rim; multicoloured print on front, green lettering "C&S X-L Ales" on back	108	40.00	45.00	20.00
Jug Watney's Barrel	White; gold rim; multicoloured print	108	40.00	45.00	20.00

QUEEN ELIZABETH II ROYAL VISITS

Compasite Ordnance Depot, 1982

The Compasite Ordnance Depot (COD) in Donnington, Shropshire, England, is one of two locations where all British military equipment is stored. The pint-sized traditional tankard, with a rolled rim, was decorated with a coat of arms and bears the inscription "To commemorate the Royal Visit of Her Majesty to COD Donnington on the 4th June 1982." The tankards were presented to the staff.

Backstamp: Red transfer print "Royal Victoria Pottery Staffordshire Wade England"

Name	Colourways	Size	U.S. $	Can. $	U.K. £
Dish	Black; gold crest and lettering	110	10.00	12.00	5.00
Tankard	White; multicoloured print	Pint/115	30.00	35.00	15.00

New Zealand, 1954

This is the same Coronation Commemorative dish as issued for the 1953 Coronation of Her Majesty Queen Elizabeth II but it has a printed inscription on the back reading "To Commemorate the visit of Her Majesty Queen Elizabeth II to New Zealand 1954.

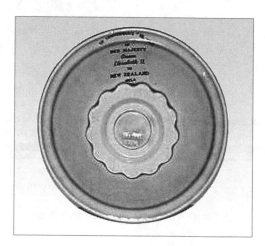

Backstamp: Impressed "Wade England" with added ink stamp inscription as above

Name	Colourways	Size	U.S. $	Can. $	U.K. £
Dish	Dark green	120	50.00	60.00	25.00
Dish	Light green	120	50.00	60.00	25.00

Redbourn Works, June 1958

This traditional tankard has a print of Buckingham Palace on the front and is inscribed on the back "Presented as a memento of the visit of H.M. Queen Elizabeth and H.R.H. Prince Philip to Redbourn Works 27th June 1958" "RTB".

Tankard, Front   Tankard, Back

Backstamp: Red printed "Wade England"

Name	Colourways	Size	U.S. $	Can. $	U.K. £
Traditional Tankard	Cream; multicoloured print; black lettering	½ pint/91	30.00	35.00	15.00

QUEEN ELIZABETH II SILVER JUBILEE, 1977

Dishes

Only a very limited quantity of commemorative ware was produced by Wade for the silver jubilee of Queen Elizabeth II on June 2, 1977.

The unusual "Silver Jubilee Beer Stein" has a pewter lid, which is lifted by pressing down on a thumb lever on the top of the handle. The tankard has a transfer print of Queen Elizabeth and Prince Philip on the front and the words "1952-1977 The Queen's Silver Jubilee."

The "Silver Jubilee Dish" is from the same mould as the 1953 "Coronation Dish." The centre design has been changed to show a crown and a scroll, with the words "The Queen's Silver Jubilee." The names of the countries above the animals have been omitted. The back of the rim is embossed with the words "Part of the proceeds from the sale of this souvenir will be donated to the Queen's Silver Jubilee Appeal." The original price was 90p.

The decanter, in the shape of the royal coach, has the words "Royal Jubilee" on the top and "25 year old Pure Malt Whisky" on the front. The cork is in the shape of a royal crown.

Backstamp:
- **A.** Red transfer print "Wade England"
- **B.** Red transfer print "Wade Ireland"
- **C.** Raised "Wade England"

Name	Colourways	Size	U.S. $	Can. $	U.K. £
Beer Stein	Dark grey; gold crest	227	60.00	70.00	30.00
Dish	Honey brown	120	20.00	25.00	10.00
Dish	Dark green	120	20.00	25.00	10.00
Dish	Light green	120	20.00	25.00	10.00
Dish	Dark blue	120	20.00	25.00	10.00
Royal Coach Decanter	White; red cork; red/black/gold decoration	165	800.00	900.00	400.00
Tankard	Amber; gold band; multicoloured print	Pint/115	60.00	70.00	30.00
Tankard	White; gold band; multicoloured print	Pint/115	60.00	70.00	30.00

COMMISSIONED COMMEMORATIVES, 1977

Lesney Ashtray

Backstamp: Raised "S42/9"

Name	Colourways	Size	U.S. $	Can. $	U.K. £
Ashtray	Silver; brown tray; black lettering: "1953 The Silver Jubilee 1977" Coat of Arms (metal)	Round/77 x 110	40.00	45.00	20.00

Murray Sons & Co. Ltd.

This jar was given as a promotional item to retailers who sold Erinmore Pipe Tobacco, it was supplied by Murray Sons & Co. Ltd. Placed on display on the shop counter, the idea was that pipe smoking customers could 'sample' the tobacco at the point of sale. On the wooden lid is a label that reads "Queen Elizabeth II Silver Jubilee".

Erinmore Tobacco Jar, Front

Erinmore Tobacco Jar, Back

Backstamp: Printed "Wade pdm England" (joined 1969-1984)

Name	Colourways	Size	U.S. $	Can. $	U.K. £
Erinmore Tobacco Jar	Yellow; multicoloured printed; red and gold lettering	112	100.00	115.00	50.00

Taunton Cider Loving Cups

A limited edition of 2,500 loving cups was produced by Wade for Taunton Cider for the 1977 Silver Jubilee. Unfortunately the first run of the cups had a mistake in the inscription. It read "Her Royal Highness Queen Elizabeth" instead of the correct title of "Her Majesty Queen Elizabeth II." The cups were immediately recalled and destroyed. Only one cup with the wrong title is known to exist. On the reverse side of the cups is a transfer print of a Taunton Dry Blackthorn Cider label.

| Loving Cup, front | Loving Cup, front "Her Royal Highness Queen Elizabeth" | Loving Cup, back "Her Majesty" Queen Elizabeth II" |

Name	Colourways	Size	U.S. $	Can. $	U.K. £
Loving Cup	White; black lettering; "Her Royal Highness Queen Elizabeth"	90	Extremely Rare		
Loving Cup	White; black lettering; "Her Majesty Queen Elizabeth II"	90	40.00	45.00	20.00

ROYAL WEDDING OF PRINCE CHARLES AND LADY DIANA, 1981

To commemorate the marriage of Prince Charles and Lady Diana Spencer on July 29, 1981, George Wade & Son Ltd. produced a quantity of commemorative ware.

Although the backstamp on the "Royal Wedding Candlesticks" only says "Wade," they were produced by Wade Ireland. They are decorated with transfer printed portraits of the couple within a floral garland.

For many years Wade Ceramics has collaborated with Arthur Bell & Sons Ltd. to produce decanters, in the shape of hand bells, to commemorate royal occasions. The first such decanter was created for the royal wedding. The multicoloured print on this 75-centilitre decanter is of a portrait of Prince Charles and Lady Diana at the time of their engagement. A limited edition of 2,000 miniature "Royal Wedding Decanters" was made to present to the staffs of the George Wade Pottery and Bell's Whisky in commemoration of the event.

The "Royal Wedding Goblet" was produced by Wade Ireland, although the backstamp only says "Wade." It is white on the outside and glazed inside with gold.

The two-handled "Royal Wedding Loving Cup" is decorated on the front with a multicoloured transfer print of Charles and Diana within two hearts, as well as the royal coat of arms. The miniature version has gold-leaf silhouettes of the heads of the couple facing each other. On the back is the inscription, "To Commemorate the Wedding of H.R.H. Prince Charles and Lady Diana Spencer at St Paul's Cathedral 29th of July 1981." The original price was £1.50.

The "Royal Wedding Napkin Ring" has gold-leaf silhouettes of the heads of the bride and groom facing each other. On the back of the ring is the inscription "To Commemorate the Wedding of H.R.H. Prince Charles and Lady Diana Spencer at St Pauls Cathedral 29th of July 1981." It was manufactured in alumina ceramic, a material usually associated with the electronics and space industries and well known for its durability. The original price for the napkin ring was £1.50.

On the front of the "Royal Wedding Tankard" there is a transfer print of the couple within two hearts, as well as the royal coat of arms. On the back is the Welsh dragon, Scottish thistle, Irish shamrock and English rose. It was produced by Wade Ireland but the backstamp reads "Wade England."

Only a small number of teapots were produced. They had a transfer print of the couple within two hearts and the royal coat of arms on the front.

Giftware

Decanter

Goblet

Backstamp:
- **A.** Black transfer print "Wade"
- **B.** Black transfer print "Wade—Commemorative Porcelain Decanter From Bell's Scotch Whisky Perth Scotland 75cl Product of Scotland 40% vol"
- **C.** Black transfer print "Wade—Commemorative Porcelain Decanter From Bell's Scotch Whisky Perth Scotland Product of Scotland"
- **D.** Black transfer print "Wade England"
- **E.** Black transfer print "Wade Made in England"
- **F.** Black transfer print "Genuine Wade Porcelain"
- **G.** Red printed "Wade"

Giftware

Loving Cup

Candlestick

Tankard

Name	Colourways	Size	U.S. $	Can. $	U.K. £
Candlesticks (pair)	White; multicoloured print	145	80.00	90.00	40.00
Decanter	White; gold rim; multicoloured print	250	120.00	135.00	60.00
Decanter	White; gold rim; multicoloured print	Miniature/105	70.00	80.00	35.00
Goblet	White/gold; multicoloured print	145	90.00	100.00	45.00
Goblet	White/gold; multicoloured print	114	90.00	100.00	45.00
Goblet, Prince of Wales	White outside; gold inside; red dragon; flowers	114	90.00	100.00	45.00
Loving Cup	White; multicoloured print	85	90.00	100.00	45.00
Loving Cup	White; gold silhouettes	Miniature/50	60.00	70.00	30.00
Napkin Ring	White; gold silhouettes	45	60.00	70.00	30.00
Napkin Ring	White ring; gold silhouettes; wood base, lid	43	30.00	35.00	15.00
Tankard	White; gold band; multicoloured print	Pint/95	60.00	70.00	30.00
Teapot	White; multicoloured print	120	90.00	100.00	45.00

Giftware

The ashtray is square, with a multicoloured transfer print of Charles and Diana within two hearts and the royal coat of arms in the centre.

Although the "Royal Wedding Bell" was backstamped "Wade," it was produced by Wade Ireland. It is decorated with a gold band around the base and transfer-printed portraits of Charles and Diana within a floral wreath.

The "Royal Wedding Plaque" was produced by Wade Ireland, although the backstamp reads only "Wade." It is white with a transfer print of Prince Charles and Lady Diana Spencer inside a garland. There is a supporting foot on the back. The portrait plaque, produced by Wade Ireland, is from the same mould as one of the Greys Art standing plaques.

In the centre of the heart shaped trinket box are the portraits of the royal couple in a heart shaped frame with the royal coat of arms. The original cost was £2.50.

One version of the "Royal Wedding Vase" has portraits of the royal couple in two yellow frames with a red 'Welsh' dragon above. The second version, which was produced by Wade Ireland even though it is backstamped Wade, has the royal couple in a heart shaped frame.

The mould for the round long necked vase was previously used in 1961 for the Disney "Fantasia" series.

| Heart-shaped Trinket Box | Portrait Plaque | Vase |

Backstamp: **A.** Black transfer print "Wade"
B. Black transfer print "Wade England"
C. Raised "Wade Porcelain Made in England"

Name	Colourways	Size	U.S. $	Can. $	U.K. £
Ashtray	White; multicoloured print	110	20.00	25.00	10.00
Bell	White; multicoloured print	145	30.00	35.00	15.00
Heart shaped trinket box	White; multicoloured print	42 x 80	70.00	80.00	35.00
Plaque	White; multicoloured print	100	70.00	80.00	35.00
Portrait Plaque Irish	White; multicoloured print	98 x 98	70.00	80.00	35.00
Trinket Box	White; multicoloured print	40	70.00	80.00	35.00
Vase	White; heart frame	220	80.00	90.00	40.00
Vase	White; two frames and red dragon		80.00	90.00	40.00

BIRTH OF PRINCE WILLIAM, 1982

This decanter was produced in partnership with Bell's Whisky to commemorate the birth of the first son of Prince Charles and Princess Diana on June 21, 1982. The 50-centilitre container is in the shape of a hand-bell and has a porcelain cap. It is decorated with a blue and gold transfer print of a crown, cherubs and ribbons.

Hand-Bell Decanter, Front

Hand-Bell Decanter, Back

Backstamp: Black transfer print "Wade—Commemorative Porcelain Decanter From Bells Scotch Whisky Perth Scotland 50cl Product of Scotland 40% vol"

Name	Colourways	Size	U.S. $	Can. $	U.K. £
Decanter	White; gold bands; blue and gold print	205	60.00	70.00	30.00

BIRTH OF PRINCE HENRY, 1984

Bell's Whisky issued this decanter to commemorate the birth of Prince Henry on September 15, 1984, the second son of Prince Charles and Princess Diana.

Backstamp: Black transfer print "Wade—Commemorative Porcelain Decanter From Bell's Scotch Whisky Perth Scotland—50cl Product of Scotland 40% vol"

Name	Colourways	Size	U.S. $	Can. $	U.K. £
Decanter	White; gold bands; red and gold print	200	60.00	70.00	30.00

60th BIRTHDAY QUEEN ELIZABETH, 1986

This decanter was produced by Bell's Whisky to commemorate the 60th birthday of Queen Elizabeth on April 21, 1986.

Backstamp: Black transfer print "Wade—Commemorative Porcelain Decanter from Bell's Scotch Whisky Perth Scotland—75cl product of Scotland 43% GL"

Name	Colourways	Size	U.S. $	Can. $	U.K. £
Decanter	White; gold bands; multicoloured print	250	60.00	70.00	30.00

MARRIAGE OF PRINCE ANDREW AND SARAH FERGUSON, 1986

This decanter, shaped like a hand-bell, was issued by Bell's Whisky to commemorate the royal wedding of Prince Andrew and Sarah Ferguson on July 23, 1986.

Backstamp: Black transfer print "Wade—Commemorative Porcelain Decanter from Bell's Scotch Whisky Perth Scotland—75cl product of Scotland 43% GL"

Name	Colourways	Size	U.S. $	Can. $	U.K. £
Decanter	White; gold bands; multicoloured print	250	60.00	70.00	30.00

BIRTH OF PRINCESS BEATRICE, 1988

In 1988 Wade and Bell's Whisky produced this decanter to commemorate the birth of Princess Beatrice on August 8, 1988, the first child of Prince Andrew and the Duchess of York.

Backstamp: Black transfer print "Genuine Wade Porcelain—Commemorative Porcelain Decanter From Bells Scotch Whisky Perth Scotland—50cl Product of Scotland 40% vol"

Name	Colourways	Size	U.S. $	Can. $	U.K. £
Decanter	White; gold/red/blue bands; blue/gold/brown print	200	60.00	70.00	30.00

BIRTH OF PRINCESS EUGENIE, 1990

Wade and Bell's Whisky issued this decanter to commemorate the birth of Princess Eugenie on March 23, 1990, the second daughter of Prince Andrew and the Duchess of York.

Backstamp: Black transfer print "Genuine Wade Porcelain—Commemorative Porcelain Decanter From Bell's Scotch Whisky Perth Scotland—50cl Product of Scotland 40% vol"

Name	Colourways	Size	U.S. $	Can. $	U.K. £
Decanter	White; gold/red/blue bands; blue/gold/brown print	200	60.00	70.00	30.00

90th BIRTHDAY QUEEN ELIZABETH THE QUEEN MOTHER, 1990

The "Church-Bell Decanter" was issued by Bell's Whisky to commemorate the Queen Mother's 90th birthday on August 4, 1990. Wade also produced 10,000 circular dishes and 10,000 circular trinket boxes for Ringtons Teas Ltd.

"Church-Bell Decanter"

Dish and Trinket Box

Backstamp: **A.** Black /red/blue transfer print "Genuine Wade Porcelain Commemorative Decanter from Arthur Bell and Son Perth Scotland—Product of Scotland 75cl—43% proof "

B. Red transfer print "Wade Ceramics "

C. Printed "Ringtons Ltd Tea Merchants Algernon Road Newcastle-On-Tyne Manufactured Exclusively for Ringtons by Wade Ceramics"

Name	Colourways	Size	U.S. $	Can. $	U.K. £
Decanter	White; gold and blue bands; multicoloured print	200	60.00	70.00	30.00
Dish	White; multicoloured print	110	20.00	25.00	10.00
Trinket Box	White; multicoloured print	44 x 95	50.00	55.00	25.00

GOLDEN WEDDING ANNIVERSARY QUEEN ELIZABETH AND PRINCE PHILIP, 1997

Bell's Whisky produced a 75cl Commemorative "Church-Bell Decanter" to celebrate the Golden Wedding Anniversary of Her Majesty Queen Elizabeth II and Prince Philip.

Backstamp: Gold printed "Extra Special Old Scotch Whiskey Arthur Bell & Sons" "Purple Genuine Wade Porcelain"

Name	Colourways	Size	U.S. $	Can. $	U.K. £
Decanter	White; gold top, bands and decoration; blue collar; multicoloured print; red and gold lettering	200	60.00	70.00	30.00

50th BIRTHDAY HRH THE PRINCE OF WALES, 1998

Bell's Whisky produced this 70cl commemorative church bell decanter to commemorate the 50th birthday of HRH The Prince of Wales on November 14, 1998.

*Photograph not
available at press time*

Name	Colourways	Size	U.S. $	Can. $	U.K. £
Decanter	Royal blue; gold portrait and lettering	200	60.00	70.00	30.00

100th BIRTHDAY HRH QUEEN ELIZABETH THE QUEEN MOTHER, 2000

Bell's Whisky produced this 70cl commemorative church bell to commemorate the 100th birthday of HRH Queen Elizabeth the Queen Mother on 4th August 2000.

*Photograph not
available at press time*

Name	Colourways	Size	U.S. $	Can. $	U.K. £
Decanter	Blue and white; gold cap and bands; multicoloured print	200	70.00	80.00	35.00

50th ANNIVERSARY QUEEN ELIZABETH II ACCESSION, 2002

Decorative Items, 2002

To celebrate the 50th anniversary of Her Majesty the Queen's accession to the throne, Wade produced four decorative items: a bud vase, a goblet, a loving cup and a trinket box. All were produced in white with blue and gold prints. The original cost direct from Wade was: bud vase £15.99, goblet £11.99, loving cup £14.99 and trinket box £21.99.

Golden Jubilee Vase

Golden Jubilee Goblet

Golden Jubilee Trinket Box

Backstamp: Gold printed "Golden Jubilee Est 1810 England" with oval 'Wade' logo

Name	Colourways	Size	U.S. $	Can. $	U.K. £
Bud vase	White; blue and gold print	135	30.00	35.00	15.00
Goblet	White; blue and gold print	90	25.00	30.00	12.00
Loving cup	White; blue and gold print	105	30.00	35.00	15.00
Trinket box	White; blue and gold print	35	50.00	55.00	25.00

COMMISSIONED COMMEMORATIVES, 2002

Ringtons Tea Ltd., 2002

This decorative tea caddy with a portrait of her Majesty the Queen at her Coronation was produced for Ringtons to celebrate the 50th anniversary of Her Majesty the Queen's accession to the throne. The design of the tea caddy was based on an original 'Maling' tea caddy produced for Ringtons for the coronation of King George VI in 1937. The teapot has a mature portrait of Her Majesty the Queen. Although both items were produced as royal commemoratives there is no reference to it in the backstamps.

Tea Caddy, front view

Tea Caddy, back view

Tea Caddy, side view

Teapot

Backstamp:
  A. Ink stamped RINGTONS; A Family Business Est. 1907; Manufactured Exclusively for Ringtons by Wade Ceramics
  B. Ink stamped RINGTONS A Family Business Est. 1907; Manufactured Exclusively for Ringtons by Wade Ceramics; RINGTONS LTD Tea Merchants

Name	Colourways	Size	U.S. $	Can. $	U.K. £
Tea Caddy	White; multicoloured prints; gold highlights	180	90.00	100.00	45.00
Teapot	White; multicoloured prints; gold highlights	140	90.00	100.00	45.00

DECORATIVE WARE

The jugs in this section are more decorative than ulitarian. They come in a large range of shapes with embossed or impressed designs, with hand-painted decoration, transfer prints or in plain or mottled colours. Sometimes with several of these components combined on one item.

Flaxman Ware jugs are usually produced with a mottled glaze, although this is not always the case. Transfer prints began to be used as decoration on jugs in the 1950s.

All of the vases produced up to World War II were made by Wade Heath. When production of decorative ware resumed following the war, it was divided between all of the Wade potteries, including Wade Ireland in the 1950s.

The jugs and vases are listed by shape number in this section.

Shape 1, Flower Handle Jugs, 1934-1935

These jugs have a large embossed seven-petal flower on the top of the handle and three large flowers on the neck. There are embossed leaves and a pebble design in the background.

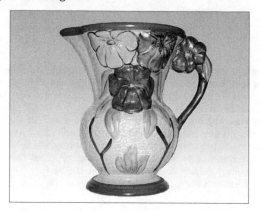

Backstamp: Black ink stamp "Wadeheath England" with a black lion and a small impressed triangle

Name	Colourways	Size	U.S. $	Can. $	U.K. £
Flower handle	Cream; yellow, brown/orange flowers; green stems	240	100.00	125.00	50.00
Flower handle	Pale yellow; pale green flowers; pale orange stems	240	100.00	125.00	50.00
Flower handle	Yellow; dark blue/pale blue flowers; brown stems	240	100.00	125.00	50.00
Flower handle	Yellow; yellow/blue/orange flowers; brown stems	240	100.00	125.00	50.00

Shape 13, Woodpecker Handle Jugs, 1933-c.1945

These waisted jugs are decorated with swirling tree branches around the bowl. A woodpecker forms the handle.

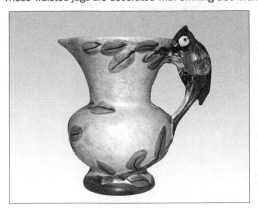

Mottled green glaze

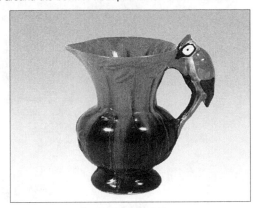

Orange and black glaze

Backstamp:
A. Red ink stamp "Wadeheath England" with a lion
B. Black ink stamp "Wadeheath England" with a lion
C. Black ink stamp "Wade Heath England"
D. Black ink stamp "Wadeheath Orcadia Ware British Made"

Name	Colourways	Size	U.S. $	Can. $	U.K. £
Woodpecker	Yellow jug; brown leaves; yellow/orange/brown bird	Small/180	125.00	150.00	60.00
Woodpecker	Yellow jug; brown/orange leaves; green /yellow/orange/blue bird	Small/180	125.00	150.00	60.00
Woodpecker	Amber/brown jug, bird	Medium/190	125.00	150.00	60.00
Woodpecker	Mottled green jug; brown/dark blue bird	Medium/190	125.00	150.00	60.00
Woodpecker	Orange/black streaked jug; orange/green/dark blue bird	Medium/190	125.00	150.00	60.00
Woodpecker	Orange/black streaked jug; orange/blue/green/yellow bird	Medium/190	125.00	150.00	60.00
Woodpecker	Yellow/orange/black jug; blue/orange bird	Medium/190	125.00	150.00	60.00
Woodpecker	Yellow/orange/brown jug; green/orange bird	Medium/190	125.00	150.00	60.00

Shape 14, Lovebirds Jugs, 1934-1935

Lovebirds

Backstamp: Black ink stamp "Wadeheath England" with a lion

Name	Colourways	Size	U.S. $	Can. $	U.K. £
Lovebirds	Yellow; brown handle; green/orange birds	Small/165	150.00	175.00	75.00
Lovebirds	Yellow; brown handle; green/orange birds	Large/193	150.00	175.00	75.00

Shape 15, Castile Jugs, 1934-1935

Butterfly and Flowers

Imari

Orcadia

Backstamp: **A.** Black ink stamp "Wadeheath England" with a lion and impressed "Castile 15"
B. Orange ink stamp "Wadeheath Orcadia Ware"

Name	Colourways	Size	U.S. $	Can. $	U.K. £
Butterfly and Flowers	Off white; brown, green; blue, orange and yellow	220	150.00	175.00	75.00
Butterfly and Flowers	Off white; green, pink and yellow	220	150.00	175.00	75.00
Imari	White; blue, gold and orange	220	150.00	175.00	75.00
Flying Bird	Off white; brown and orange	220	150.00	175.00	75.00
Orcadia	Turquoise; orange and yellow	220	150.00	175.00	75.00

Shape 16 and 24, Pyramid Jugs, 1933-1935

These jugs have been reported with both 16 and 24 as the shape number. The long, straight handle steps in at the bottom of the jug. The hand-painted 'Imari' decoration was a popular 1930s design used many times by Wade on decorative and tableware products.

Abstract

Abstract and flower

Imari

Backstamp: **A.** Black ink stamp "Wadeheath England" with a lion and impressed "16" (1934-1935)
B. Black ink stamp "Flaxman Ware Hand Made Pottery by Wadeheath" (1935-1937)

Name	Colourways	Size	U.S. $	Can. $	U.K. £
Imari	White; cobalt blue spout/handle/panels; white/orange/gold decoration	185	150.00	175.00	75.00
Abstract	Brown handle; brown/orange/yellow abstract design	215	150.00	175.00	75.00
Abstract/Flower	Orange handle; black/orange/yellow design; black/orange flower	215	150.00	175.00	75.00
Imari	White; blue handle, spout; blue/gold/orange design	215	150.00	175.00	75.00
Rose	Green; orange spout, handle; pink rose; cream centre panel	215	150.00	175.00	75.00

Shape 18, Orcadia Ware Vases, 1933-1937

Bands

Marigolds

Sponged Shell

Backstamp: **A.** Orange ink stamp "Wades Orcadia Ware" with a lion, 1933-1934
B. Black ink stamp "WadeHeath England" with a lion and impressed "18, 1933-1935"
D. Black ink stamp "Wadeheath, England" with impressed "18"

Name	Colourways	Size	U.S. $	Can. $	U.K. £
Bands	Orange, yellow and brown	171	75.00	85.00	40.00
Orcadia	Orange, brown and yellow	171	75.00	85.00	40.00
Splash	Orange, turquoise and yellow	171	75.00	85.00	40.00
Sponged shells	Mottled blue, blue, green, yellow and orange	171	75.00	85.00	40.00
Sponged shells	Mottled purple, purple, green, yellow and orange	171	75.00	85.00	40.00
Sponged shells marigolds	Brown, orange and yellow	171	75.00	85.00	40.00

Shape 19, Flaxman and Orcadia Ware Vases, 1933-1937

Orcadia ware vases were produced between 1933 and 1935.

Art Nouveau

Orcadia ware

Sponged shells

Backstamp:
- **A.** Orange ink stamp "Wades Orcadia Ware" with a lion, 1933
- **B.** Orange ink stamp "Wadeheath Orcadia Ware", 1933-1934
- **C.** Black ink stamp "WadeHeath England" with a lion and impressed "19", 1933-1935
- **D.** Black ink stamp "Flaxman Ware Hand Made Pottery by Wadeheath, England" with impressed "19", 1935-1937

Name	Colourways	Size	U.S. $	Can. $	U.K. £
Art Nouveau	Orange; brown leaf design	120	100.00	115.00	50.00
Bird	Cream; brown rim, handles, tree stump; orange bird	120	100.00	115.00	50.00
Bird	Green/cream; orange/mauve flowers; brown bird	120	100.00	115.00	50.00
Bird	Yellow; blue flower; brown bird (tube lined)	120	100.00	115.00	50.00
Flowers	Brown; orange/yellow flowers	120	100.00	115.00	50.00
Flowers	Green handles; brown flecks; pink flowers; green leaves	120	100.00	115.00	50.00
Flowers	Orange; blue flowers; green leaves	120	100.00	115.00	50.00
Leaves	Mustard; brown leaves	120	100.00	115.00	50.00
Mottled	Mottled orange	120	50.00	60.00	25.00
Mottled	Turquoise; brown/turquoise/green design	120	75.00	85.00	40.00
Orcadia	Green/orange	120	75.00	85.00	40.00
Orcadia	Orange/yellow	120	75.00	85.00	40.00
Orcadia	Orange/yellow/brown streaks	120	75.00	85.00	40.00
Sponged shells	Blue handles; blue/yellow/green/orange shells	120	100.00	115.00	50.00
Stripes	Orange top, handles; bright blue/orange/green/yellow/purple stripes	120	75.00	85.00	40.00

Shape 23, Flaxman And Orcadia Ware Vases, 1935-1937

These vases with moulded feet were previously catalogued as shape number 11. A new example has been found with a clearly impressed "23."

Art Nouveau

Heron

Backstamp: **A.** Black ink stamp "Flaxman Ware Hand Made Pottery by Wadeheath, England" with impressed "23"
B. Orange ink stamp "Wadeheath Orcadia Ware"

Name	Colourways	Size	U.S. $	Can. $	U.K. £
Art Nouveau	Amber; brown/green foliage; orange/brown flowers	150	100.00	115.00	50.00
Heron	Cream; green foliage; orange/blue flowers brown outline of heron	150	100.00	115.00	50.00
Orcadia	Green streaked top, base; orange streaked middle	150	100.00	115.00	50.00

Shape 36, British Roskyl Vase, 1935-c.1952

This vase with an orb-shaped body, and a round foot, has the unusual British Roskyl Pottery backstamp.

Tree and flowers

Backstamp: Black ink stamp "British Roskyl Pottery" with impressed "36"

Name	Colourways	Size	U.S. $	Can. $	U.K. £
Tree and flowers	Cream; green tree; orange/yellow blue flowers	190	70.00	80.00	35.00

Shape 55, Wide-Mouth Jugs, 1933-1935

A number of these jugs were produced in Orcadia Ware a design of vivid streaked glazes which were allowed to run over the rims and down the inside and outside of the item. They have been found in two sizes.

Orcadia Flowers Leaves

Backstamp: **A.** Orange ink stamp "Wadeheath Orcadia Ware"
B. Black ink stamp "Wadeheath Orcadia Ware British Made"
C. Black ink stamp "Made in England"with impressed "55"
D. Black ink stamp "Wadeheath England" with lion

Name	Colourways	Size	U.S. $	Can. $	U.K. £
Orcadia	Brown/orange/brown streaks; brown base	180	90.00	100.00	45.00
Orcadia	Orange/dark green streaks; grey base	180	90.00	100.00	45.00
Orcadia	Orange/yellow/brown streaks; brown base	180	90.00	100.00	45.00
Orcadia	Orange/yellow/green; grey-blue base; wide-mouth	180	90.00	100.00	45.00
Flowers	Large orange/blue flowers; yellow lines; black panel, foot	195	100.00	115.00	50.00
Leaves	Large orange leaves; black seeds, rim	195	100.00	115.00	50.00

Shape 69, Flaxman, Harvest and Orcadia Ware Vases, 1935-c.1952

Orcadia ware vases were produced between 1933 and 1935. The Flaxman ware vases were produced from 1935 to 1939. The peony design vases were produced between the late 1940s and the early 1950s. The brightly coloured splash design looks almost like crocus flowers.

Blue Tulip

Splash

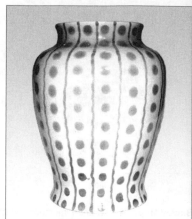
Spots

Backstamp:
A. Black ink stamp "Harvest Ware Wade England" with impressed "69," late 1940s-early 1950s
B. Black ink stamp "Flaxman Ware Hand Made Pottery by Wadeheath England" with impressed "69," 1935-1937
C. Black ink stamp "Flaxman Wade Heath England" with impressed "69," 1937-1939
D. Green ink stamp "Wade England" with impressed "69," late 1940s-early 1950
E. Orange ink stamp "Wadeheath Orcadia Ware"

Name	Colourways	Size	U.S. $	Can. $	U.K. £
Orcadia	Green/brown/yellow streaks; dark brown base	Small/125	70.00	80.00	35.00
Blue tulip	Cream; blue tulips	Large/200	80.00	90.00	40.00
Peony	Cream; multicoloured flowers	Large/200	100.00	115.00	50.00
Splash	Orange; mauve/blue/green splashes; brown base	Large/200	70.00	80.00	35.00
Speckled	Blue/yellow brown speckles	Large/200	70.00	80.00	35.00
Sponged shell	Cream; green/mauve shells; orange base	Large/200	70.00	80.00	35.00
Spots	White; blue spots; grey lines	Large/200	70.00	80.00	35.00

Shape 88, Jugs, 1934-1937

Most of these jugs are hand-painted and have a spout that is moulded in a V shape.

Flowers and Streaks

Flowers

Backstamp:
A. Black ink stamp "WadeHeath England" with a lion and impressed shape number
B. Black ink stamp "Flaxman Ware Hand Made Pottery by Wadeheath, England" with impressed shape number
C. Black ink stamp "Wadeheath Ware England" with impressed shape number

Shape Nos.: 88M — Miniature
88MS — Medium
88 — Large

Name	Colourways	Size	U.S. $	Can. $	U.K. £
Flower	Yellow; large orange flower	Miniature/140	60.00	70.00	30.00
Flowers	Cream; pink/blue flowers; green leaves	Miniature/140	60.00	70.00	30.00
Flowers	Cream; pink/mauve flowers	Miniature/140	60.00	70.00	30.00
Flowers	Cream; blue handle; pink flowers	Miniature/140	60.00	70.00	30.00
Flowers	Cream; large orange/blue flowers	Miniature/140	60.00	70.00	30.00
Flowers	Cream; yellow/orange flowers; grey cross stripes	Miniature/140	60.00	70.00	30.00
Flowers	Cream; yellow/red flowers	Miniature/140	60.00	70.00	30.00
Mottled	Mottled brown/light brown neck	Miniature/140	50.00	60.00	25.00
Mottled	Mottled greens	Miniature/140	50.00	60.00	25.00
Mottled	Mottled yellow/brown	Miniature/140	50.00	60.00	25.00
Solid colour	Green	Miniature/140	50.00	60.00	25.00
Streaks	Cream; dark brown/light brown streaks	Miniature/140	50.00	60.00	25.00
Streaks	Cream; orange/yellow/brown streaks	Miniature/140	50.00	60.00	25.00
Flowers	Cream; blue/yellow flowers	Medium/185	60.00	70.00	30.00
Streaks	Streaked orange/yellow/brown; orange handle, bowl; brown base	Medium/185	60.00	70.00	30.00
Windmill	Off white; red/yellow windmill; green trees	Medium/185	60.00	70.00	30.00
Flowers	Cream; blue spout, handle; grey base; red/blue flowers	Large/210	60.00	70.00	30.00
Flying Heron	Green/yellow; blue/yellow flowers; brown flying Heron	Large/215	75.00	85.00	40.00

Shape 89, Jug, 1934-1935

This jug has a long pointed spout and an impressed and embossed triangle design around the neck.

Photograph not available
at press time

Backstamp: **A.** Black ink stamp "WadeHeath England" with a lion and impressed 89
B. Orange ink stamp "Wadeheath Orcadia Ware"

Name	Colourways	Size	U.S. $	Can. $	U.K. £
Flowers	Cream; blue/yellow/orange flowers; green leaves	160	100.00	115.00	50.00
Orcadia	Orange/brown	155	100.00	115.00	50.00

Shape 90, Jugs, 1934-1935

These jugs are similar to shape 89, but the spout extends down to the waist of the jug and the triangle design is around the waist.

Backstamp: **A.** Black ink stamp "WadeHeath England" with a lion and embossed "90," 1934-1935
B. Black ink stamp "Flaxman Ware Hand Made Pottery by Wadeheath England," 1935-1937

Name	Colourways	Size	U.S. $	Can. $	U.K. £
Bird	Cream; blue/yellow flowers; brown trees, bird	215	125.00	150.00	60.00
Butterflies	Green; brown flowers, green leaves (top); blue/brown flowers; black outlined butterflies	215	125.00	150.00	60.00
Flowers	Cream/green; blue/brown/yellow flowers	215	125.00	150.00	60.00
Flowers	Cream/orange; orange/yellow flowers	215	125.00	150.00	60.00
Flowers	Cream; yellow/blue flowers; green leaves	215	125.00	150.00	60.00
Flowers	Green; blue flowers; brown/green leaves	215	125.00	150.00	60.00
Hummingbirds	Green; brown flowers (top); blue flowers; brown tree outline, hummingbirds	215	130.00	160.00	65.00
Streaks	Orange/brown/yellow streaks; orange band	215	60.00	70.00	30.00
Triangles	Green; blue spout, handle; blue/brown flowers; brown triangles	225	125.00	150.00	60.00

Shape 92, Jugs, 1935-c.1945

Backstamp: **A.** Black ink stamp "Wadeheath Ware England" with impressed "92"
B. Black ink stamp "Made in England" with impressed "92"

Name	Colourways	Size	U.S. $	Can. $	U.K. £
Flowers	Mottled brown foot, handle; yellow/orange bowl, flowers	204	70.00	80.00	35.00
Streaks	Brown foot, handle; blue/yellow/orange streaks	204	70.00	80.00	35.00
Streaks	Brown foot, handle; yellow/orange/grey streaks	204	70.00	80.00	35.00
Streaks	Yellow foot, handle; orange/brown/yellow streaks	204	70.00	80.00	35.00

Shape 93, Elite Jugs, 1934-1937, c.1948-c.1952, 1955

Various Decoration, 1934-1937

The shape name for these jugs is 'Elite,' they were issued over a twenty year period with many different decorations.

| Bird | Flowers | Leaves | Leaves |

Backstamp: **A.** Black ink stamp "WadeHeath England" with a lion and embossed "Elite No 93," 1934-1935
B. Black ink stamp "Flaxman Ware Hand Made Pottery by Wadeheath England" with embossed "Elite 93"\

Name	Colourways	Size	U.S. $	Can. $	U.K. £
Flowers	Cream; brown striped jug, handle; large orange flower; green/black/brown leaves	285	140.00	160.00	70.00
Flowers	Cream; green/brown base, handle; maroon/mauve flowers	285	140.00	160.00	70.00
Bird	Cream; green handle; blue/yellow flowers;brown/green tree; bird outline is brown	295	140.00	160.00	70.00
Flames	Cream; orange spout, handle; blue/orange/brown flames	295	140.00	160.00	70.00
Leaves	Yellow; orange spout, base; brown handle; green leaves	295	140.00	160.00	70.00
Peony	Cream; multicoloured flowers	280	140.00	160.00	70.00

Shape 94, Richmond Vases With Handles, 1934-1935, 1937-1939

These vases have horizontal ribs on the neck. One vase has been found that is slightly larger than the others.

Art Nouveau

Feather and flowers

Heron

Backstamp: **A.** Black ink stamp "WadeHeath England" with a lion and embossed "94 Richmond," 1934-1935
B. Black ink stamped "Flaxman Ware Hand Made Pottery by Wadeheath England" (1935-1937)
C. Black ink stamp "Flaxman Wade Heath England" 1937-1939
D. Black ink stamped "Flaxman Wade Heath England" embossed "94" impressed "M" (1937-1939)

Name	Colourways	Size	U.S. $	Can. $	U.K. £
Art Nouveau	Brown neck/base; yellow handle; brown/yellow/green leaves	160	75.00	85.00	40.00
Bands	Yellow; orange bands; blue/orange streaks; blue dots, cross lines	160	75.00	85.00	40.00
Circles	Yellow; orange rim, handle, base, circles; blue/green leaves	160	75.00	85.00	40.00
Feather/flowers	Orange, black bands; orange/blue feather; orange/mauve flowers	160	75.00	85.00	40.00
Flowers	Blue/green with chevron, flowers	160	75.00	85.00	40.00
Flowers	Blue/green; blue handle, flower; golden brown triangles	160	75.00	85.00	40.00
Flowers	Off white; pink/blue/yellow flowers	160	75.00	85.00	40.00
Orcadia	Green/yellow; brown streaks at base	160	75.00	85.00	40.00
Squares	Green/blue; brown fan; blue/brown squares	160	75.00	85.00	40.00
Heron	Cream; green trees; orange, mauve flowers; brown flying heron	172	75.00	85.00	40.00

Shape 95, Richmond Vase Without Handles, 1934-1935

*Photograph not available
at press time*

Backstamp: Black ink stamp "WadeHeath England" with a lion and embossed "95 Richmond"

Name	Colourways	Size	U.S. $	Can. $	U.K. £
Stripes	Green; green/yellow top stripe; brown bottom stripe	Unknown		Rare	

Shape 99, Pine Vases, 1935-1937

Art Deco

Streaks

Backstamp: Black ink stamp "Flaxman Ware Hand Made Pottery by Wadeheath England" with impressed "99 Pine"

Name	Colourways	Size	U.S. $	Can. $	U.K. £
Art Deco	Green; blue flowers; brown deco triangles	140	75.00	85.00	40.00
Streaks	Brown/green/yellow streaks	140	60.00	70.00	30.00

Shape 100, Art Deco Jugs, 1934-c.1948

These jugs were either decorated with hand-painted designs or produced in all-over mottled colours.

Cream, with large orange flower

Mottled blue and brown

Backstamp: **A.** Black ink stamp "Wadeheath England" with a lion and impressed "100"
B. Impressed "Streamline 100 "

Name	Colourways	Size	U.S. $	Can. $	U.K. £
Flowers	Cream; orange handle, base; large orange flower	180	150.00	175.00	75.00
Mottled	Mottled blue and brown	180	125.00	150.00	60.00

Shape 106, Jugs, 1934-c.1948

These jugs were either decorated with hand-painted designs or produced in an all-over mottled colours. There is a drainage hole inside the base under the handle.

Imari

Flowers

Art Deco

Parrot

Backstamp:
- **A.** Black ink stamp "Wadeheath England" with a lion and impressed "106/30"
- **B.** Black ink stamp "Flaxman Ware Hand Made Pottery by Wadeheath England" with impressed "106"
- **C.** Black ink stamp "Flaxman Wade Heath England" with impressed "106"
- **D.** Black ink stamp "Wadeheath Ware England" with impressed "106"
- **E.** Black ink stamp "Made in England" with impressed "106"

Shape No.: 106 — Miniature, large; 106/30 — Medium

Name	Colourways	Size	U.S. $	Can. $	U.K. £
Flowers	Cream; green base, handle; large blue/yellow/orange flowers	Miniature/140	60.00	70.00	30.00
Flowers	Cream; green base, handle; light brown leaves; small pink flower	Miniature/140	60.00	70.00	30.00
Flowers	Cream; grey base; brown handle; large blue/yellow/orange flowers	Miniature/140	60.00	70.00	30.00
Flowers	Cream; orange base; pink/mauve/blue flowers	Miniature/140	60.00	70.00	30.00
Flowers	Cream; orange base; red/yellow/orange flowers	Miniature/140	60.00	70.00	30.00
Flowers	Cream; pink base; brown/mauve flowers	Miniature/140	60.00	70.00	30.00
Mottled	Mottled blue	Miniature/140	60.00	70.00	30.00
Mottled	Mottled green	Miniature/140	60.00	70.00	30.00
Mottled	Mottled orange/grey	Miniature/140	60.00	70.00	30.00
Solid colour	Dark blue	Miniature/140	60.00	70.00	30.00
Solid colour	Orange	Miniature/140	60.00	70.00	30.00
Imari	White; dark blue handle; orange/dark blue flowers; gold lustre	Medium/190	100.00	115.00	50.00
Flowers	Cream; three multicoloured flowers	Medium/190	100.00	115.00	50.00
Flowers	Cream; yellow flowers; green leaves	Medium/190	100.00	115.00	50.00
Flowers	Cream; yellow/orange flowers; green leaves	Medium/190	100.00	115.00	50.00
Mottled	Mottled dark green	Medium/190	60.00	70.00	30.00
Mottled	Mottled cream/blue	Medium/190	60.00	70.00	30.00
Streaks	Blue; brown streaks on base	Medium/190	60.00	70.00	30.00
Tree's	Blue; brown trees	Medium/190	60.00	70.00	30.00
Art Deco	Yellow/orange; orange handle; black/green/yellow squares	Large/222	125.00	150.00	60.00
Flowers	Yellow; orange handle; orange/brown flowers; green leaves	Large/222	125.00	150.00	60.00
Mottled	Mottled mustard/green/yellow; orange bands	Large/222	100.00	115.00	50.00
Mottled	Mottled orange and yellow	Large/222	100.00	115.00	50.00
Parrot	Cream; orange handle, parrot; green leaves	Large/222	125.00	150.00	60.00
Parrot	Yellow; orange handle; orange/green parrot; green leaves	Large/222	125.00	150.00	60.00
Trees	Blue; brown base, handle; brown/blue trees	Large/222	125.00	150.00	60.00

Shape 107, Vases, 1934-1935

This vase has two handles that end on the round footed base.

Birds and flowers

Flowers

Backstamp: **A.** Black ink stamp "Wadeheath England" with a lion and embossed "107"
B. Black ink stamp "Flaxman Ware Hand Made Pottery by Wadeheath England" with embossed "107"

Name	Colourways	Size	U.S. $	Can. $	U.K. £
Bird and Flowers	White; orange bird; blue flowers; brown handles/foot/tree	225	75.00	85.00	40.00
Flowers and triangles	White; pink/blue/yellow triangles and flowers	225	75.00	85.00	40.00
Flower	Cream; pink flower; green leaves; grey trees/base	225	75.00	85.00	40.00
Mottled	Yellow/brown/orange	225	50.00	60.00	25.00

Shape 110, Jugs, 1934-1935

There are four ribbed bands around the waist of these jugs.

Cottage

Mottled

Flowers

Backstamp: **A.** Black ink stamp "Wadeheath England" with a lion and embossed "110"
B. Orange ink stamp "Wadeheath Orcadia Ware"

Name	Colourways	Size	U.S. $	Can. $	U.K. £
Butterfly	Beige; rust spout; green flowers; outlined butterfly	230	100.00	115.00	50.00
Cottage	Cream; grey rim, spout, handle, base; mauve flowers; brown gate, cottage	230	100.00	115.00	50.00
Flowers	Cream; large orange/blue/green flowers	230	100.00	115.00	50.00
Flowers	Cream; large orange/green flowers; brown/silver and green/silver leaves	230	100.00	115.00	50.00
Flowers	Cream; purple/lilac/grey/yellow flowers; green grass; orange-lustre spout/handle	230	100.00	115.00	50.00
Mottled	Mottled yellow/green	230	70.00	80.00	35.00
Orcadia	Orange/yellow/brown streaks; brown base	230	70.00	80.00	35.00
Orcadia	Yellow; brown streaks	230	70.00	80.00	35.00
Scrolls	Yellow; orange scrolls	230	70.00	80.00	35.00

Shape 113, Jugs, 1934-c.1945

The body of these jugs is ribbed, which is hard to see on the mottled versions.

Backstamp: **A.** Black ink stamp "Wadeheath England" with a lion and impressed "113"
B. Black ink stamp "Flaxman Ware Hand Made—Pottery by Wadeheath England"
C. Black ink stamp "Made in England" with impressed "113"

Name	Colourways	Size	U.S. $	Can. $	U.K. £
Flowers	Cream, green, pink and yellow	Miniature/130	60.00	70.00	30.00
Flowers	Cream, orange and green	Miniature/130	60.00	70.00	30.00
Flowers	Cream, orange, black, blue and green	Miniature/130	60.00	70.00	30.00
Flowers	Cream, pearlised orange, orange, red, blue and silver lustre	Miniature/130	60.00	70.00	30.00
Flowers	Off white and orange	Miniature/130	60.00	70.00	30.00
Mottled	Green and mottled brown	Miniature/130	60.00	70.00	30.00
Plain	Green	Miniature/130	40.00	50.00	20.00
Plain	Orange and green	Miniature/130	40.00	50.00	20.00
Plain	Yellow and mottled brown	Miniature/130	40.00	50.00	20.00
Flower	Cream, black, orange and green	Large/190	90.00	100.00	45.00
Flowers	Cream, orange and green	Large/190	90.00	100.00	45.00
Flowers	Cream, orange, blue, yellow and green	Large/190	90.00	100.00	45.00
Fruit	Green, yellow and blue	Large/190	90.00	100.00	45.00
Mottled	Mottled Green	Large/190	90.00	100.00	45.00

Shape 114, Long-Tailed Bird Jug, 1934-1935

The tail of the moulded bird on the bowl of these jugs extends upward to form the handle.

Backstamp: Black ink stamp "Wadeheath England" with a lion

Name	Colourways	Size	U.S. $	Can. $	U.K. £
Long-tailed bird	Yellow, orange and green	180	140.00	160.00	70.00
Long-tailed bird	Yellow, orange, mauve and light green	180	140.00	160.00	70.00

Shape 119, Jugs, 1935-1937

Mottled

Tree

Silver flower

Backstamp:
A. Black ink stamp "Flaxman Ware Hand Made Pottery by Wadeheath England" with embossed "119" and black ink stamp "Wadeheath England Registration No 812659"
B. Black ink stamp "Flaxman Ware Hand Made Pottery by Wadeheath England" with impressed "119"
C. Black ink stamp "Wadeheath England" with impressed "119"

Name	Colourways	Size	U.S. $	Can. $	U.K. £
Cottage	Yellow; green handle; brown/grey cottage; blue/yellow flowers	229	100.00	115.00	50.00
Fruit	Green; blue/yellow/green fruit	229	100.00	115.00	50.00
Mottled	Mottled cream/green	229	100.00	115.00	50.00
Silver flower	Cream; green bands; silver lustre flower, lines	229	100.00	115.00	50.00
Tree	White; blue/yellow tree, flowers	229	100.00	115.00	50.00

Shape 121, Jugs, 1934-1940

Bands

Cottage

Flowers

Backstamp:
A. Grey ink stamp "Wadeheath England Registration No 812930" and embossed "121A"
B. Black ink stamp "Wadeheath England" with a lion and impressed "121A"
C. Black ink stamp "Flaxman Ware Hand Made Pottery by Wadeheath England" with embossed "121"
D. Black ink stamp "Wade Heath England" with embossed "121"

Name	Colourways	Size	U.S. $	Can. $	U.K. £
Bands	Cream; yellow, green, black and orange	230	120.00	140.00	60.00
Cottage	Cream; brown, grey, green, orange and blue	230	120.00	140.00	60.00
Flowers	Cream; orange, blue and yellow	230	120.00	140.00	60.00
Flowers	Cream; yellow, green, orange and blue	230	120.00	140.00	60.00
Flowers	Cream; grey and orange	230	120.00	140.00	60.00
Mottled	Mottled blue	230	120.00	140.00	60.00
Mottled	Mottled cream and turquoise	230	120.00	140.00	60.00
Mottled	Mottled green	230	120.00	140.00	60.00
Mottled	Mottled orang	230	120.00	140.00	60.00
Mottled	Mottled yellow and golden brown	230	120.00	140.00	60.00

Shape 129, Jugs, 1934-1935

This art deco-shaped vase has two half handles, one on the upper section, the other on the opposite lower section.

Backstamp: Black ink stamp "Wadeheath England" with a lion and embossed "129"

Name	Colourways	Size	U.S. $	Can. $	U.K. £
Flowers	White; blue/orange/yellow flowers; orange handles/foot	135	200.00	225.00	100.00
Leaves	Mottled yellow; green/grey/yellow leaves	135	200.00	225.00	100.00
Trees and rectangles	Cream; cream trees; multicoloured flowers/rectangles	135	200.00	225.00	100.00

Shape 131, Jugs, 1934-1940

These jugs have horizontal ribs running around the body and base.

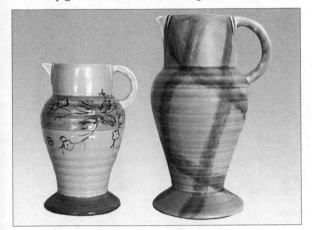

Backstamp: **A.** Black ink stamp "WadeHeath England" with a lion and impressed "131"

B. Black ink stamp "Flaxman Ware Hand Made Pottery by Wadeheath, England" and impressed "131MIN" or "131MS"

Name	Colourways	Size	U.S. $	Can. $	U.K. £
Flowers	Cream; blue base; green band; blue flowers; brown branches	Miniature/135	75.00	85.00	40.00
Mottled	Mottled blue	Miniature/135	60.00	70.00	30.00
Mottled	Mottled green	Miniature/135	60.00	70.00	30.00
Mottled	Mottled grey	Miniature/135	60.00	70.00	30.00
Bands	Yellow; green crossed bands	Medium/184	60.00	70.00	30.00
Cross bands	Grey; blue/brown crossed bands	Medium/184	60.00	70.00	30.00
Mottled	Mottled blue	Medium/184	60.00	70.00	30.00
Mottled	Mottled green/orange on yellow	Medium/184	60.00	70.00	30.00
Bird	Light green; green/brown trees; brown bird	Large/215	125.00	150.00	60.00
Cottage	Off white; bright orange base, handle, cottage; brown tree	Large/215	125.00	150.00	60.00
Flowers	Cream; bright yellow base, handle; multicoloured flowers	Large/215	125.00	150.00	60.00
Mottled	Mottled grey/mauve; mottled brown handle, base	Large/215	60.00	70.00	30.00
Mottled	Mottled yellow/green/orange	Large/215	60.00	70.00	30.00
Trees and sun	Green; orange sun; blue/green/orange trees	Large/215	60.00	70.00	30.00

Shape 134, Jugs, 1935-1937

These six-sided jugs have four panels of raised lines and two framed panels on either side.

Cottage

Mottled

Windmill

Backstamp: **A.** Black ink stamp "Wadeheath England" with a lion and embossed "134"
B. "Flaxman Ware Hand Made Pottery by Wadeheath England" with embossed "134"

Name	Colourways	Size	U.S. $	Can. $	U.K. £
Cottage	Cream; brown cottage, tree	215	100.00	115.00	50.00
Mottled	Mottled blue-green	215	100.00	115.00	50.00
Mottled	Mottled brown/green	215	100.00	115.00	50.00
Mottled	Mottled green	215	100.00	115.00	50.00
Mottled	Mottled orange bands; mottled turquoise bands	215	100.00	115.00	50.00
Mottled	Mottled orange/brown	215	100.00	115.00	50.00
Windmill	Mottled green; blue/black windmill	215	100.00	115.00	50.00

Shape 135, Jugs, 1934-1937

These unusual jugs have four spouts around the rim.

Cottage

Flowers

Plain

Backstamp: **A.** Black ink stamp "Wadeheath England" with a lion and embossed "135"
B. Black ink stamp "Flaxman Ware Hand Made Pottery by Wadeheath, England" with embossed "135"

Name	Colourways	Size	U.S. $	Can. $	U.K. £
Cottage	Pale green; brown handle, tree; brown/black cottage; multicoloured fruit	216	110.00	125.00	55.00
Flowers	Pale yellow; large mauve flower, small red/yellow flowers	216	100.00	115.00	50.00
Flowers	Pale yellow; large orange flowers; brown leaves	216	100.00	115.00	50.00
Plain	Pale yellow top; light green bottom	216	75.00	85.00	40.00
Rabbits	Pale blue; brown trees, rabbits	216	110.00	125.00	55.00

Shape 147, Jugs, 1933-c.1940

These jugs have wavy, ribbed lines around the bowl.

Backstamp: **A.** Black ink stamp "Wadeheath England" with a lion and embossed "147"
  B. Black ink stamp "Flaxman Wade Heath England"
  C. Green ink stamp "Wade Heath England" with embossed "147"
  D. Black ink stamp "Flaxman Ware Hand Made Pottery Wadeheath England" and impressed "147MIN"

Name	Colourways	Size	U.S. $	Can. $	U.K. £
Flowers	Green base; green/yellow/cream handles; yellow/green flowers; black leaves	Miniature/145	70.00	80.00	35.00
Flowers	Grey base; orange/cream handles; orange/grey flowers; black leaves	Miniature/145	70.00	80.00	35.00
Mottled	Mottled brown/green/cream	Miniature/145	60.00	70.00	30.00
Mottled	Mottled green	Miniature/145	60.00	70.00	30.00
Mottled	Mottled turquoise/brown	Miniature/145	60.00	70.00	30.00
Plain	Green/purple	Miniature/145	60.00	70.00	30.00
Butterfly	Cream; blue/pink flowers; orange butterfly	Medium/185	100.00	115.00	50.00
Flowers	Blue base; blue/yellow/cream handles; blue/yellow flowers; black leaves	Medium/185	100.00	115.00	50.00
Flowers	Cream; orange band; orange/black flowers; black leaves	Medium/185	100.00	115.00	50.00
Budgie	Yellow	Medium/195	60.00	70.00	30.00
Budgie	Blue	Large/225	70.00	80.00	35.00
Budgie	Green	Large/225	70.00	80.00	35.00
Budgie	Turquoise	Large/225	70.00	80.00	35.00
Budgie	Turquoise; dark blue handle	Large/225	70.00	80.00	35.00
Budgie	Yellow	Large/225	70.00	80.00	35.00
Budgie	Green	Extra large/266	70.00	80.00	35.00

Shape 154, Squirrel / Birds Jugs, 1936-c.1948

Type one jugs have a moulded squirrel sitting under a tree holding a nut. A pair of loverbirds are perched on top of the tree branch that forms the handle.

Type two jugs were issued in the late 1940s. They were produced in one-colour glazes and do not have the lovebirds on the handle.

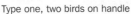

Type one, two birds on handle

Type two, no birds on handle

Backstamp:
- **A.** "Flaxman Wade Heath England" with impressed "154"
- **B.** Brown ink stamp "Flaxman Wade Heath England" with impressed "154"
- **C.** Black ink stamp "Wade Heath England"
- **D.** Black print "Wade England"

Type One: Squirrel and Lovebirds

Name	Colourways	Size	U.S. $	Can. $	U.K. £
Squirrel/birds	Amber; honey-brown squirrel, birds; green leaves	220	125.00	150.00	60.00
Squirrel/birds	Beige jug; brown squirrel, birds	220	125.00	150.00	60.00
Squirrel/birds	Blue jug; blue/brown squirrel, birds	220	125.00	150.00	60.00
Squirrel/birds	Green jug; green/brown squirrel	220	125.00	150.00	60.00
Squirrel/birds	Honey-brown jug; honey/dark brown squirrel, birds	220	125.00	150.00	60.00
Squirrel/birds	Orange jug; grey squirrel, birds	220	125.00	150.00	60.00
Squirrel/birds	Turquoise jug; light brown squirrel, birds	220	125.00	150.00	60.00

Type Two: Squirrel

Name	Colourways	Size	U.S. $	Can. $	U.K. £
Squirrel	Blue	215	100.00	115.00	50.00
Squirrel	Brown	215	100.00	115.00	50.00
Squirrel	Green	215	100.00	115.00	50.00
Squirrel	Orange	215	100.00	115.00	50.00
Squirrel	Pale orange	215	100.00	115.00	50.00
Squirrel	Yellow	215	100.00	115.00	50.00

Shape 168, Dovecote Jugs, 1936-1940

These jugs were moulded in the shape of a wooden dovecote on a pole; the bird forms the top of the handle. Large lupins grow under the birdhouse; one flower forming the bottom of the handle.

Backstamp: **A.** Black ink stamp "Flaxman Wade Heath England" with impressed "168"
B. Black ink stamp "Wade Heath England" with impressed "168"

Name	Colourways	Size	U.S. $	Can. $	U.K. £
Dovecote	Cream, brown, pink and lilac (high gloss glaze)	223	150.00	175.00	70.00
Dovecote	Blue, dark brown, yellow and dark blue	223	150.00	175.00	70.00
Dovecote	Green, brown, pale blue, blue and yellow	216	150.00	175.00	70.00
Dovecote	Green, dark brown, blue, yellow and green	223	150.00	175.00	70.00
Dovecote	Green, yellow, brown and blue	223	150.00	175.00	70.00
Dovecote	Yellow, brown and blue	223	150.00	175.00	70.00
Dovecote	Yellow, golden brown, pink, blue and yellow	223	150.00	175.00	70.00

Shape 169, Jugs, 1936-c.1948

Type One, the handle is shaped like a tree branch with a moulded bird feeding chicks in a nest. Type Two jugs were issued in the late 1940s in one-colour glazes; they do not have the bird on the handle.

Bird on handle

No bird on handle

Backstamp: **A.** Green ink stamp "Wade Heath England" with impressed "169"
B. Black ink stamp "Wade England"

Type One: Handle With Bird

Name	Colourways	Size	U.S. $	Can. $	U.K. £
Rabbit/bird	Yellow; brown leaves, rabbit; blue/brown bird	190	150.00	175.00	70.00
Rabbit/bird	Yellow jug, rabbit; green leaves; blue/yellow bird	190	150.00	175.00	70.00
Rabbit/bird	Blue jug, bird; green leaves; grey rabbit	190	150.00	175.00	70.00
Rabbit/bird	Orange; grey rabbit; blue bird	190	150.00	175.00	70 .00

Type Two: Handle Without Bird

Name	Colourways	Size	U.S. $	Can. $	U.K. £
Rabbit	Blue	190	100.00	115.00	50.00
Rabbit	Dark blue	190	100.00	115.00	50.00
Rabbit	Green	190	100.00	115.00	50.00
Rabbit	Orange	190	100.00	115.00	50.00
Rabbit	Yellow	190	100.00	115.00	50.00
Rabbit	Crea	190	100.00	115.00	50.00

Shape 212, Vases, 1934-1935

Backstamp: A. Black ink stamp "WadeHeath England" with a lion and impressed "212"
       B. Black ink stamp "Flaxman Wade Heath England" with impressed "212"

Name	Colourways	Size	U.S. $	Can. $	U.K. £
Castle	Cream; grey rim; yellow turrets; mauve/purple flowers	165	100.00	115.00	50.00
Flowers	Brown; orange/yellow flowers; green leaves	165	100.00	115.00	50.00
Solid colour	Pale blue	165	100.00	115.00	50.00

Shape 213, Vases, 1934-1935

Flowers

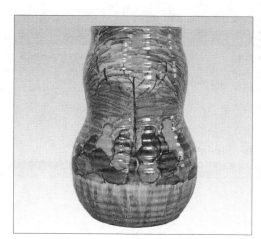

Tree

Backstamp: Black ink stamp "WadeHeath England" with a lion and impressed "213"

Name	Colourways	Size	U.S. $	Can. $	U.K. £
Flowers	Fawn; orange leaves; blue/red flowers	184	90.00	100.00	45.00
Flowers	Mottled blue/mauve; large orange flowers; brown flying birds/trees	184	90.00	100.00	45.00
Tree	Cream/brown; brown/green tree; brown rocks; green grass	184	90.00	100.00	45.00

Shape 214, Vases, 1934-1935

Backstamp: Black ink stamp "WadeHeath England"with a lion and impressed "214"

Name	Colourways	Size	U.S. $	Can. $	U.K. £
Flowers	Mottled cream/brown; yellow leaves; orange/blue flowers	184	90.00	100.00	45.00
Mottled	Mottled green	184	60.00	70.00	30.00
Two tone	Pale blue/light brown	184	60.00	70.00	30.00

Shape 215, Vases, 1934-1937

The hand painted vase has a cottage and trees design often seen on Wadeheath items of this era. The mottled V vase has a background of turquoise with a broad band of orange in a V shape.

Cottage and trees

Mottles V

Backstamp: Black ink stamp "Flaxman Ware Hand Made Pottery by Wadeheath England" with impressed "215"
1935-1937

Name	Colourways	Size	U.S. $	Can. $	U.K. £
Cottage and trees	Cream/brown;/green;/grey/orange/blue flowers; green handles	190	100.00	115.00	50.00
Mottled stripe	Pale blue; yellow stripe	190	90.00	100.00	45.00
Mottled V	Turquoise; orange	190	90.00	100.00	45.00

Shape 217, Vases, 1934-1937

There are several holes for flowers on top of the scalloped ledge in the middle of the vase.

Backstamp: **A.** Black ink stamp "WadeHeath England" with a lion and impressed "217", 1934-1935
B. Black ink stamp "Flaxman Ware Hand Made Pottery by Wadeheath England" with impressed "217", 1935-1937

Name	Colourways	Size	U.S. $	Can. $	U.K. £
Flowers	Cream; orange flowers; grey shields; orange rim	225	100.00	115.00	50.00
Flowers	Cream; yellow/mauve/orange flowers; green handles, shields; orange rim	225	100.00	115.00	50.00
Mottled	Mottled blue	225	90.00	100.00	45.00
Mottled	Mottled grey/pale blue	225	90.00	100.00	45.00

Shape 310, Vases, 1934-1937

This tapered vase has an embossed Art Nouveau leaf design wrapped around the body from top to bottom. The design on the flowered vase obscures the embossed leaf.

Flowers

Silver flower, leaf

Backstamp: Black ink stamped Wadeheath England with Lion and embossed No 219

Name	Colourways	Size	U.S. $	Can. $	U.K. £
Flowers	Cream; multicoloured flowers	220	100.00	115.00	50.00
Silver flower /leaf	Cream; light green rim/base; silver leaf and flower	220	100.00	115.00	50.00

Shape 359, Gothic Ware Vases, 1940, c.1947-c.1953

The 1940 issue was produced in matt colours. Shape 359 was reissued from 1947 to 1953 in new gloss colours, with the embossed design highlighted in pastel colours and gold lustre.

Flaxenware, matt

Gold lustre, high gloss

Backstamp: **A.** Black ink stamp "Gothic Wade Heath England" with impressed "359"
B. Green ink stamp "Wade England Gothic" with impressed "359"

Name	Colourways	Size	U.S. $	Can. $	U.K. £
Gothic	Orange; matt	170	90.00	100.00	45.00
Gothic	Pale orange; pale pink flowers; pale green leaves; gloss	170	90.00	100.00	45.00
Gothic	Cream; pink/yellow flowers; blue/green leaves; gold lustre; gloss	170	90.00	100.00	45.00
Gothic	Cream; lilac/pink flowers; green/gold leaves; gloss	160	90.00	100.00	45.00

Shape 362, Harvest Ware Vases, c.1948-c.1952

The large daisy and peony designs are hand-painted, so no two are identical. A Canadian store advertised the peony vase for sale in June 1951.

Daisies

Daisy with bands

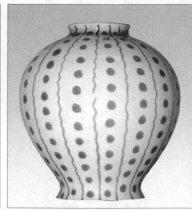

Spots and wavy lines

Backstamp: **A.** Black ink stamp "Harvest Ware Wade England" with impressed "362"
B. Black ink stamp "Wade England" with impressed "362"

Name	Colourways	Size	U.S. $	Can. $	U.K. £
Daisies	Cream; purple/maroon flowers	225	100.00	115.00	50.00
Daisy and bands	Grey; white band; blue/grey flowers	225	100.00	115.00	50.00
Leaves	Cream; long brown / coffee leaves; grey speckles	225	100.00	115.00	50.00
Peony	Cream; multicoloured flowers	225	100.00	115.00	50.00
Spots, wavy lines	White; blue spots; grey lines	225	100.00	115.00	50.00

DISNEY

A small number of Walt Disney character models were produced by Wade Heath Ltd. for approximately three years before giftware production ceased at the onset of World War II. In the early 1960s, Wade again produced Disney figures under license to Walt Disney.

Disney Money Boxes

Please see the Money Box Section Page 260 for the complete listing of "Hat Box" Figure Money Boxes.

BROOCHES

Snow White and the Seven Dwarfs, c.1938

Miniature lapel brooches were produced in the cellulose glaze used by the Wadeheath pottery during the mid-late 1930s, one of Snow White's face and full figure brooches of the dwarfs. The brooches have only been found in Canada and the USA. They were probably produced for Walt Disney staff during the North American promotion of the film *Snow White and the Seven Dwarfs.* They have an unusual "Wade Burslem England" backstamp, which adds to the belief that they were a special promotion.

Backstamp: Embossed "[name of character] Made in England Wade Burslem England"

Name	Colourways	Size	U.S. $	Can. $	U.K. £
Snow White	Black hair and eyes; red bow and mouth	40			
Bashful	Green hat; orange coat; blue trousers; brown shoes	35			
Doc	Green hat; orange coat; maroon trousers; yellow belt buckle; blue shoes	35		All Are	
Dopey	Unknown	35		Considered	
Grumpy	Orange hat; orange-brown coat; blue trousers; orange brown shoes	37		Very Rare	
Happy	Light blue hat; brown coat; green trousers; red-brown shoes	35			
Sleepy	Green hat; brown coat; purple trousers; red shoes	35			
Sneezy	Green hat; blue coat; orange-red trousers; orange shoes	35			

CLOCK

Happy (Seven Dwarfs), c.1938

A rare find is a *Happy Clock* in the cellulose glaze used by the Wade Heath pottery during the mid-late 1930s. The eyes move from side to side as the clock ticks. Although not marked "Wade," this unusual piece has the same cellulose colours used on the 1930's *Snow White Dwarfs*. More interesting is that the paper label has a BCM/OWL mark which is a known backstamp used on a number of the early Wade Lady Figures.

| Happy Clock, Front | Happy Clock, Back | Happy Clock, Base |

Backstamp: Impressed "Made in England" on back of hat, Paper Label on base with black printed "By permission Walt Disney Mickey Mouse Ltd., Made in England" BCM/OWL Foreign Movement is ink stamped on the wood back plate.

Name	Colourways	Size	U.S. $	Can. $	U.K. £
Happy Clock	Yellow hat and jacket; orange trousers; green shoes	Unknown	Extremely Rare		

FIGURINES

Blow Ups, 1961-1965

Disney Blow Ups is a set of ten characters from the Disney films *Lady and the Tramp* and *Bambi*. They are referred to as blow-ups because they are larger slip cast versions of the miniature *Hat Box Series* that preceded them. "Tramp," "Jock," "Thumper" and "Dachie" are the hardest of these models to find.

Name	Issue Price	Issue Date
Tramp	17/6d	January 1961
Lady	15/-	January 1961
Bambi	13/6d	January 1961
Scamp	12/6d	January 1961
Si	15/-	Autumn 1961
Am	15/-	Autumn 1961
Thumper	12/6d	Autumn 1961
Trusty	17/6d	Autumn 1961
Jock	13/6d	Autumn 1962
Dachie	15/-	Autumn 1962

Backstamp: **A.**   Black transfer "Wade Porcelain—Copyright Walt Disney Productions—Made in England" (1-10)
             B.   Black transfer "Wade Porcelain—Copyright Walt Disney Productions—Made in Ireland" (7)

Name	Colourways	Size	U.S. $	Can. $	U.K. £
Tramp	Grey; white face, neck, chest; red tongue	160 x 105	400.00	450.00	200.00
Lady	Beige; honey ears; blue collar	110 x 140	150.00	175.00	80.00
Bambi	Beige; white spots; pink ears; red tongue	110 x 120	150.00	175.00	80.00
Scamp	Grey; pink ears; white/maroon paws	110 x 115	150.00	175.00	80.00
Si	Brown; black/lilac ears; blue eyes; red mouth	140 x 110	150.00	175.00	80.00
Am	Brown; black/lilac ears; black nose, tail, legs	147 x 85	150.00	175.00	80.00
Thumper	Blue; white/yellow, white/red flowers	130 x 80	600.00	700.00	300.00
Trusty	Beige; red-brown ears; gold medallion	135 x 80	600.00	700.00	300.00
Jock	Grey; pink/mauve ears; gold medallion	100 x 115	600.00	700.00	300.00
Dachie	Beige; brown ears, eyes; red tongue	125 x 105	600.00	700.00	300.00

Bulldogs, c.1968

Two model bulldogs have been found, possibly representing Pluto's arch enemy "Butch" and his nephew "Bull." The models are slip cast (hollow). Both bulldogs are sitting and smiling; "Butch" scratches his ribs with his hind leg.

Butch

Backstamp: Black printed "Wade Porcelain Copyright Walt Disney Productions Made in England"

Name	Colourways	Size	U.S. $	Can. $	U.K. £
Bull	Cream; grey muzzle, nose	85 x 100	250.00	300.00	130.00
Butch	Beige; grey muzzle, nose	90 x 110	250.00	300.00	130.00

Donald Duck, 1937

A Japanese copy of the Wade Donald Duck has been reported in a slightly different colourway.

Backstamp: Black ink stamp "WadeHeath England with lion" (1934-1937)

Name	Colourways	Size	U.S. $	Can. $	U.K. £
Donald Duck	White body; yellow beak, legs; blue hat, coat; red bow tie	127		Rare	

Dopey (Seven Dwarfs), 1939

This cellulose model of Dopey is a different model than the one used for the 1938 *Snow White* set. He was the only model produced in an intended *Snow White* set for F.W. Woolworth, England during Christmas 1939, but with the onset of World War II, the order for the rest of the models was cancelled.

Backstamp: None

Name	Colourways	Size	U.S. $	Can. $	U.K. £
Dopey	Mauve hat; yellow coat; brown shoes	110 x 53	400.00	450.00	200.00

HAT BOX SERIES

First Issue, 1956-1965

These charming Walt Disney cartoon characters were sold in round, striped cardboard boxes which resemble hat boxes, from which this series takes its name. The boxes each had a colour print of the enclosed model on the lid. There are 26 models in this long-running series. The last ten models had only a short production run and are considered scarce. The hardest of all to find are the models from *The Sword in the Stone*, especially the Merlin models.

Three variations of "Jock" can be found. When first produced in 1956, he was not wearing a coat. After Wade was advised that he wore one in the film, he was produced with a blue tartan coat in early 1957. Later that year the coat was changed to green tartan.

The original price for all the models was 2/11d, except for the figures from *The Sword in the Stone*, which sold for 3/6d. The films from which the models were taken are as follows:

Film	Model	Date of Issue
Lady and the Tramp	Lady	January 1956
	Jock, No Coat	January 1956
	Jock, Blue Coat	Early 1957
	Jock, Green Coat	Late 1957
	Tramp	January 1956
	Trusty	January 1956
	Peg	February 1957
	Scamp	February 1957
	Dachie	January 1958
	Si	August 1958
	Am	August 1958
	Boris	February 1960
	Toughy	February 1960
Bambi	Bambi	December 1957
	Flower	December 1957
	Thumper	December 1957
Dumbo	Dumbo	December 1957
Fantasia	Baby Pegasus	January 1958
101 Dalmatians	The Colonel	September 1961
	Lucky	September 1961
	Rolly	September 1961
	Sergeant Tibbs	September 1961
The Sword in the Stone	Archimedes	Autumn 1962
	Madam Mim	Autumn 1962
	Merlin as a Caterpillar	Autumn 1962
	Merlin as a Hare	Autumn 1962
	Merlin as a Turtle	Autumn 1962
	The Girl Squirrel	Autumn 1962

Set One, 1956-1965

Backstamp: **A.** Black and gold "Wade England" Label
B. Blue transfer "Wade England"
C. Unmarked

Name	Colourways	Size	U.S. $	Can. $	U.K. £
Lady	Beige; light brown ears; blue collar	40 x 35	30.00	35.00	15.00
Jock, no coat	Blue-grey; purple mouth	40 x 25	60.00	70.00	30.00
Jock, blue tartan coat	Blue coat; purple mouth	40 x 25	60.00	70.00	30.00
Jock, green tartan coat	Green coat; purple mouth	40 x 25	50.00	60.00	25.00
Tramp, standing	Grey/white; red tongue	50 x 50	70.00	80.00	35.00
Trusty	Brown; brown nose	55 x 35	60.00	70.00	30.00
Trusty	Brown; black nose	55 x 35	70.00	80.00	35.00
Peg	Yellow fringe; red nose, mouth	40 x 35	30.00	35.00	15.00
Scamp	Grey; mauve ears, mouth; brown toes	40 x 35	30.00	35.00	15.00

Set Two

Backstamp: **A.** Black and gold "Wade England" label
B. Unmarked

Name	Colourways	Size	U.S. $	Can. $	U.K. £
Bambi	Beige; tan/white patches; dark brown eyes	40 x 35	40.00	45.00	20.00
Flower	Black/white; blue eyes; red tongue	40 x 25	70.00	80.00	35.00
Thumper	Blue-grey; pink cheeks; red mouth	60 x 35	70.00	80.00	35.00
Thumper	Blue-grey; white cheeks; red mouth	60 x 35	70.00	80.00	35.00
Dumbo	Grey/white; pink ears	40 x 38	90.00	100.00	45.00
Baby Pegasus	Blue-grey; blue eyes; pink nose, mouth	40 x 30	90.00	100.00	45.00
Dachie	Brown; light brown ears; red mouth	60 x 30	40.00	45.00	20.00
Si	Beige; black tail, legs, ears; blue eyes	60 x 30	70.00	80.00	35.00
Am	Beige; black tail, legs, ears; eyes closed	60 x 25	60.00	70.00	30.00
Boris	Grey; white chest, tail tip; pink in ears	60 x 28	70.00	80.00	35.00
Toughy	Brown; white chest, face; red tongue	55 x 30	100.00	115.00	50.00

Set Three

Backstamp: **A.** Black and gold "Wade England" label
B. Unmarked

Name	Colourways	Size	U.S. $	Can. $	U.K. £
The Colonel	Beige/white; black streak across eye	50 x 34	100.00	115.00	50.00
Sergeant Tibbs	Beige; white chest, nose, paws; blue in ears	55 x 30	100.00	115.00	50.00
Rolly	White; black spots; red collar; sitting	40 x 30	100.00	115.00	50.00
Lucky	White; black spots, ears; red collar; standing	30 x 35	100.00	115.00	50.00
Madam Mim	Honey/brown; black neck, wing tips	30 x 28	175.00	200.00	90.00
Merlin as a Turtle	Brown-grey; black/white eyes	30 x 45	300.00	325.00	145.00
Archimedes	Brown head, back, wings, log	50 x 35	150.00	175.00	80.00
Merlin as a Hare	Blue; white tail, chest	55 x 35	150.00	175.00	80.00
The Girl Squirrel	Beige; honey brown tail	50 x 30	100.00	115.00	50.00
Merlin as a Caterpillar	White/pink/mauve; black/yellow eyes	20 x 45	300.00	325.00	145.00

Hat Box Derivatives, First Issues

Butter Dish, c.1960

From 1955 to 1956, the George Wade Pottery produced a butter dish, to which "Jock" was later added on the back rim.

Backstamp: Embossed "Wade England"

Name	Colourways	Size	U.S. $	Can. $	U.K. £
Jock	No coat; blue dish	65 x 80	60.00	70.00	30.00
Jock	No coat; grey dish	65 x 80	60.00	70.00	30.00
Jock	No coat; white dish	65 x 80	60.00	70.00	30.00
Jock	Blue coat, dish	65 x 80	60.00	70.00	30.00
Jock	Green coat; blue dish	65 x 80	60.00	70.00	30.00

Card Trumps, c.1960

These unusual pieces are of "Merlin as a Hare." One is glued onto a Bakerlite stand which has plastic playing card trumps hanging from the frame, and the other is fixed to a Bouldray tray which has a brass card trump frame on it.

Backstamp: Raised "Bouldray Wade Porcelain 2 Made in England"

Name	Colourways	Size	U.S. $	Can. $	U.K. £
Merlin as a Hare	Bakerlite brown stand, frame; blue/grey Merlin; white plastic cards	90 x 75		Rare	
Merlin as a Hare	Brass frame; blue tray; blue/grey Merlin; white plastic cards	90 x 75		Rare	

Hat Box Derivatives, First Issues (cont.)

Disney Lights (Candle Holders), c.1960

This set is similar in appearance to the 1959-1960 *Zoo Lights*, but the triangular base is much larger, thicker and heavier, and it has an original issue *Hat Box* model sitting on the front edge of the candle holder. The holders are all black and were made for cake-size candles, which stand in a hole on the back edge. These models are rarely found. Examples other than those listed below are believed to exist.

Flower Candle Holder

Lady Candle Holder

Scamp Candle Holder

Backstamp: Embossed "Wade"

Name	Colourways	Size	U.S. $	Can. $	U.K. £
Bambi	Beige; black holder	60 x 50	100.00	115.00	55.00
Dumbo	White/pink; black holder	60 x 50	100.00	115.00	55.00
Flower	Black/white; black holder	60 x 50	100.00	115.00	55.00
Jock	Blue-grey/white; green coat; black holder	60 x 50	100.00	115.00	55.00
Lady	Beige/white; black holder	60 x 50	100.00	115.00	55.00
Lucky	White; black spots, holder	50 x 50	100.00	115.00	55.00
Rolly	White; black spots, holder	60 x 50	100.00	115.00	55.00
Thumper	Blue-grey/white; black holder	80 x 50	100.00	115.00	55.00

Hat Box Series Second Issue, 1981-1985

In spring 1981 George Wade and Son renewed its license with Walt Disney Productions Ltd. and reissued six models from the *Hat Box* series, using the original moulds. The new series was named "Disneys."

At first glance the reissues are hard to distinguish from the earlier figures. As the original moulds were used, some of which were worn, the model features are flat compared to the originals which is most noticeable on the "Scamp" model. There is only a slight variation in colour on the reissued models. The name of "Dachie" was changed to "Dachsie."

Four new models from the Disney film, *The Fox and the Hound,*— "Tod," "Copper," "Chief" and "Big Mama"— were added in February 1982. In 1985 the last two models in the set, a new shape "Tramp" and a reissued "Peg" were issued.

When first issued the models were sold in round, numbered plastic hat box-shaped containers, later the plastic boxes were discontinued and the Disneys were then sold in oblong numbered cardboard boxes, which had two types of labels: type one — a long label that sealed the box flap, type two — a short 'name' label. "Tramp" and "Peg," were only issued in cardboard boxes. Models are listed in chronological order.

Backstamp: Black and gold label "Walt Disney Productions Wade England"

Name	Colourways	Size	U.S. $	Can. $	U.K. £
Lady	Dark brown ears; light blue collar	40 x 35	50.00	60.00	25.00
Scamp	Pink mouth, ears; facial markings flat	40 x 35	50.00	60.00	25.00
Jock, green tartan coat	Green coat; pink mouth; orange collar	40 x 25	50.00	60.00	25.00
Dachsie	Dark brown ears; pink mouth	60 x 30	50.00	60.00	25.00
Bambi	Light brown eyes	40 x 35	50.00	60.00	25.00
Thumper	Light grey; pink mouth, cheeks; pale orange flower	60 x 35	50.00	60.00	25.00
Copper	Beige; brown patch, ears; white chest, paws	45 x 50	60.00	70.00	30.00
Tod	Red-brown; dark brown paws	45 x 50	60.00	70.00	30.00
Big Mama	Beige head, back, wings; orange beak	45 x 45	60.00	70.00	30.00
Chief	Grey; white chest; black eyes; red tongue	50 x 20	60.00	70.00	30.00
Tramp, seated	Grey; red tongue	47 x 30	60.00	70.00	30.00
Peg	Beige fringe; brown nose; pink mouth	40 x 35	50.00	60.00	25.00

Note: Prices listed are for pieces only or pieces in cardboard boxes. Models that are found in their original round plastic boxes will command a premium of 10-20% above list price.

Little Hiawatha and his Forest Friends, 1937

These models are from Walt Disney's cartoon *Little Hiawatha*. The models shown can be seen in a Wade Heath advertisement dated August 2nd, 1937. Along side Hiawatha are a deer, a bear cub and another character which has not been identified, but is thought to be an opossum or possum. In the cartoon Little Hiawatha goes on a hunting trip in the forest and meets many small animals he cannot bear to shoot with his bow and arrow. In a conversation with Tony Wade, he referred to the four models in the advertisment as "Hiawatha and his Forest Friends." "Hiawatha" was produced with a cellulose glaze, so it is difficult to find in mint condition.

Little Hiawatha

Little Hiawatha's friend Opossum

Advertisement from August 1937 issue of *Pottery and Glass Trade Review*,
Little Hiawatha, Deer, Bear Cub, Opossum (Possum) and Pluto

Backstamp: **A.** Black hand-painted "'Hiawatha' Wade England"
B. Unmarked

Name	Colourways	Size	U.S. $	Can. $	U.K. £
Bear Cub	Unknown	Unknown		Rare	
Deer	Unknown	Unknown		Rare	
Little Hiawatha	Yellow feather; red trousers	100 x 50	200.00	225.00	100.00
Little Hiawatha	Red feather; blue trousers	100 x 50	200.00	225.00	100.00
Opossum / Possum	Beige; black eyebrows, eyes, nose	90	200.00	225.00	100.00

Mickey Mouse, 1935

A rare model of *Mickey Mouse* was produced by the Wadeheath Pottery at the same time as a children's toy Mickey Mouse tea set. This model was first advertised along with the toy tea set in March 1935.

Backstamp: Black ink stamp "Wadeheath Ware by Permission Walt Disney Mickey Mouse Ltd Made in England" (1935)

Colourways	Size	U.S. $	Can. $	U.K. £
Black and white body; yellow gloves; blue shorts; orange shoes; brown suitcase	90	2,000.00	2,250.00	1,000.00
Black and white body; yellow gloves; green shorts; orange shoes; brown suitcase	90	2,000.00	2,250.00	1,000.00
Black and white body; yellow gloves; orange shorts and shoes; brown suitcase	95	2,000.00	2,250.00	1,000.00
Black and white body; yellow gloves and shoes; blue shorts; brown suitcase	90	2,000.00	2,250.00	1,000.00

Pluto, 1937-1938

Some *Pluto* models may have the impressed shape number 205.

Backstamp: **A.** Black ink stamp "Wadeheath by permission of Walt Disney, England"
B. Black ink stamp "Flaxman Ware Hand Made Pottery by Wadeheath England"

Name	Colourways	Size	U.S. $	Can. $	U.K. £
Pluto	Grey; black ears, nose, eyes	100 x 162	450.00	500.00	225.00
Pluto	Orange-brown; black ears, nose, eyes	100 x 162	450.00	500.00	225.00
Pluto	White; black ears, nose and eyes	100 x 162	450.00	500.00	225.00

Pluto's Pups, 1937

Pluto's puppies, the "Quinpuplets," were from the Walt Disney cartoon film of the same name. In the film they were not given names, but one pup reappeared in a 1942 Disney cartoon as "Pluto Junior."

Pup sitting, front paws up and Puppy, lying on back

Pup, sitting

Pup, sniffing ground

Pup, looking back

Backstamp: **A.** Black ink stamp "Flaxman Wadeheath England"
B. Black ink stamp "Wadeheath by permission of Walt Disney, England"

Name	Colourways	Size	U.S. $	Can. $	U.K. £
Pup, lying on back	Beige	62 x 112	450.00	500.00	225.00
Pup, lying on back	Green	62 x 112	450.00	500.00	225.00
Pup, lying on back	Orange	62 x 112	450.00	500.00	225.00
Pup, sitting	Grey; blue ears, eyes, nose	100 x 62	450.00	500.00	225.00
Pup, sitting	Orange	100 x 62	450.00	500.00	225.00
Pup, sitting, front paws up	Beige	95 x 85	450.00	500.00	225.00
Pup, sitting, front paws up	Grey; blue ears, eyes, nose	95 x 85	450.00	500.00	225.00
Pup, sitting, front paws up	Light blue; dark blue ears, eyes	95 x 85	450.00	500.00	225.00
Pup, sitting, front paws up	Light grey; dark blue ears, eyes	95 x 85	450.00	500.00	225.00
Pup, sitting, front paws up	Orange	95 x 85	450.00	500.00	225.00
Pup, sitting, front paws up	Orange; blue ears, eyes, nose	95 x 85	450.00	500.00	225.00
Pup, sniffing ground	Beige	62 x 112	450.00	500.00	225.00
Pup, sniffing ground	Orange	62 x 112	450.00	500.00	225.00
Pup, looking back	Grey; blue ears, eyes, nose	100 x 62	450.00	500.00	225.00
Pup, looking back	Orange	100 x 62	450.00	500.00	225.00

Sammy Seal, 1937

Sammy Seal is believed to have appeared in a Disney Short in which *Mickey Mouse* carries him home unknowingly in his picnic basket after a visit to the zoo. A miniature model of *Sammy* has been found which is approximately 85 mm in height and has no backstamp.

Backstamp: Black ink stamp "Wadeheath England by permission Walt Disney"

Name	Colourways	Size	U.S. $	Can. $	U.K. £
Sammy	Beige	Large/150 x 150	450.00	500.00	225.00
Sammy	Grey; black eyes, nose	Large/150 x 150	450.00	500.00	225.00
Sammy	Off white; brown eyes	Large/150 x 150	450.00	500.00	225.00
Sammy	Orange	Large/150 x 150	450.00	500.00	225.00
Sammy	Orange, black eyes, nose	Large/150 x 150	450.00	500.00	225.00
Sammy	Pink; black eyes, nose	Large/150 x 150	450.00	500.00	225.00
Sammy	White; black eyes, nose	Large/150 x 150	450.00	500.00	225.00
Sammy	Orange, black eyes, nose	Small/110 x 110	450.00	500.00	225.00
Sammy	Beige; black eyes, nose	Miniature/85	400.00	450.00	200.00
Sammy	Orange; black eyes, nose	Miniature/85	400.00	450.00	200.00

Snow White and the Seven Dwarfs

Style One, 1938

The George Wade Pottery held a Walt Disney license to produce Disney models, and the Wade Heath Royal Victoria Pottery issued this first *Snow White* set to coincide with the release of the Walt Disney film, *Snow White and the Seven Dwarfs*. These models were produced with a cellulose glaze.

Backstamp: **A.** Black hand-painted "Wade [name of model]," plus red ink stamp with a leaping deer and "Made in England"

B. Black hand-painted "Wade [name of model]," plus red ink stamp "Made in England"

C. Unmarked

Name	Colourways	Size	U.S. $	Can. $	U.K. £
Snow white	Yellow dress; red bodice	180 x 65	500.00	575.00	250.00
Bashful	Orange coat; blue trousers	100 x 45	275.00	300.00	135.00
Doc	Orange jacket; maroon trousers	110 x 55	275.00	300.00	135.00
Dopey	Red coat; green trousers	110 x 45	275.00	300.00	135.00
Grumpy	Maroon jacket; green trousers	100 x 60	275.00	300.00	135.00
Happy	Orange jacket; red trousers	125 x 55	275.00	300.00	135.00
Sleepy	Orange-brown jacket; blue trousers	100 x 35	275.00	300.00	135.00
Sneezy	Blue jacket; red trousers	100 x 35	275.00	300.00	135.00
Set (8 pieces)	Boxed	—	4,000.00	4,500.00	2,000.00

Style Two, 1981-1984

This issue of *Snow White and the Seven Dwarfs*, modelled by Alan Maslankowski, was first offered through mail order by Harper's Direct Mail Marketing just before Christmas 1981, then distributed in stores during the next spring.

Snow White, First Version

Snow White, Second Version

Backstamp:
A. Black and gold label "© Walt Disney Productions Wade England"
B. Black transfer "© Walt Disney Productions Wade England"
C. Black transfer "Wade Made in England"

Name	Colourways	Size	U.S. $	Can. $	U.K. £
Snow White, First Version	Head straight; smiling; pink, light blue, pale yellow	95 x 100	225.00	250.00	115.00
Snow White, Second Version	Head back; pink, light blue, pale yellow	95 x 100	225.00	250.00	115.00
Bashful	Orange coat; grey hat; beige shoes	80 x 45	200.00	225.00	95.00
Doc	Blue coat; grey trousers; beige hat, shoes	80 x 50	200.00	225.00	95.00
Dopey	Beige coat; red hat; pale blue shoes	80 x 50	200.00	225.00	95.00
Grumpy	Red coat; beige hat; brown shoes	75 x 45	200.00	225.00	95.00
Happy	Brown vest; beige hat; blue trousers	85 x 50	200.00	225.00	95.00
Sleepy	Pale green coat, shoes; orange hat	80 x 50	200.00	225.00	95.00
Sneezy	Navy coat; blue trousers; brown hat, shoes	80 x 45	200.00	225.00	95.00
8 pce set	Boxed	—	1,500.00	1,700.00	750.00

MUSICAL JUGS

Big Bad Wolf and the Three Little Pigs Jugs, 1937-1939

The Big Bad Wolf forms the handle of these cartoon jugs, which can be found with or without a musical box fitted in the base. The jug is hand painted, so no two are identicle (for example, the top of the door on the pig's house is square on one jug, rounded on another). The musical jug plays "Whose Afraid of the Big Bad Wolf" or "The Teddy Bear's Picnic."

Musical Jug, round door

Musical jug, square door

Backstamp: Black hand painted "Wadeheath England"

Name	Colourways	Size	U.S. $	Can. $	U.K. £
Jug	Cream/multicoloured; brown wolf; orange and green	245	850.00	950.00	425.00
Musical jug, round door	Cream/multicoloured; brown wolf; orange and green	260	1,000.00	1,150.00	500.00
Musical jug, square door	Cream/multicoloured; brown wolf; orange amd green	260	1,000.00	1,150.00	500.00

Snow White and the Seven Dwarfs, 1938

This musical jug has Snow White and the Seven Dwarfs moulded around the front with the dwarfs' cottage on the back. A squirrel and a pair of bluebirds sit on the handle. Two tunes have been reported, "Whistle While You Work" and "Someday My Prince Will Come."

Snow White Musical Jug, face

Snow White Musical Jug, back

Backstamp: Black ink stamp "Wade Heath England"

Name	Colourways	Size	U.S. $	Can. $	U.K. £
Snow White	Cream; multicoloured figures	225	1,000.00	1,150.00	500.00

NURSERY WARES

Mickey Mouse and Friends Nursery Ware, c.1934

Although Wadeheath advertising shows these items as a boxed set of four pieces, a heavy baby plate, a clipped-corner plate and a cup and saucer, a fifth piece, an oatmeal bowl with clipped corners has been found. With each four piece boxed set the purchaser received a free babies mug.

Produced in two background colours, cream or white, each set has different Mickey and Minnie Mouse, Donald Duck, Pluto and other Disney character transfer prints.

Transfer Prints

Mickey and Horsecollar
Mickey looking at puppy
Minnie looking in hand mirror
Minnie reading letter
Mickey and Minnie

Mickey holding out hand to barking Pluto
Mickey walking
Minnie with Horsecollar holding scatter gun
Pluto looking sad

Mickey and Minnie
Plate, Clipped Corners

Mickey Walking
Oatmeal Bowl

Mickey Mouse Conducting Orchestra
Plate, Clipped corners

Backstamp: **A.** Ink stamp "Wadeheath Ware made in England manufactured by permission Walt Disney Mickey Mouse LTD"
B. Ink stamp "Wadeheath Ware by Permission Walt Disney Mickey Mouse LTD made in England"
C. Unmarked

Name	Colourways	Size	U.S. $	Can. $	U.K. £
Baby plate	Cream or white; orange rim; multicoloured print	169	70.00	80.00	35.00
Cup and saucer	Crean or white; orange rim; multicoloured print	77 / 144	70.00	80.00	35.00
Beaker, without handle	Cream or white; orange rim; multicoloured print	60	70.00	80.00	35.00
Beaker, with handle	Cream or white; orange rim; multicoloured print	82	70.00	80.00	35.00
Mug	Cream or white; orange rim; multicoloured print	77	70.00	80.00	35.00
Oatmeal bowl, clipped corners	Cream or white; orange rim; multicoloured print	159	70.00	80.00	35.00
Plate, clipped corners	Cream or white; orange rim; multicoloured print	152	70.00	80.00	35.00
Plate, round	Cream or white; orange rim; multicoloured print	165	70.00	80.00	35.00

Mickey's Circus Nursery Ware, c.1937

Although the transfers are from scenes in the Disney short entitled 'Mickey's Circus', the majority of the transfers feature Donald Duck and Baby seal. In the cartoon Donald's performing seals escape and are chased by an angry Donald. One transfer shows Baby Seal blowing a horn so loudly that Donald, dressed as a bandsman is blown across the circus ring.

Transfer Prints

Baby Seal Blowing Horn
Donald as Bandsman
Donald as Peanut Vendor
Donald with whip
Mickey Mouse Ringmaster

Baby Seal Juggling
Donald Blown Over
Donald and Pluto
Mickey Mouse Conducting orchestra
Mickey Mouse Ringmaster on bicycle

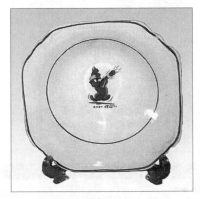

Baby Seal Blowing Horn

Backstamp: Ink stamped "Wadeheath By Permission Walt Disney England"

Name	Colourways	Size	U.S. $	Can. $	U.K. £
Baby plate	White; orange rim; multicoloured print	169	70.00	80.00	35.00
Cup / saucer	White; orange rim; multicoloured print	77 / 144	70.00	80.00	35.00
Beaker, without handle	White; orange rim; multicoloured print	60	70.00	80.00	35.00
Beaker, with handle	White; orange rim; multicoloured print	82	70.00	80.00	35.00
Mug	White; orange rim; multicoloured print	77	70.00	80.00	35.00
Oatmeal bowl, clipped corners	White; orange rim; multicoloured print	159	70.00	80.00	35.00
Plate, clipped corners	White; orange rim; multicoloured print	152	70.00	80.00	35.00
Plate, round	White; orange rim; multicoloured print	165	70.00	80.00	35.00

Nursery Ryhmes Nursery Ware, c.1937

Only one example of the Nursery Ryhmes Nursery Ware set has been found to date. It has a print of Clara bell as Miss Muffet.

Clarabell as Miss Muffett

Backstamp: Ink stamped "Wadeheath By Permission Walt Disney England"

Name	Colourways	Size	U.S. $	Can. $	U.K. £
Mug	White; orange rim; multicoloured print	77	70.00	80.00	35.00

Pinocchio Nursery Ware, c.1937

The baby plate has a thick raised rim and is heavy so that it stays in place more easily.

Transfer Prints

Blue Fairy	Donkey	Figaro the Cat
Gepetto	Jiminy Cricket	Pinocchio
Stromboli's Parrot		

Jiminy Cricket and Blue Fairy   Gepetto and Blue Fairy

Backstamp: **A.** Ink stamp "Wadeheath by permission Walt Disney England"
              B. Black ink stamp "Made in England"

Name	Colourways	Size	U.S. $	Can. $	U.K. £
Baby plate	White; orange rim; multicoloured print	169	70.00	80.00	35.00
Cup and saucer	White; orange rim; multicoloured print	77 / 144	70.00	80.00	35.00
Beaker, without handle	White; orange rim; multicoloured print	60	70.00	80.00	35.00
Beaker, with handle	White; orange rim; multicoloured print	82	70.00	80.00	35.00
Mug	White; orange rim; multicoloured print	77	70.00	80.00	35.00
Oatmeal bowl, clipped corners	White; orange rim; multicoloured print	159	70.00	80.00	35.00
Plate, clipped corners	White; orange rim; multicoloured print	152	70.00	80.00	35.00
Plate, round	White; orange rim; multicoloured print	165	70.00	80.00	35.00

Snow White and the Seven Dwarfs Nursery Ware, 1938

The baby plate has a thick raised rim and is heavy so that it stays in place more easily. Snow White is the most collectable of the Walt Disney items.

Transfer Prints

Bashful	Doc	Dopey
Grumpy	Happy	Sleepy
Sneezy	Snow White	

| Baby plate, 'Snow White' and 'Grumpy' | Beaker with handle, 'Sneezy' | Oatmeal bowl, 'Grumpy' |

Backstamp: Ink stamp "Wadeheath by Permission Walt Disney England"

Name	Colourways	Size	U.S. $	Can. $	U.K. £
Baby plate	White; orange rim; multicoloured print	169	90.00	100.00	45.00
Cup and saucer	White; orange rim; multicoloured print	77 / 144	90.00	100.00	45.00
Beaker, without handle	White; orange rim; multicoloured print	60	90.00	100.00	45.00
Beaker, with handle	White; orange rim; multicoloured print	82	90.00	100.00	45.00
Mug, large	White; orange rim; multicoloured print	77	90.00	100.00	45.00
Mug, small	White; orange rim; multicoloured print	65	90.00	100.00	45.00
Oatmeal bowl, clipped corners	White; orange rim; multicoloured print	159	90.00	100.00	45.00
Plate, clipped corners	White; orange rim; multicoloured print	152	90.00	100.00	45.00
Plate, round	White; orange rim; multicoloured print	165	90.00	100.00	45.00

TABLEWARE

Donald Duck

Large 4-cup teapot

Milk Jug and 2-cup Teapot

Backstamp: **A.** Black ink stamp "Wadeheath By Permission Walt Disney England"
B. Black ink stamp "Wadeheath England By Permission Walt Disney"

Name	Colourways	Size	U.S. $	Can. $	U.K. £
Cream / milk jug	Dark yellow	approx 60		Rare	
Cream / milk jug	White; blue hat/jacket; yellow beak/hands/legs/buttons	approx 60		Rare	
Sugar	Dark yellow	approx 60		Rare	
Sugar	White; blue hat/jacket; yellow beak/hands/legs/buttons	approx 60		Rare	
Teapot, 4-cup	White; blue hat/jacket; yellow beak/hands/legs/buttons	160 x 220	300.00	350.00	150.00
Teapot, 2-cup	White; blur hat/jacket; yellow beak/hands/legs/buttons	101 x 140	250.00	275.00	125.00
Teapot, 2-cup	Dark Yellow	101 x 140	250.00	275.00	125.00

Snow White and the Seven Dwarfs Breakfast Set, 1938

Each item in this series has an embossed background design of bark and embossed multicoloured Snow White figures, Happy and Sleepy are the pepper and salt sitting with their backs to a tree stump which is the mustard pot. The butter dish has a boxed base and the cheese dish has a flat base.

The egg cups were produced with a base which had four receses in which the egg cups stood.

Buscuit Barrel (Snow White)

Butter Dish, round (Dopey)

Butter Dish, square (Dopey)

Cheese Dish (Dwarf's Cottage)

Backstamp: Ink stamp "Wadeheath by permission Walt Disney England"

Name	Colourways	Size	U.S. $	Can. $	U.K. £
Biscuit barrel	Cream/brown/yellow/maroon/green	180	400.00	450.00	200.00
Butter dish, round	Cream/brown/purple/orange/green	115 x 170	250.00	275.00	120.00
Butter dish, round	Blue	115 x 170	200.00	225.00	100.00
Butter dish, round	Pink	115 x 170	200.00	225.00	100.00
Butter dish, square	Cream/brown/maroon/orange/blue	100	200.00	225.00	100.00
Cheese dish	Yellow/brown/green	130 x 180	600.00	675.00	300.00

Cruet

Hot Water Jug

Milk Jug

Sugar Bowl

Teapot

Name	Colourways	Size	U.S. $	Can. $	U.K. £
Cruet set	Cream/green/brown/maroon/yellow	60 x 76	150.00	175.00	80.00
Egg cups / tray	Cream/brown/green	63	200.00	225.00	100.00
Fruit bowl	Cream/brown/green/yellow	229	150.00	175.00	80.00
Honey / Jam pot	Cream/brown/purple	110	100.00	115.00	50.00
Hot water jug	Cream/brown/purple/green/blue	195	400.00	450.00	200.00
Hot water jug	Green	195	300.00	350.00	150.00
Milk jug,	Cream/brown/maroon/green	93	150.00	175.00	80.00
Sandwich plate	Cream/green/purple/yellow/brown	229	150.00	175.00	80.00
Sugar bowl	Cream/brown/maroon/green	101	100.00	115.00	50.00
Sugar bowl	Green	101	80.00	90.00	40.00
Teapot	Cream/brown/maroon/purple/green	165	400.00	450.00	200.00
Toast rack	Cream/brown	65 x 110	150.00	175.00	80.00

Snow White and the Seven Dwarfs Derivatives

Happy Ashtray c.1938-1939

The "Happy" figure, seated on the edge of the ashtray, is the same as that used for the "Sleepy and Happy" Cruet Set, which was produced in 1938 for the Snow White Breakfast Set. Sir George Wade's policy of using up unsold or left over stock by ordering that they be attached to another Wade Heath item was known in the Pottery as a "Stick-em-on-Something". This practice produced many interesting items during the 1930s–1950s. To date this is the only example reported and as such is considered rare.

Backstamp: Ink stamp "Flaxman Ware Hand Made pottery By Wadeheath England"

Name	Colourways	Size	U.S. $	Can. $	U.K. £
Happy Ashtray	Mottled cream tray; green dwarf	40 x 115		Rare	

TOY TEA and DINNER SETS

Lullaby Land Toy Tea Set, c.1940s

The plate has three Walt Disney characters depicted on it with the name "Walt Disney" printed underneath each print. The plate does not have a Walt Disney backstamp.

Transfer Prints

Funny Little Bunnies   Little Hiawatha   Three Little Kittens

Backstamp: Black ink stamp "Wade Heath England" with "A" added (round W 1939-1945)

Name	Colourways	Size	U.S. $	Can. $	U.K. £
Cup / saucer	Cream; orange rim; multicoloured print	46/95	30.00	35.00	15.00
Milk jug	Cream; orange rim; multicoloured print	50	30.00	35.00	15.00
Plate, large	Cream; orange rim; multicoloured print	127	30.00	35.00	15.00
Teapot, small	Cream; orange rim; multicoloured print	76	30.00	35.00	15.00

Mickey Mouse Toy Tea Set, 1935

This set could be purchased with two, four or six cups / saucers and plates. Two size plates in this set have been reported which suggests the set also sold as a 'Dinner' set.

Transfer prints

Horsecollar with scatter gun	Mickey Mouse dancing	Mickey Mouse digging
Mickey Mouse with envelope	Mickey Mouse walking	Mickey Mouse sitting
Minnie Mouse with Horsecollar holding scatter gun	Minnie Mouse reading letter	Minnie Mouse with mirror
Pluto barking	Pluto looking sad	

Backstamp: **A.** Black circular ink stamp "Wadeheath Ware by permission Walt Disney Mickey Mouse Ltd. Made in England"
B. Ink stamp "Wadeheath by permission Walt Disney England"

Name	Colourways	Size	U.S. $	Can. $	U.K. £
Cup / Saucer	White; orange rim; multicoloured print	46 / 95	30.00	35.00	15.00
Milk jug	White; orange rim; multicoloured print	50	30.00	35.00	15.00
Plate, large	White; orange rim; multicoloured print	130	30.00	35.00	15.00
Plate, small	White; orange rim; multicoloured print	105	30.00	35.00	15.00
Sugar bowl	White; orange rim; multicoloured print	38	30.00	35.00	15.00
Teapot, large	White; orange rim; multicoloured print	82	30.00	35.00	15.00
Teapot, small	White; orange rim; multicoloured print	72	30.00	35.00	15.00
Boxed Set for 4	White; orange rim; multicoloured print	—	600.00	700.00	300.00
Boxed Set for 6	White; orange rim; multicoloured print	—	800.00	900.00	400.00

Mickey Mouse and Friends as Nursery Ryhmes Characters, Toy Tea Set

Tea set items have been reported that have transfers of Donald Duck and Mickey and Minnie Mouse as Nursery Rhyme characters.

Photograph not available
at press time

Transfer prints

Donald, Mickey and Minnie dancing Ring a Ring of Roses
Mickey as Jack

Donald as Little Boy Blue
Minnie as Jill

Name	Colourways	Size	U.S. $	Can. $	U.K. £
Baby Beaker	White; orange rim; multicoloured print	77	30.00	35.00	15.00
Cup / Saucer	White; orange rim; multicoloured print	46 / 95	30.00	35.00	15.00
Milk jug	White; orange rim; multicoloured print	50	30.00	35.00	15.00
Plate, small	White; orange rim; multicoloured print	105	30.00	35.00	15.00
Sugar bowl	White; orange rim; multicoloured print	38	30.00	35.00	15.00
Teapot, large	White; orange rim; multicoloured print	85	30.00	35.00	15.00

Mickey's Circus Toy Tea and Dinner Set, c.1937

Although the transfers are from scenes in the Disney short entitled 'Mickey's Circus', the majority of the images feature Donald Duck and Baby Seal. In the cartoon Donald's performing seals escape and cause havoc while being chased by an angry Donald. One transfer shows Baby Seal blowing a horn so loudly that Donald dressed as a bandsman is blown across the circus ring.

Transfer prints

Plate

Cup and Saucer

Donal Duck Teapot

Baby Seal Blowing Horn
Donald Blown over
Donald with whip

Baby Seal Juggling
Donald as Peanut Vendor

Donald as Bandsman
Donald and Pluto

Name	Colourways	Size	U.S. $	Can. $	U.K. £
Cup / Saucer	White; orange rim; multicoloured print	46 / 95	20.00	30.00	15.00
Milk jug	White; orange rim; multicoloured print	50	20.00	30.00	15.00
Plate, small	White; orange rim; multicoloured print	105	20.00	30.00	15.00
Plate, large	White; orange rim; multicoloured print	127	20.00	30.00	15.00
Sugar bowl	White; orange rim; multicoloured print	38	20.00	30.00	15.00
Teapot, large	White; orange rim; multicoloured print	85	20.00	30.00	15.00

Pinocchio Toy Tea and Dinner Sets, 1940

This set was advertised in April 1940. A children's nursery ware set was available at the same time, both sets have transfer prints of characters from the Walt Disney cartoon film *Pinocchio*.

Different sizes of cups /saucers, and sugar bowls have been reported which suggests that this set was also produced as a larger 'dinner' set. The Pinocchio pieces are seldom seen

Transfer prints

Blue Fairy	Donkey	Figaro the Cat and Cleo the Godlfish
Geppetto	Jiminy Cricket	Pinocchio
Strombolis Parrot		

Small cup left, 'Stromboli'; large cup right, 'Pinocchio'

Geppetti large plate left; small plate right

Backstamp: Ink stamp "Wadeheath by permission Walt Disney England"

Name	Colourways	Size	U.S. $	Can. $	U.K. £
Cup / saucer, large	White; orange band; multicoloured print	46/95	30.00	35.00	15.00
Cup / saucer, small	White; orange band; multicoloured print	40	30.00	35.00	15.00
Milk jug,, large	White; orange band; multicoloured print	50	30.00	35.00	15.00
Milk jug,, small	White; orange band; multicoloured print	40	30.00	35.00	15.00
Plate, large	White; orange band; multicoloured print	130	30.00	35.00	15.00
Plate, small	White; orange band; multicoloured print	103	30.00	35.00	15.00
Platter	White; orange band; multicoloured print	159	30.00	35.00	15.00
Sugar bowl, large	White; orange band; multicoloured print	38	30.00	35.00	15.00
Sugar bowl, small	White; orange band; multicoloured print	28	30.00	35.00	15.00
Teapot, small	White; orange band; multicoloured print	76	30.00	35.00	15.00
Teapot, large	White; orange band; multicoloured print	89	30.00	35.00	15.00

Snow White and the Seven Dwarfs Toy Tea Set, 1930s

The eight-piece boxed set illustrated may be one of the first *Snow White and the Seven Dwarfs* children's tea set issued. The teapot illustrates Snow White and Dopey; the two cups and saucers show four of the seven dwarfs; the sugar bowl has a dancing rabbit, and the milk jug a fawn.

Later sets contained four cups and saucers, teapot, sugar bowl and a milk jug, allowing for transter prints of all the dwarfs. Although the box refers to the contents as "Nursery ware" the set is a child's toy tea set.

Transfer Prints

Bashful	Dancing Rabbit	Doc
Dopey	Fawn	Grumpy
Happy	Sleepy	Sneezy
Snow White		

Lid for eight piece Tea Set

Eight piece Tea Set

Lid for twelve piece Tea Set

Twelve piece Tea Set

Backstamp: Ink stamp "Wadeheath by Permission Walt Disney England"

Name	Colourways	Size	U.S. $	Can. $	U.K. £
Cup / Saucer	White; orange band; multicoloured print	46/95	30.00	35.00	15.00
Milk jug	White; orange band; multicoloured print	50	30.00	35.00	15.00
Plate	White; orange band; multicoloured print	130	30.00	35.00	15.00
Sugar bowl	White; orange band; multicoloured print	35	30.00	35.00	15.00
Teapot	White; orange band; multicoloured print	85	30.00	35.00	15.00

Snow White and the Seven Dwarfs Toy Dinner Set

To date only four pieces have been reported that appear to be from the Disney *Snow White and the Seven Dwarfs* dinner set, they are listed below.

Transfer prints

Dancing Rabbit

Fawn

Vegetable Tureen

Sugar Bowl

Backstamp: **A.** Ink stamp "Wade Heath England"
  B. Ink stamp "Wadeheath by Permission Walt Disney England"

Name	Colourways	Size	U.S. $	Can. $	U.K. £
Milk jug	Cream; orange rim; multicoloured print	50	85.00	115.00	58.00
Sugar bowl	Cream; orange rim; multicoloured print	38 x 63	85.00	115.00	58.00
Vegetable tureen	Cream; orange rim; multicoloured print	76 x 130	Rare		
Platter	Cream; orange rim; multicoloured print	125	Rare		

FIGURES

The production of Wade figures began in late 1927. "Pavlova" was the first Wade figure to be produced followed by "Curtsey" and "Romance." In 1930 a talented modeller, Jessie Van Hallen, was employed by the company to increase their production. With her input Wade figures started to appear in large numbers at various trade shows and retail outlets. Original cost of the figures was 10/6d.

All Wade figures are slip cast and therefore hollow, with a circular casting hole in the base. Initially they were glazed with what was at that time a new Scintillite cellulose glaze. In 1939 and again in the late 1940s to the mid 1950s, a number of models were produced in high-gloss glaze. These figures command a much higher price than the cellulose-glazed figures and are considered extremely rare.

The figures are divided into three sections—Cellulose Figures, 1927-1939; High-Gloss Figures, 1939 to the the mid 1950s; Sets and Series, c.1948-1991. The models are listed alphabetically within the cellulose and high-gloss sections. The sets and series are presented in chronological order.

Three new figures have been found: 'Dora' is a wonderful nude figure putting on a robe: 'Sleepyhead' is a baby lying on a pillow: the third figure is the bust of a woman's head and shoulders.

A new version of Curtsey has been found on which the head is turned upward looking above the left shoulder. This model has a BCM Owl backstamp which was the earliest known Wade backstamp used on these figures, therefore the tilted head version is considered to be the first version.

When originally issued the 'Madonna and Child' figure had a brass halo, which attached to the back of her head, it is rare to find a model complete with halo.

For 'Alice and the Dodo' in cellulose glaze see the *Charlton Standard Catalogue of Wade Whimsical Collectables*

Care and Handling

The Scintillite glaze easily chips and flakes off models that have been kept in direct sunlight or in damp conditions. Most of these figures now have varying degrees of flaking. On no account should the collector try to touch up these models as it will detract from their value. If models have more white porcelain exposed than glazing, the job of restoration should be done by a professional.

Pricing

The degree of flaking on the cellulose figures will affect the price. Prices in this catalogue are for figures with a moderate degree of flaking. Mint figures with no flaking will command higher prices than those listed here, while figures with excessive flaking will be worth much less.

BACKSTAMPS

Cellulose Figures

The earliest Wade figures were produced with a rarely seen backstamp that included a grey ink-stamped owl. Because some models were reissued once or twice, they can be found with two or three different backstamps on the base. The following backstamps can be found on the cellulose figures:

1927-1930

Paper label "Scintillite Ware," grey ink stamp "BCM/OWL Made in England" and owl's head, with the name of the model hand painted in red

1927-1930

Grey ink stamp of an owl over "British Scintillite REGD" and "Made in England" (or British Make with the name of the model hand painted in red (some include "Red - Ashay" and registration number)

1930-c.1935

Grey ink stamp of an owl over "British Scintillite REGD," black handwritten Wade Figures," black ink stamp "Made in England" and the name of the model hand painted in black (with and without Jessie Van Hallen's signature hand painted in black)

Mid 1930s

Black hand painted Wade Figures, a red ink stamp of a leaping deer with "Made in England" and the name of the figure handwritten in black

c.1930-c.1939

Black hand painted "Wade," a red ink stamp of a leaping deer over "Made in England" and the name of the figure handwritten in black

1938-1939

1) Black hand painted "Wade," black ink stamp "Made in England" (may include Great Britain) and the name of the figure handwritten in black
2) Black handwritten "Pageant Made in England" and black handwritten name of the figure

1939

1) Black hand painted "Wade England" with the name of the figure handwritten in black
2) The name of the figure handwritten in black

Numbers or a letter written in black on the base along with the backstamp do not signify the order in which the models were produced. Instead, they identify the decorator or that it is a second version of the model.

High-Gloss Figures

The following backstamps are found on the high-gloss figures:

1939:

1) Blue handwritten "Wade England 1939" and the figure name
2) Black handwritten "Wade England"

c.1948-c.1952:

Blue handwritten "Wade England" and the figure name

c.1948-c.1955:

Black or green ink stamp "Wade England" (sometimes includes the name of the figure)

Sets and Series

The figures of the sets and series were backstamped as follows:

c.1945-c.1952

Black ink stamp "Wade England"

1990-1992

Red or grey transfer print "My Fair Ladies, fine porcelain, Wade Made in England" with the figure name

1991

1) Red transfer print "Wade England"
2) Green ink stamp "Seagoe Ceramics Wade Ireland 1991"

CELLULOSE FIGURES, 1927-1939

Alfie and Peggy

Anita

Ann

Anton

Argentina, no bracelets

Argentina, with bracelets

Name	Colourways	Size	U.S. $	Can. $	U.K. £
Alfie and Peggy	Grey wall; green shawl; yellow clothes	150	375.00	425.00	190.00
Alfie and Peggy	Green wall, shawl; yellow clothes	150	375.00	425.00	190.00
Alfie and Peggy	Green wall; red shawl; green clothes	150	375.00	425.00	190.00
Anita	Grey ruff; multicoloured suit; yellow wall	170	375.00	425.00	190.00
Anita	Orange ruff; multicoloured suit; grey wall	170	375.00	425.00	190.00
Ann	Yellow top; red/brown skirt	145	325.00	350.00	160.00
Anna	Black hair band, tutu, ballet slippers	160		Rare	
Anna	Green hair band; yellow/green/orange tutu; black slippers	160		Rare	
Anton	Black cape; black/yellow/red suit; red hat	135	325.00	350.00	160.00
Anton	Red cape; black/yellow/pink suit; black hat	135	325.00	350.00	160.00
Anton	Red cape, hat; black/yellow/green suit	135	325.00	350.00	160.00
Anton	Green cape; black/yellow/red suit; red hat	135	325.00	350.00	160.00
Argentina, bracelets	Mauve dress; black scarf	240	800.00	900.00	400.00
Argentina, bracelets	Black/red/orange dress; orange scarf	240	800.00	900.00	400.00
Argentina, bracelets	Black/red/green/yellow dress; yellow scarf	240	800.00	900.00	400.00
Argentina, without bracelets	Yellow/red/orange dress; black/yellow scarf	240	800.00	900.00	400.00
Argentina, without bracelets	Red dress; black scarf	240	800.00	900.00	400.00

Barbara

Betty, Style One

Betty, Style Two

Betty, Style Three

Name	Colourways	Size	U.S. $	Can. $	U.K. £
Barbara	Pink/yellow bonnet; pink ribbons; yellow/green dress	210	325.00	350.00	160.00
Barbara	Black/pink bonnet; green ribbons, pink/yellow dress	210	325.00	350.00	160.00
Barbara	Orange bonnet; black/orange ribbons, pale orange dress	210	325.00	350.00	160.00
Betty, Style One	Black hair; yellow/orange dress; yellow/black fan	115	275.00	300.00	135.00
Betty, Style Two	Black hair; yellow/maroon dress; yellow flowers	125	275.00	300.00	135.00
Betty, Style Two	Black hair; pink/red dress; pink/yellow flowers	125	275.00	300.00	135.00
Betty, Style Two	Black hair; yellow dress	125	275.00	300.00	135.00
Betty, Style Three	Black hair/cat; grey blue dress; pink/blue flowers	125	375.00	425.00	190.00
Betty, Style Three	Black hair; grey cat; grey blue dress; pink/blue flowers	125	375.00	425.00	190.00

Blossoms with Mirror

Bride

Carmen

Carnival

Name	Colourways	Size	U.S. $	Can. $	U.K. £
Blossoms with Mirror	Black hair; pink shawl	210	Extremely Rare		
Blossoms with Mirror	Blonde hair; orange and yellow shawl	210	Extremely Rare		
Boy Scout	Beige uniform; green base	Unkn.	Extremely Rare		
Bride	Cream dress, lilies; pink garland in hair	190	450.00	500.00	225.00
Carmen	Orange dress; red shoes; red/yellow earrings	265	800.00	900.00	400.00
Carmen	Orange dress; black shoes; gold earrings	265	800.00	900.00	400.00
Carmen	Green/yellow dress; gold earrings	265	800.00	900.00	400.00
Carmen	Red dress, earrings	265	800.00	900.00	400.00
Carmen	Yellow/orange/black dress; yellow earrings	265	800.00	900.00	400.00
Carnival	Maroon bodice; yellow skirt; brown hat, pompon	245	325.00	350.00	160.00
Carnival	Green dress, pompon; black hat	245	325.00	350.00	160.00
Carnival	Orange/black dress; black hat; orange pompon	245	325.00	350.00	160.00

Carole

Cherry with Cherries

Choir Boy

Christina

Claude with Coin

Name	Colourways	Size	U.S. $	Can. $	U.K. £
Carole	Black/red dress; red shoes	215	450.00	500.00	225.00
Carole	Red/yellow dress; red shoes	215	450.00	500.00	225.00
Cherry with Cherries	Red dress; yellow/green sash; black hair	250	450.00	500.00	225.00
Cherry with Cherries	Red/yellow dress; green sash; black hair	250	450.00	500.00	225.00
Choir Boy	White smock; brown cassock; black shoes	190	450.00	500.00	225.00
Choir Boy	White smock; red cassock; black shoes	190	450.00	500.00	225.00
Christina	Black hair; pink shirt; yellow trousers; yellow dog	275	800.00	900.00	400.00
Christina	Black hair; yellow shirt; brown trousers; black/brown dog	275	800.00	900.00	400.00
Christina	Yellow hair, shirt; gold/brown trousers; grey/yellow dog	275	800.00	900.00	400.00
Claude with Cards	Green coat, trousers; red waistcoat; brown cloak	200	450.00	500.00	225.00
Claude with Coin	Black/brown coat; green trousers; maroon/brown cloak	200	450.00	500.00	225.00
Claude with Coin	Black/brown coat; yellow trousers; black cloak	200	450.00	500.00	225.00
Claude with Coin	Black coat; pink waistcoat; yellow trousers; green cloak	200	450.00	500.00	225.00
Claude with Coin	Green coat; yellow waistcoat; gold trousers; black cloaks	200	450.00	500.00	225.00

Colorado

Conchita

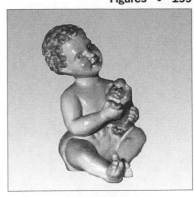

Curls

Curtsey, Style One

Cynthia

Daisette

Name	Colourways	Size	U.S. $	Can. $	U.K. £
Colorado	Man: red and black; Woman: red and yellow	245	1,400.00	1,600.00	700.00
Colorado	Man: black and yellow; Woman: yellow dress	245	1,400.00	1,600.00	700.00
Colorado	Man: black and yellow; Woman: red dress	245	1,400.00	1,600.00	700.00
Conchita	Green, yellow and orange	220	450.00	500.00	225.00
Curls	Dark brown hair, puppy	120	450.00	500.00	225.00
Curls	Pale yellow hair, puppy; pale green nappy	120	450.00	500.00	225.00
Curls	Light brown hair, puppy; blue eyes; yellow/green nappy	120	450.00	500.00	225.00
Curtsey, Style One	Black bonnet; mottled orange dress	125	275.00	300.00	135.00
Curtsey, Style Two	Yellow bonnet, ribbon; green and yellow dress	125	275.00	300.00	135.00
Curtsey, Style Two	Yellow, red and black	125	275.00	300.00	135.00
Curtsey, Style Two	Black, yellow and pink	125	275.00	300.00	135.00
Curtsey, Style Two	Black, yellow and red	125	275.00	300.00	135.00
Curtsey, Style Two	Black and pink	125	275.00	300.00	135.00
Curtsey, Style Two	Black, green, yellow and maroon	125	275.00	300.00	135.00
Curtsey, Style Two	Black, pink and blue	125	275.00	300.00	135.00
Curtsey, Style Three	Pale blue and pink	120	275.00	300.00	135.00
Cynthia	Yellow, green and cream	110	350.00	400.00	175.00
Cynthia	Green, red and cream	110	350.00	400.00	175.00
Cynthia	Black, orange and cream	110	350.00	400.00	175.00
Cynthia	Black, pink, green and yellow	110 x 45	350.00	400.00	175.00
Cynthia	Pink and pale green	110 x 45	800.00	900.00	400.00

Dawn, Version One

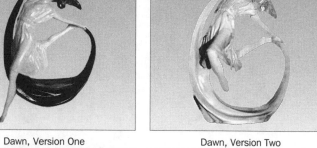

Dawn, Version Two

Dolly Varden

Dora

Elf

Ginger

Name	Colourways	Size	U.S. $	Can. $	U.K. £
Daisette	Multicoloured dress; silver petticoat, shoes	250	900.00	1,000.00	450.00
Dawn, Version One	Green dress, scarf	205	550.00	625.00	275.00
Dawn, Version One	Yellow dress; maroon scarf	205	550.00	625.00	275.00
Dawn, Version One	Yellow dress, scarf	205	550.00	625.00	275.00
Dawn, Version Two	Yellow/red dress, scarf	205	550.00	625.00	275.00
Delight	Yellow hair; multicoloured flowers; green base	75	550.00	625.00	275.00
Dolly Varden	Maroon hat; yellow/orange dress, bows; green shoes	265	375.00	425.00	190.00
Dolly Varden	Yellow hat, dress, bows; mauve shoes	265	375.00	425.00	190.00
Dolly Varden	Yellow hat, dress; black bows; red shoes	265	375.00	425.00	190.00
Dolly Varden	Brown hat; yellow dress, shoes	260	375.00	425.00	190.00
Dolly Varden	Brown hat; yellow dress, shoes	260	375.00	425.00	190.00
Dora	Nude; black hair; long pink/maroon robe	190	550.00	625.00	275.00
Elf	Dark green butterfly, base	100	550.00	625.00	275.00
Elf	Yellow butterfly; light green base	100	550.00	625.00	275.00
Elf	Blue/red butterfly; pink base	100	550.00	625.00	275.00
Elf	Pink/yellow butterfly; pink base	100	550.00	625.00	275.00
Ginger	Silver hat, shoes; silver/lilac suit	245	800.00	900.00	400.00
Ginger	Black hat, suit, shoes	245	800.00	900.00	400.00
Ginger	Black hat; orange/yellow suit	245	800.00	900.00	400.00

Gloria, Version Two

Grace, Long-stemmed flowers

Grace, short-stemmed flowers

Greta

Harriet with flowers

Harriet with fruit

Name	Colourways	Size	U.S. $	Can. $	U.K. £
Gloria, Version One	Maroon, yellow and orange (hand out)	135	325.00	375.00	160.00
Gloria, Version Two	Yellow, orange, black and maroon (hand on fan)	135	325.00	375.00	160.00
Gloria, Version Two	Maroon, red and yellow (hand on fan)	135	325.00	375.00	160.00
Gloria, Version Two	Yellow, red, black, green and orange (hand on fan)	135	325.00	375.00	160.00
Gloria, Version Two	Maroon, red and black (hand on fan)	135	325.00	375.00	160.00
Grace, Version One	Pink and yellow	245	375.00	425.00	190.00
Grace, Version Two	Green, yellow and orange	245	375.00	425.00	190.00
Greta	Green	198	600.00	700.00	300.00
Greta	Yellow, green and pink	198	600.00	700.00	300.00
Harriet with Flowers	Black, red, yellow and green	210	450.00	500.00	225.00
Harriet with Flowers	Black, yellow and green	210	450.00	500.00	225.00
Harriet with Fruit	Green, yellow and black	210	450.00	500.00	225.00
Harriet with Fruit	Black, red, maroon and yellow	210	450.00	500.00	225.00

Helga

Hille Bobbe

Humoresque

Iris

Name	Colourways	Size	U.S. $	Can. $	U.K. £
Helga	Yellow hair; yellow/orange dress; black scarf, shoes	230	450.00	500.00	225.00
Helga	Yellow hair, scarf, shoes; yellow/red dress	230	450.00	500.00	225.00
Helga	Black hair; yellow/green dress, scarf	230	450.00	500.00	225.00
Helga	Black hair; red/black dress; black scarf	230	450.00	500.00	225.00
Hille Bobbe	Green/yellow/black dress; brown table	255	375.00	425.00	190.00
Hille Bobbe	Blue dress; cream collar, apron	255	375.00	425.00	190.00
Hille Bobbe	Brown dress; yellow bonnet	255	375.00	425.00	190.00
Hille Bobbe	Green dress; yellow bonnet	255	375.00	425.00	190.00
Humoresque	Green hat, pompon, shoes, bobbles; yellow/orange dress	200	325.00	375.00	160.00
Humoresque	Black hat, shoes, bobbles; red pompon; red dress	200	325.00	375.00	160.00
Humoresque	Red hat, bobbles; black pompon, shoes; yellow/green dress	200	325.00	375.00	160.00
Humoresque	Black hat, shoes; red pompon, bobbles; black/red dress	200	325.00	375.00	160.00
Iris	Black dress with yellow/green/orange splashes; light brown hair	190	375.00	425.00	190.00

Jean

Jeanette

Jose

Joy

Name	Colourways	Size	U.S. $	Can. $	U.K. £
Jean	Yellow hat; yellow/green dress; black base	170	375.00	425.00	190.00
Jeanette	Yellow flowered dress; yellow gloves; black hat	145	375.00	425.00	190.00
Jeanette	Yellow/orange/black dress; yellow gloves; black hat	145	375.00	425.00	190.00
Jeanette	Green/yellow dress; yellow gloves; black hat	145	375.00	425.00	190.00
Jeanette	Red dress; black hat, gloves	145	375.00	425.00	190.00
Joie Ballerina	Yellow tutu/shoes	110	Rare		
Jose	Pink/yellow/lilac dress	110	200.00	225.00	100.00
Jose	Green/yellow dress	110	200.00	225.00	100.00
Jose	Green/blue dress	110	200.00	225.00	100.00
Jose	Yellow/orange dress	110	200.00	225.00	100.00
Jose	Yellow dress	110	200.00	225.00	100.00
Joy	Yellow/orange dress; orange shoes; floral cap	245	800.00	900.00	400.00
Joy	Yellow/red dress; green shoes; floral cap	245	800.00	900.00	400.00
Joy	Yellow flowered dress; green shoes; floral cap	245	800.00	900.00	400.00

Joyce

June

Kay

Lady Gay

Lotus/Anna May Wong

Madonna and Child

Name	Colourways	Size	U.S. $	Can. $	U.K. £
Joyce	Yellow, green, black and red	185	375.00	425.00	190.00
Joyce	Black, yellow and green	185	375.00	425.00	190.00
Joyce	Black and gold	185	375.00	425.00	190.00
June	Yellow and maroon	180	375.00	425.00	190.00
June	Yellow and green	180	375.00	425.00	190.00
June	Green, yellow and red	180	375.00	425.00	190.00
June	Green, yellow and black	180	375.00	425.00	190.00
June	Yellow, red and green	180	375.00	425.00	190.00
Kay	Black, red, orange, and yellow	265	375.00	425.00	190.00
Lady Gay	Grey, brown, yellow and red	230	450.00	500.00	225.00
Lady Gay	Grey, brown hat, red and yellow	230	450.00	500.00	225.00
Lady Gay	Brown, black, green and yellow	230	450.00	500.00	225.00
Lady Gay	Yellow and green	225	450.00	500.00	225.00
Lotus/Anna May Wong	Orange and green	245	550.00	600.00	270.00
Lotus/Anna May Wong	Yellow and green	245	550.00	600.00	270.00
Lupino Lane	Red and white	100	250.00	275.00	125.00
Madonna and Child	Cream and green	340	1,400.00	1,600.00	700.00

Maria Theresa

Midnight

Mimi

Mother and Child

Pavlova

Name	Colourways	Size	U.S. $	Can. $	U.K. £
Maria Theresa	Maroon, orange and green dress	195	600.00	675.00	300.00
Midnight	Grey hair; black and cream tutu	175	600.00	675.00	300.00
Mimi	Mottled red dress; yellow top; black shoes	190	450.00	500.00	225.00
Mimi	Black dress and shoes	190	450.00	500.00	225.00
Mimi	Red and yellow dress; red shoes	190	450.00	500.00	225.00
Mimi	Green dress; brown shoes	190	450.00	500.00	225.00
Mother and Child	Mother: brown hair; yellow dress	229	450.00	500.00	225.00
Pavlova, Large	Orange and yellow dress; orange hat, shoes	240	375.00	425.00	190.00
Pavlova, Large	Green and yellow dress; yellow hat, shoes	240	375.00	425.00	190.00
Pavlova, Large	Yellow dress; black hat, shoes	240	375.00	425.00	190.00
Pavlova, Large	Red dress; black hat, shoes	240	375.00	425.00	190.00
Pavlova, Large	Pink dress; black hat, shoes	240	375.00	425.00	190.00
Pavlova, Large	Black and orange dress, hat	240	375.00	425.00	190.00
Pavlova, Large	Green dress and hat	240	375.00	425.00	190.00
Pavlova, Large	Red and yellow dress; black hat, shoes	240	375.00	425.00	190.00
Pavlova, Large	Yellow and maroon dress; maroon hat	240	375.00	425.00	190.00
Pavlova, Large	Black and orange hat; yellow and orange dress	240	375.00	425.00	190.00
Pavlova, Large	Black and yellow hat; yellow and turquoise blue dress	240	375.00	425.00	190.00
Pavlova, Small	Red and yellow dress; yellow hat	110	325.00	350.00	160.00

Peggy

Phyllis

Pompadour

Princess Elizabeth

Name	Colourways	Size	U.S. $	Can. $	U.K. £
Pavlova, Small	Green dress; black hat	110	325.00	350.00	160.00
Pavlova, Small	Pink dress; black hat	110	325.00	350.00	160.00
Pavlova, Small	Black dress and hat	110	325.00	350.00	160.00
Pavlova, Small	Blue, yellow and orange dress; black hat	110	325.00	350.00	160.00
Peggy	Yellow and pink dress; black hat and shoes	175	375.00	425.00	190.00
Peggy	Yellow dress; green hat, shoes	175	375.00	425.00	190.00
Peggy	Yellow dress, hat; black shoes	175	375.00	425.00	190.00
Phyllis	Yellow/orange dress; pink bustle; black hat, shoes	180	325.00	350.00	160.00
Phyllis	Pink dress; brown bustle; black hat, shoes	180	325.00	350.00	160.00
Pompadour	Yellow and maroon dress; maroon fan	150	325.00	350.00	160.00
Pompadour	Cream, yellow and orange dress; green fan	150	325.00	350.00	160.00
Pompadour	Yellow and maroon dress; red fan	150	325.00	350.00	160.00
Pompadour	Yellow, orange and black dress; orange fan	150	325.00	350.00	160.00
Pompadour	Orange dress; green fan	150	325.00	350.00	160.00
Princess Elizabeth	Yellow and orange dress; grey shoes; black stool	150	325.00	350.00	160.00
Princess Elizabeth	Pink dress; white shoes; brown stool	150	325.00	350.00	160.00
Princess Elizabeth	Green dress; black shoes	150	325.00	350.00	160.00
Princess Elizabeth	Yellow dress; green shoes	150	325.00	350.00	160.00

Queenie

Rhythm

Romance

Sadie

Sleepyhead

Name	Colourways	Size	U.S. $	Can. $	U.K. £
Queenie	Pink/yellow dress; green hair band; pink/black fan	100	350.00	400.00	175.00
Queenie	Yellow/pink dress; pink hair band; pink fan	100	350.00	400.00	175.00
Queenie	Yellow/red dress; green hair band; green/red fan	100	350.00	400.00	175.00
Rhythm	Red dress; black hair	230	600.00	675.00	300.00
Rhythm	Yellow and green dress; black hair	230	600.00	675.00	300.00
Rhythm	Green mottled dress; black hair	230	600.00	675.00	300.00
Rhythm	Red and black dress; black hair	230	600.00	675.00	300.00
Romance	Yellow, orange and black dress; yellow parasol	165	325.00	350.00	160.00
Romance	Yellow and green dress	165	325.00	350.00	160.00
Romance	Orange dress, parasol	165	325.00	350.00	160.00
Romance	Yellow and green all over	165	325.00	350.00	160.00
Sadie	Yellow wall; maroon hat; orange suit	350	450.00	500.00	225.00
Sadie	Yellow wall, hat; green suit	350	450.00	500.00	225.00
Sadie	Brown wall; red suit	350	450.00	500.00	225.00
Sandra	Green scarf, bolero, skirt	230	450.00	500.00	225.00
Sleepyhead, eyes closed	Yellow pillow; dull yellow all over	110 x 195	375.00	425.00	190.00
Sleepyhead, eyes closed	Orange and yellow pillow; green and yellow coat	110 x 195	375.00	425.00	190.00
Sleepyhead, eyes open	Orange and yellow pillow; green and yellow coat	110 x 195	375.00	425.00	190.00

Springtime

Strawberry Girl

Sunshine

Susan

Sylvia

Name	Colourways	Size	U.S. $	Can. $	U.K. £
Springtime	Red shoes; yellow dress; green base	235	600.00	675.00	300.00
Springtime	Yellow shoes, dress; green base	235	600.00	675.00	300.00
Springtime	Green shoes; yellow dress; green base	235	600.00	675.00	300.00
Strawberry Girl	Red hat; green/yellow dress; brown basket	135	275.00	300.00	135.00
Strawberry Girl	Blue hat; orange dress; brown basket	135	275.00	300.00	135.00
Sunshine	Green and orange jacket, green and yellow dress	165	275.00	300.00	135.00
Sunshine	Black and green jacket; yellow and orange dress	165	275.00	300.00	135.00
Sunshine	Maroon jacket; orange and yellow dress	165	275.00	300.00	135.00
Sunshine	Green dress	165	275.00	300.00	135.00
Sunshine	Yellow jacket; yellow and orange dress	165	275.00	300.00	135.00
Sunshine	Green and yellow jacket; yellow and orange dress	165	275.00	300.00	135.00
Sunshine	Blue and yellow streaked dress	165	275.00	300.00	135.00
Susan	Orange and yellow dress; green belt; yellow daffodils	165	450.00	500.00	225.00
Sylvia	Yellow and green dress; silver sandals	200	600.00	675.00	300.00
Sylvia	Yellow dress; brown sandals	200	600.00	675.00	300.00
Sylvia	Black dress with red/yellow/green patches; silver sandals	200	600.00	675.00	300.00
Sylvia	Red and yellow dress; gold sandals	200	600.00	675.00	300.00
Sylvia	Black dress with red/yellow/green patches; green sandals	200	600.00	675.00	300.00

Tessa

Tony

Trixie

Woman, bust

Zena

Name	Colourways	Size	U.S. $	Can. $	U.K. £
Tessa	Yellow dress; green bow; black shoes	120	350.00	400.00	175.00
Tessa	Green flowered dress; pink bow; black shoes	120	350.00	400.00	175.00
Tessa	Green and yellow dress; pink bow; black shoes	120	350.00	400.00	175.00
Tessa	Pink dress, bow; black shoes; brown bench	120	350.00	400.00	175.00
Tony	Cream suit; black hat, shoes	120	350.00	400.00	175.00
Trixie	Cream and red hat; brown and cream suit; red gloves, shoes	255	600.00	675.00	300.00
Woman, bust	Black hair and eyebrows; red lips; yellow blouse	Unk.		Rare	
Zena, Large	Green hat; yellow and orange dress	220	450.00	500.00	225.00
Zena, Large	Maroon and green hat; red and yellow dress	220	450.00	500.00	225.00
Zena, Large	Black/green hat; black, green, red and yellow dress	220	450.00	500.00	225.00
Zena, Small	Yellow hat; yellow and orange dress; red shoes	105	275.00	300.00	135.00
Zena, Small	Green hat; green and yellow dress	105	275.00	300.00	135.00
Zena, Small	Pink and yellow hat, dress	105	275.00	300.00	135.00
Zena, Small	Blue and green hat and dress	105	275.00	300.00	135.00

Pageant Figures, 1938-1939

The *Pageant Figures* series is a small set of models based on historical figures, all hand decorated in the cellulose Scintillite glaze. Advertising material suggests that they were produced and offered for sale at the same time as "Barbara," "Zena," "Rhythm," "Daisette" and others created in the late 1930s.

Henry VIII and Elizabeth I

Backstamp: **A.** Ink stamp "Henry VIII Wade England"
B. Ink stamp "Queen Elizabeth Pageant Made in England"

Name	Colourways	Size	U.S. $	Can. $	U.K. £
Cardinal Wolsey	Red hat, cloak, tunic	115			
Elizabeth I	Green and white dress; yellow fan; gold highlights	115			
Henry VIII	Black and white hat, cloak; yellow tunic, shoes	115		All are	
James I	Yellow cloak; green suit	115		considered	
John Knox	Black coat; yellow vest	115		extremely	
Mary, Queen of Scots	White hat; black and white dress	115		rare	
Richard the Lionheart	Silver grey chain mail; red cross on white tunic	110			
Robert the Bruce	Silver grey; dark blue	110			

Derivatives

Models on Bookends and Floral Bases, c.1939

Wade did not attach models to bookends or floral bases; this was done by an outside company marketing such products.

Photograph not available
at press time

Name	Colourways	Size	U.S. $	Can. $	U.K. £
Cynthia	Porcelain floral base; Green, yellow and brown	110	325.00	375.00	160.00
Strawberry Girl	Bookends; Blue , orange and brown	135	325.00	375.00	160.00

Models on Mirrors, c.1935-1939

Some figures have been found mounted on a base with an oval or round mirror. In the 1938 trade papers, Wade advertised the model "Blossoms" attached to a mirror decorated in porcelain flowers. Mirrors that were not incorporated into the design and had no floral decoration were not produced by Wade. Models found mounted with a plain mirror were attached by another company. Backstamps are unavailable on attached figures. The Pavlova mirror model has a moulded wall, pillar, shrubs and flowers on a three stepped base; Pavlova stands to one side of the circular mirror.

Sunshine and Mirror

Pavlova and Mirror

Backstamp: Unknown

Name	Colourways	Size	U.S. $	Can. $	U.K. £
Curtsey	Yellow bonnet, ribbon; green and yellow dress	125	375.00	425.00	190.00
Pavlova	Maroon hat; yellow and maroon dress	240	450.00	500.00	225.00
Pavlova	Green bonnet; yellow dress and shoes	350	450.00	500.00	225.00
Pavlova	apink bonnet; pink and green streaked dress	350	450.00	500.00	225.00
Sunshine	Yellow parasol; yellow and green dress	165	250.00	300.00	130.00
Tessa	Yellow dress and bench; pink flowers on base	165	325.00	350.00	160.00

Note: The dog on "Sunshine and Mirror" is not a Wade model.

Models on Table Lamps, c.1935-1939

Figures have been found mounted on wooden table lamp bases. The wooden bases are usually black. The model of "Phyllis" is moulded in one piece as a table lamp: the tree stump of the original model has been extended to form the tree trunk lamp holder. There are no moulded flowers on the "Phyllis" model.

Curtsey

Pavlova

Phyllis

Backstamp:
A. Black ink stamped "Made in England" handwritten "Phyllis 3. L" with incised letter *H*
B. Black hand written "Phyllis, 4L"

Name	Colourways	Size	U.S. $	Can. $	U.K. £
Barbara	Yellow bonnet and dress	210	325.00	375.00	160.00
Carnival	Black hat; yellowand green balloons, pompon dress	245	260.00	300.00	130.00
Curtsey	Black and yellow bonnet; yellow ribbon; red and yellow dress	125	260.00	300.00	130.00
Curtsey	Yellow bonnet; light orange dress	125	260.00	300.00	130.00
Conchita	Yellow dress	220	275.00	325.00	135.00
Pavlova	Green bonnet; black, yellow and orange dress	240	275.00	325.00	135.00
Phyllis	Black hat; yellow and orange dress; brown tree trunk	177	275.00	325.00	135.00
Phyllis	Black hat; yellow and green dress; brown tree trunk	177	275.00	325.00	135.00
Pompadour	Orange flowered dress; green fan	150	275.00	325.00	135.00
Sunshine	Black and orange bonnet; yellow jacket; yellow and orange dress	165	260.00	300.00	130.00

HIGH GLOSS FIGURES, 1939-c.1955

Anita

Choir Boy, blue cassock

Curtsey

Elf

Fay

Hille Bobbe

Name	Colourways	Size	U.S. $	Can. $	U.K. £
Anita	Black, green ruff; multicoloured suit; yellow wall	170	700.00	775.00	350.00
Betty, Style Two	White, green and yellow dress; pink flowers	125	600.00	675.00	300.00
Betty, Style Two	Pink dress; yellow and blue garland, flowers	125	600.00	675.00	300.00
Bride	White	190	700.00	800.00	350.00
Choir Boy	White smock; red cassock	205	700.00	800.00	350.00
Choir Boy	White smock; blue cassock; black shoes	200	700.00	800.00	350.00
Curtsey	Cream bonnet, ribbon; green/yellow dress	125	500.00	575.00	250.00
Curtsey	Maroon bonnet, dress; yellow ribbon	125	500.00	575.00	250.00
Curtsey	Grey, green; multicoloured flowers	125	500.00	575.00	250.00
Curtsey	Black, pale pink; multicoloured flowers	125	500.00	575.00	250.00
Curtsey	Blue bonnet, dress; pink ribbon	125	500.00	575.00	250.00
Cynthia	Black hat, pale pink; multicoloured flowers	110	500.00	575.00	250.00
Cynthia	Black, green, pale pink; multicoloured flowers	110	500.00	575.00	250.00
Cynthia	Yellow, pink, pale pink; multicoloured flowers	110	500.00	575.00	250.00
Elf	Light brown, pink , dark blue, maroon and yellow	100	900.00	1,000.00	450.00
Fay	Red hair; lilac dress; small multicoloured flowers	165	700.00	800.00	350.00
Grace	Green hat; maroon dress; short stemmed flowers		700.00	800.00	350.00
Harriet with Flowers	Green shawl; white apron; yellow dress	210	700.00	800.00	350.00
Hille Bobbe	White, pastel green and pale blue	255	700.00	800.00	350.00

Joy

Madonna and Child with Halo

Madonna and Child on base

Lady in Armchair

Lady in Armchair

Name	Colourways	Size	U.S. $	Can. $	U.K. £
Iris	Pale blue, blue, pink, green and gold	190	700.00	800.00	350.00
Iris	Pale green and pink dress; gold design	190	700.00	800.00	350.00
Jose	Cream and yellow dress; pink flowers	110	600.00	675.00	300.00
Joy	Pastel green	245	900.00	1,000.00	450.00
Joy	Pastel blue	245	900.00	1,000.00	450.00
Juliet	Sage green, pink and brown	240	900.00	1,000.00	450.00
Juliet	White, blue and yellow	240	900.00	1,000.00	450.00
Juliet	Mottled pastel green, blue and gold	240	900.00	1,000.00	450.00
Knight Templer	White robes, red cross, silver shield	240	300.00	350.00	150.00
Knight Templer	White robes, red cross, white/red shield	240	200.00	225.00	100.00
Lady in Armchair	Pale green dress	200 x 250	950.00	1,100.00	475.00
Lady in Armchair with Budgerigar	White and gold; multicoloured flowers	200 x 250	950.00	1,100.00	475.00
Lady in Armchair with Budgerigar	Maroon, yellow and gold	200 x 250	950.00	1,100.00	475.00
Madonna and Child with Halo	Blue and cream	340	1,500.00	1,700.00	800.00
Madonna and Child with Halo	Green and cream	340	1,500.00	1,700.00	800.00
Madonna and Child on base	Ivory and black	415	1,500.00	1,700.00	800.00

Old Nannie

Spirit of Britain

The Swan Dancer

Zena

Name	Colourways	Size	U.S. $	Can. $	U.K. £
Old Nannie	Pale blue and white	230	700.00	800.00	350.00
Old Nannie	White, blue and grey	230	700.00	800.00	350.00
Pavlova, Large	Black hat with multicoloured flowers; mauve dress	240	700.00	800.00	350.00
Pavlova, Small	Orange hat with multicoloured flowers; mauve dress	110	500.00	575.00	250.00
Queenie	Cream and pink	100	500.00	575.00	250.00
Romance	Green, pink, blue and yellow	170	700.00	800.00	350.00
Spirit of Britain	Blue uniform; blue and fawn mottled base	190		Extremely	Rare
Sunshine	Black, pink, white and blue	165	500.00	575.00	250.00
Sunshine	Black, pink, light grey, maroon and pale blue	165	500.00	575.00	250.00
The Swan Dancer	Black, pale green, white and gold	210	1,000.00	1,150.00	500.00
The Swan Dancer	Black, pink and white	210	1,000.00	1,150.00	500.00
The Swan Dancer	Black, white and gold	210	1,000.00	1,150.00	500.00
Zena, Large	Pastel blue, blue, green and pink	220	700.00	800.00	350.00
Zena, Large	Grey-blue and dark red	220	700.00	800.00	350.00
Zena, Large	Light to dark blue, pink and gold highlights	220	500.00	575.00	250.00
Zena, Small	Lilac, blue and green	100	500.00	575.00	250.00

SETS AND SERIES, c.1948-1991

Canterbury Tales Figures, c.1948-c.1952

These four characters from *The Canterbury Tales* were produced in a limited edition of 100 each. The exact date of production is not known; however the backstamp suggests the period indicated above. A paper label was pasted on the front of the base with a short quote from the poem relating to the model. Each figure was produced in two sizes.

The Nun's Priest
label on base reads: "Just look what brawn he has this Gentle Priest."

The Prioress

The Reeve
label on base reads: "Feared like the Plague he was by those beneath"

The Squire
label on base reads: "As Fresh as in the month of May"

Name	Colourways	Size	U.S. $	Can. $	U.K. £
The Nun's Priest	White hat; pale blue cloak; pink robe; beige horse	150			
The Nun's Priest	Pink hat, robe; grey/blue cloak; beige horse	150			
The Nun's Priest	White hat; pale blue cloak; pink robe; beige horse	95			
The Prioress	Dark/light brown habit; grey horse	150		All are	
The Prioress	Dark/light brown habit; grey horse	95		considered	
The Reeve	Grey collar; blue robe; white hair; orange-brown horse	150		extremely	
The Reeve	Pink collar; blue robe; white hair; orange-brown horse	150		rare	
The Reeve	Grey collar; blue robe; white hair; orange-brown horse	95			
The Squire	Dark blue hat; silver-grey tunic; white hose, horse	150			
The Squire	Dark blue hat; silver-grey tunic; white hose, horse	95			

My Fair Ladies, 1990-1991

A series of 16 Victorian-style lady figures was produced in Wade's Royal Victoria Pottery from 1990 to 1991. They were issued in two sets of eight, although only four moulds were used for each set.

A number of these models were also used by Hebrides Scotch Whiskey in late 1992 as decanters. "Natalie" has been found wrongly named "Belinda. "

The grey transfer print backstamp was first used on Set 1 and the red transfer print on Set 2, but because of firing difficulties with the red transfer, the second set was later produced with the grey backstamp.

Set 1, 1990

"Sarah" is from the same mould as "Marie"; "Lisa" is from the same mould as "Hannah"; "Rebecca" is from the same mould as "Caroline" ; "Kate" is from the same mould as "Rachel."

Marie/Sarah and Hannah/Lisa

Caroline/Rebecca and Rachel/Kate

Backstamp: **A.** Grey printed "My Fair Ladies Wade Made in England"
B. Red printed "My Fair Ladies Wade Made in England"

Name	Colourways	Size	U.S. $	Can. $	U.K. £
Caroline	Dark blue hat; yellow flower; dark blue bodice; grey-blue skirt; yellow bow	94	40.00	45.00	20.00
Hannah	Brown hair; green/grey/white dress	94	40.00	45.00	20.00
Kate	Off white/grey/white dress with red roses; grey hat	96	40.00	45.00	20.00
Lisa	Brown hair; pastel blue/white dress	94	40.00	45.00	20.00
Marie	Dark green hat; dark green/grey-green dress	92	40.00	45.00	20.00
Rachel	White/grey-blue dress; grey-blue hat	96	40.00	45.00	20.00
Rebecca	Yellow/beige hat; pink flower; grey bodice; white skirt; pink bow	94	40.00	45.00	20.00
Sarah	Greenish grey hat; greenish grey/white dress; pink flowers	92	40.00	45.00	20.00

Set 2, 1991

"Amanda" is from the same mould as "Melissa"; "Anita" is from the same mould as "Belinda"; "Natalie" is from the same mould as "Emma"; "Diane" is from the same mould as "Lucy."

Melissa/Amanda and Belinda/Anita

Emma/Natalie and Lucy/Diane

Backstamp: **A.**   Red printed "My Fair ladies Wade Made in England"
               B.   Grey printed "My Fair ladies Wade Made in England"

Name	Colourways	Size	U.S. $	Can. $	U.K. £
Amanda	Dark brown jacket; pink skirt; white petticoat	95	40.00	45.00	20.00
Anita	Shell pink dress	90	40.00	45.00	20.00
Belinda	Pearl, white and yellow dress	90	40.00	45.00	20.00
Diane	Pale blue and white hat, jacket, handbag; off-white skirt	90	40.00	45.00	20.00
Emma	White dress; creamy yellow shawl, ribbons, bows	90	40.00	45.00	20.00
Lucy	Grey hat, skirt; dark brown jacket, handbag	90	40.00	45.00	20.00
Melissa	Light brown hat; dark blue jacket; pale blue skirt; white petticoat	95	40.00	45.00	20.00
Natalie	Pale pink dress; light grey scarf, ribbons, bows	90	40.00	45.00	20.00

Sophisticated Ladies, 1991

This is a limited edition of four hand-decorated lady figures in the style of *My Fair Ladies*. The same four figures were also issued in an all-over, white porcelain glaze.

Some of the first models were mistakenly marked "My Fair Ladies Fine Porcelain Wade England" using a grey transfer print. Later models have a red transfer print which reads "Wade England."

Emily

Felicity

Roxanne

Susannah

Name	Colourways	Size	U.S. $	Can. $	U.K. £
Emily	Blonde hair; pink and white dress; white petticoat	145	100.00	115.00	50.00
Emily	White all over	145	40.00	45.00	20.00
Felicity	Brown hair; dark green jacket; pale yellow skirt	150	100.00	115.00	50.00
Felicity	White all ove	150	40.00	45.00	20.00
Roxanne	Blonde hair; pale blue/lilac dress	145	100.00	115.00	50.00
Roxanne	White all over	145	40.00	45.00	20.00
Susannah	Brown hair; orange and yellow dress; white	150	100.00	115.00	50.00
Susannah	White all over	150	40.00	45.00	20.00

Derivatives

Pincushion Dolls, 1939

Pincushion dolls are a very popular collectable. They comprise the top half of a lady model, with small holes around the hips with which to attach a dress. The purchaser of the doll sewed, knitted or crocheted a padded dress which formed a pincushion.

The models are hollow and are marked around the rim of the base. Only four varieties of Pincushion dolls have been reported.

Welsh Lady

Spanish Lady

Backstamp: **A.** Black hand written "Wade England"
B. Green ink stamp "Wade England"

Name	Colourways	Size	U.S. $	Can. $	U.K. £
Gypsy Girl	Black hair, shawl; gold earrings	95	325.00	350.00	160.00
Spanish Lady	Blue dress; pink hair comb	105	325.00	350.00	160.00
Spanish Lady	White, yellow, green, blue, maroon, black and red	105	325.00	350.00	160.00
Spanish Lady	White, yellow, green, blue, maroon and red	105	325.00	350.00	160.00
Welsh Lady	Black hat; red shawl	90	325.00	350.00	160.00
Welsh Lady	Black hat; green shawl	90	325.00	350.00	160.00
Woman with Bonnet	Yellow bonnet; cream and yellow dress	90	325.00	350.00	160.00

FLOWERS

At the same time they were producing the lady figures, the George Wade and Wade Heath potteries issued a long series of hand-made earthenware and china flowers in bowls, pots, vases, baskets, miniature jugs and other containers. Included in this range are flowers that were produced without containers. Over a hundred variations of flowers, pots and bowls are known to exist.

Wade produced two types of containers for the flower centres, low bowls and dishes in small, medium and large sizes, which could be purchased separately from the flowers. Apparently there were 79 models in the earthenware set, although information is not available for numbers 66 to 79.

The first series of flowers was made of earthenware. Ninety percent of the bowls, baskets, vases and pots, etc., that contain the flowers are black, but a few examples were also produced in mottled greens and yellows and in plain yellow. The earthenware flower colours can be easily recognised, as they were all hand painted in dark blue, dark red, dark pink, maroon, purple, mauve and deep yellow with bright green leaves.

The second series was produced in china and includes a variety of spring flowers. These flowers were produced in natural pastel shades of pale blues, pinks, mauves and yellows. Unfortunately these flowers are rarely found undamaged. With so many edges to chip and snap off, it is the fortunate collector who finds a perfect example. The price guide is for flowers in mint or near-mint condition; damaged models are worth 50 to 75 percent less. In 1939 the original price for the china flowers ranged from 1/- to 25/-.

When an item is described as miniature, small, medium, large or extra large, that refers to the container only, not the size of the flowers. Because all the flowers are hand made, their sizes vary.

BACKSTAMPS

Handwritten Backstamps

Handwritten marks can be found on both series of flowers. They all say "Wade England."

Ink Stamps

Flaxman Ware ink stamps, as well as "Wade Made in England" and "Wade England," can be found on series one and series two flowers.

Embossed Backstamps

Almost all the embossed backstamps found on series one and two flowers include the words, "British Made."

Some flowers have two handwritten numbers and a handwritten letter on them. One of the numbers corresponds to the Wade catalogue number, the other number is the code for the variety of flower. A letter refers to the size and type of container.

FLOWER CODE NUMBERS

1.	Primula	13.	Unknown
2.	Poppy	14.	Stock elsa
3.	Tulip	15.	Blossom
4	Primrose also Spring Flowers	16.	Violet
5	Narcissus	17.	Wild rose
6	Forget-me-not / Tulip	18.	Carnation
7	Unknown	19.	Unknown
8	Anemone or daffodil	20.	Unknown
9	Rose	21.	Unknown
10	Pansy	22.	Unknown
11	Rosebud	23.	Unknown
12	Oleander		

Some of the flowers are hard to distinguish from one another because of their similarity and the colours used. For example, it is difficult to tell a tulip and rosebud apart, but on close inspection you will see that the central petals of the tulip come to a point, while the rosebud petals have a swirl with a small central hole. The difference between the anemone and the wild rose is that the anemone has long black stamens.

To date 23 flower types are known, but the code numbers for the buttercup, campanula, daisy, delphinium, hibiscus, shamrock and water lily have not yet been identified. We would welcome any further information on this. the following flowers have been found with the same number on the base: Anemone and daffodil with #8 on the base; Forget-me-Not and Tulip with #6 on the base; Primrose and Spring Blossoms with #4 on the base. The reason for this number conflict is unknown.

CONTAINER CODE LETTERS

D.	Medium	J.	Large
E.	Small	K.	Extra large
G.	Miniature	SB.	Small basket
H.	Flower centre, long stem, no container		

EARTHENWARE FLOWERS

Two types of flower centres were produced:

1. Flowers on long stems with no container
Miniature—three flowers
Small—four flowers
Medium—six flowers
Large—eight or more flowers, approximately 130 x 100 mm
Extra large—eight or more flowers, approximately 175 x 150 mm

2. Flowers on short stems with no container
Large—eight or more flowers, approximately 110 x 110mm
Extra large—12 or more flowers, approximately 135 x 155 mm

FLOWER CENTRES

Flower Centres (Earthenware), c.1930-c.1935

Delphiniums, long stemmed

Anemones, long stemmed

Wild roses, short stemmed

Backstamp:
A. Raised "British Made"
B. Raised "British Made" and black handwritten "Wade England"
C. Raised "British Made" and black handwritten "Made in England"
D. Black handwritten "Wade England"
E. Black handwritten "No 29 Wade England"
F. Black handwritten "Wade England No 47 Dell (E)"

Long Stem:

Name	Colourways	Size	U.S. $	Can. $	U.K. £
Tulips	Blue/dark pink/yellow flowers	Miniature/60 x 50	30.00	35.00	15.00
Wild roses	Purple/pink/yellow/blue flowers	Small/70 x 60	30.00	35.00	15.00
Delphiniums/wild roses	Blue/pink flowers	Medium/100 x 60	40.00	45.00	20.00
Rose bud	Yellow/blue/dark pink flowers	Medium/95 x 50	40.00	45.00	20.00
Anemones	Maroon/mauve/yellow/pink flowers	Large/146 x 170	50.00	60.00	25.00
Delphiniums	Blue/pink flowers	Large/150 x 120	50.00	60.00	25.00
Delphiniums	Blue/pink flowers	Large/150 x 120	50.00	60.00	25.00
Pansies	Blue/maroon/yellow flowers	Large/145 x 120	50.00	60.00	25.00
Poppies	Blue/maroon/yellow flowers	Large/140 x 120	50.00	60.00	25.00
Tulips	Yellow/blue/dark pink flowers	Large/146 x 78	50.00	60.00	25.00
Wild rose	Yellow/blue/dark pink flowers	Large/146 x 78	50.00	60.00	25.00

Short Stem:

Catalogue numbers for short stem earthenware flower centres are 38, 42 and 50.

Name	Colourways	Size	U.S. $	Can. $	U.K. £
Anemone.pansy/poppy	Pink/yellow/blue flowers	Large/145 x 140	50.00	60.00	25.00
Anemone/rose/wide rose	Pink/yellow/blue flowers	Large/145 x 140	50.00	60.00	25.00
Roses.wild roses	Pink/yellow/blue flowers	Large/105 x 120	50.00	60.00	25.00
Wild Roses	Pink/yellow/blue flowers	Large/145 x 140	50.00	60.00	25.00

Flower Centres (China), c.1935-1939

Catalogue numbers for china flower centres are: 81-82, 96-98, and 101-102.

Tulips, long stemmed

Anemones, pansies and poppies
short stemmed

Backstamp: **A.** Handwritten "Wade England"
B. Black ink stamp "Wade Made in England"

Flower	Colourways	Size	U.S. $	Can. $	U.K. £
Tulips/long stem	Palue blue/pale pink/pale yellow flowers	Miniature/60 x 50	30.00	35.00	15.00
Anemones/long stem	Mauve/white flowers	Small/60 x 60	40.00	45.00	20.00
Daffodils/long stem	Pale yellow/orange flowers	Small/60 x 50	40.00	45.00	20.00
Anemones/pansies/poppies/short stem	Orange/pink/mauve/yellow flowers	Large/130 x 220	50.00	60.00	25.00

HOLDERS WITH FLOWERS

ARCHES

Arches (Earthenware), c.1930-c.1935

Catalogue numbers for the arches are 56 and 57.

Pansies, roses, wild roses

Violets

Roses

Backstamp:
- **A.** Black handwritten "Wade England"
- **B.** Black ink stamp "Wade England"
- **C.** Black handwritten "Wade England No. 57 Stock"
- **D.** Black handwritten "Wade England No. 57 Violet"

Flower	Colourways	Size	U.S. $	Can. $	U.K. £
Assorted flowers	Red/blue/yellow flowers; dark green arch	Small/130 x 145	70.00	80.00	35.00
Pansies	Yellow/maroon/mauve/blue flowers; pale green arch	Small/130 x 145	70.00	80.00	35.00
Stock	Yellow/maroon/mauve/blue flowers; yellow arch	Small/130 x 145	70.00	80.00	35.00
Violets	Yellow/maroon/mauve/blue flowers; yellow arch	Small/130 x 145	70.00	80.00	35.00
Wild roses	Yellow/maroon/mauve/blue flowers; yellow arch	Small/130 x 145	70.00	80.00	35.00
Anemones	Blue/maroon/red, pink/yellow flowers; yellow arch	Large/170 x 190	100.00	115.00	50.00
Anemones	Blue/maroon/red/pink/yellow flowers; cream/green arch	Large/170 x 190	100.00	115.00	50.00
Pansies/roses/stock	Pink/yellow flowers; yellow arch	Large/170 x 190	100.00	115.00	50.00
Roses	Pink/yellow flowers; pale green arch	Large/170 x 190	100.00	115.00	50.00

BASKETS

Baskets With Handles (Earthenware), c.1930-c.1935

Catalogue number for the basket with handle is 54.

Wild roses   Stock flowers

Backstamp: Black ink stamp "Wade England"

Flower	Colourways	Size	U.S. $	Can. $	U.K. £
Pansies	Yellow/pink flowers; yellow basket	75 x 86	50.00	55.00	25.00
Stock	Yellow/pink flowers; yellow basket	75 x 86	50.00	55.00	25.00
Wild roses	Blue/yellow/pink/maroon flowers; black basket	75 x 86	50.00	55.00	25.00
Wild roses	Blue/yellow/pink/maroon flowers; yellow basket	75 x 86	50.00	55.00	25.00

Oval Wicker Baskets, Without Handles (Earthenware), c.1930-c.1935

Catalogue numbers for the large oval wicker baskets are 4, 5 and 6, but catalogue numbers for the small baskets have not been found.

Unknown flower   Spring Blossoms   Wild roses

Backstamp: Black handwritten "Wade England"

Flower	Colourways	Size	U.S. $	Can. $	U.K. £
Primroses	Yellow flowers; black basket	Small/40 x 70	35.00	40.00	18.00
Rosebuds	Yellow/pink/blue flowers; black basket	Small/40 x 70	35.00	40.00	18.00
Roses	Yellow/pink/blue flowers; black basket	Small/40 x 70	35.00	40.00	18.00
Roses/rosebuds	Yellow/pink flowers; yellow baskets	Small/40 x 70	35.00	40.00	18.00
Wild roses	Yellow/pink/blue flowers; black basket	Small/37 x 70	35.00	40.00	18.00
Wild roses	Yellow/pink/blue flowers; yellow basket	Small/37 x 70	35.00	40.00	18.00
Pansies	Yellow/blue/maroon flowers; black basket	Large/70 x 105	50.00	55.00	25.00
Pansies	Yellow/blue/dark pink flowers; yellow basket	Large/70 x 105	50.00	55.00	25.00
Spring Blossoms	Pink flowers; black basket	Large/65 x 105	50.00	55.00	25.00
Tulips	Yellow/blue/maroon flowers; black basket	Large/70 x 105	50.00	55.00	25.00
Unknown	Yellow/pink/maroon/ blue flowers; black basket	Large/65 x 105	50.00	55.00	25.00
Wild roses	Yellow/pink/maroon/blue flowers; black basket	Large/65 x 105	50.00	55.00	25.00

Oval Wicker Baskets, Without Handles (China), c.1935-c.1939

Primroses

Roses

Backstamp: Black ink stamp "Wade Made in England"

Flower	Colourways	Size	U.S. $	Can. $	U.K. £
Pansies	Pale pink/mauve flowers; black basket	Small/37 x 70	40.00	45.00	20.00
Primroses	Pale yellow flowers; black basket	Small/37 x 70	40.00	45.00	20.00
Prinrose/pansy/rose	Pale yellow/pink/mauve flowers; black basket	Small/37 x 70	40.00	45.00	20.00
Roses	Pale yellow/pink flowers; black basket	Small/37 x 70	40.00	45.00	20.00

Round Baskets Without Handles (Earthenware), c.1930-c.1935

These round baskets have a hollow base. The catalogue numbers are 20, 26 and 27.

Assorted flowers

Wild roses

Backstamp:
- **A.** Raised "British Made" and black handwritten "Wade England"
- **B.** Raised "British Made"
- **C.** Black handwritten "Wade England"
- **D.** Raised "Made in England" and model number
- **E.** Black handwritten "Wade England No.20 W. Rose"

Flower	Colourways	Size	U.S. $	Can. $	U.K. £
Assorted flowers	Yellow/blue/pink/maroon flowers; black basket	66 x 50	40.00	45.00	20.00
Oleanders	Yellow/maroon/mauve flowers; black basket	66 x 50	40.00	45.00	20.00
Roses	Yellow/blue/red/pink flowers; black basket	66 x 50	40.00	45.00	20.00
Tulips	Yellow/pink/maroon flowers; black basket	66 x 50	40.00	45.00	20.00
Wild roses	Blue/yellow/pink/maroon flowers; black basket	66 x 50	40.00	45.00	20.00
Wild roses	Blue/yellow/pink/maroon flowers; yellow basket	66 x 50	40.00	45.00	20.00

BOWLS AND POTS

Ajax Bowl (Earthenware), c.1930-c.1935

Catalogue numbers for the Ajax bowls are 39-41.

Tulips

Wild Roses

Backstamp: A. Black handwritten "Wade England"
B. Black handwritten "Wade England Camelia E" with embossed "British"

Flower	Colourways	Size	U.S. $	Can. $	U.K. £
Roses	Purple/pink/yellow/blue flowers; black bowl	130 x 110	40.00	45.00	20.00
Tulips	Purple/pink/yellow/blue flowers; black bowl	130 x 110	40.00	45.00	20.00
Wild roses	Purple/pink/yellow/blue flowers; black bowl	130 x 110	40.00	45.00	20.00
Wild roses	Purple/pink/yellow/blue flowers; yellow bowl	130 x 110	40.00	45.00	20.00

Basket-Weave Footed Bowl (Earthenware), c.1930-c.1935

The catalogue number for the Basket-weave bowl is unknown.

Wild roses

Pansies, roses, wild roses

Backstamp: A. Black ink stamp "Wade England GAY"
B. Black ink stamp "Wade England GWEN Mixed"

Name	Colourways	Size	U.S. $	Can. $	U.K. £
Anemones	Blue/red/maroon/yellow flowers; black bowl	Small/116 x 60	40.00	45.00	20.00
Assorted	Blue/red/maroon/yellow flowers; green/brown bowl	Small/116 x 60	40.00	45.00	20.00
Pansies	Blue/red/maroon/yellow flowers; black bowl	Small/116 x 60	40.00	45.00	20.00
Poppies/roses	Blue/pink/yellow flowers; yellow bowl	Small/116 x 60	40.00	45.00	20.00
Wild roses	Blue/red/maroon/yellow flowers; black bowl	Small/116 x 60	40.00	45.00	20.00
Pansies/rose/wild rose	Blue/red/maroon/yellow flowers; green bowl	Large/210 x 120	50.00	55.00	25.00

Binnie Pots (Earthenware), c.1930-c.1935

The Binnie Pots are Wade catalogue number 64.

Pansies

Pansies, roses, wild roses

Wild roses

Backstamp: **A.** Black ink stamp "Wade England"
B. Black ink stamp "L Wade England No. 64 Mixed"

Flower	Colourways	Size	U.S. $	Can. $	U.K. £
Pansies	Purple/blue/yellow flowers; black pot	145 x 77	40.00	45.00	20.00
Pansy/rose/wild rose	Purple/blue/yellow flowers; black pot	155 x 77	40.00	45.00	20.00
Wild roses	Purple/blue/yellow flowers; yellow pot	145 x 77	40.00	45.00	20.00

Footed Bowl (Earthenware), c.1930-c.1935

This footed bowl has catalogue number 115 on the base, no information has been found as to the Wade catalogue number for this item.

Backstamp: Black ink stamp "L Wade England No. 115"

Flower	Colourways	Size	U.S. $	Can. $	U.K. £
Anemone/carnation/dahlia	Maroon/purple/yellow flowers; creamy yellow bowl	140 x 150	50.00	55.00	25.00

Moss Covered Pots (Earthenware), c.1930-c.1935

These flowers are in a moss covered flowerpot, with a round base. The Wade sales catalogue number is 104.

Poppies, large and medium sizes

Backstamp: Black handwritten "M Wade England No. 104"

Flower	Colourways	Size	U.S. $	Can. $	U.K. £
Assorted	White/mauve/dark pink flowers; green pot	Small/60 x 60	40.00	45.00	20.00
Poppies	Purple/blue/yellow flowers; green pot	Medium/90 x 110	40.00	45.00	20.00
Poppies	Purple/blue/yellow flowers; green pot	Large/125 x 130	50.00	55.00	25.00

Octagonal Bowls (Earthenware), c.1930-c.1935

Pansies, roses, wild roses

Poppies

Backstamp:
A. Raised "British Made" and "Wade England Made in England"
B. Raised "British Made" and black handwritten "Wade England"
C. Raised "British Made"
D. Black handwritten "Wade England"
E. Black ink stamp "Wade England"
F. Black ink stamp "14 Wade England No. 55" with impressed "England"

Flower	Colourways	Size	U.S. $	Can. $	U.K. £
Poppies/roses/wildroses	Yellow/mauve/purple flowers; black bowl	70 x 60	50.00	55.00	25.00
Poppies	Yellow/mauve/purple flowers; yellow bowl	70 x 60	50.00	55.00	25.00
Stock	Yellow/mauve/purple flowers; yellow bowl	70 x 60	50.00	55.00	25.00

Octagonal Bowls (China), c.1935-1939

Forget-me-nots

Narcissus

Flower	Colourways	Size	U.S. $	Can. $	U.K. £
Forget-me-nots	Pale blue /pink flowers; black bowl	Miniature/60 x 60	60.00	70.00	30.00
Narcissus	White/yellow flowers; black bowl	Large/60 x 75	60.00	70.00	30.00
Primula	Blue/yellow/pink flowers; black bowl	Extra large/75 x 90	60.00	70.00	30.00

Oval Bowls (Earthenware), c.1930-c.1935

Although this bowl has the number 14 on the base it does not correspond with the Wade catalogue number or flower type.

Pansies, roses, wild roses

Anemones, wild roses

Backstamp: Raised "New Oval Bowl 14 Wade England"

Flower	Colourways	Size	U.S. $	Can. $	U.K. £
Anemones/wild roses	Yellow/mauve/purple flowers; mottled cream/green bowl	140 x 160	75.00	85.00	40.00
Pansies/roses/wild roses	Yellow/mauve/purple flowers; green bowl	140 x 160	75.00	85.00	40.00

Posy Pot (Earthenware), c.1930-c.1935

Assorted flowers

Oleander

Backstamp: **A.** Black handwritten "Wade England"
B. Raised "British Made"
C. Raised "British Made" and black handwritten "Wade England"
D. Raised "British Made," black handwritten "Wade England" and " Made in England"

Flower	Colourways	Size	U.S. $	Can. $	U.K. £
Assorted	Blue/pink/yellow flowers; yellow bowl	Large/65 x 57	40.00	45.00	20.00
Orleander	Blue/pink/yellow flowers; black bowl	Large/65 x 57	40.00	45.00	20.00
Wild rose	Blue/pink/yellow flowers; yellow bowl	Large/65 x 57	40.00	45.00	20.00
Assorted	Blue/pink/yellow flowers; yellow bowl	Small/58 x 45	40.00	45.00	20.00
Rose Buds	Mauve/pink/yellow flowers; black bowl	Small/58 x 45	40.00	45.00	20.00
Tulips	Pink/blue/yellow/flowers; black bowl	Small/58 x 45	40.00	45.00	20.00

Powder Bowl (China), c.1935-1939

This bowl has been produced from the base of one of the Wadeheath powder bowls and has been filled with china roses.

Backstamp: Black handwritten "Wade Made in England"

Flower	Colourways	Size	U.S. $	Can. $	U.K. £
Roses	Pink/yellow/white flowers; brown bowl	140 x 160	70.00	80.00	35.00

Shallow Bowls (Earthenware), c.1930-c.1935

Listed as Posy Pots in the Wade sales catalogues these shallow bowls have been found in three sizes; miniature, catalogue numbers 1, 2 and 9; small, numbers 8, 10 and 47; and medium, numbers 18, 19 and 28.

Anemones, rosebuds - Eathenware

Primroses - China

Roses, rosebuds - China

Backstamp:
A. Raised "British Made" with an impressed code letter (sometimes includes a black handwritten "Wade England" or "Made in England"
B. Raised "British Made" and "Wade England"
C. Raised "British Made" and "Made in England"
D. Handwritten "Wade England"

Flower	Colourways	Size	U.S. $	Can. $	U.K. £
Anemone/rosebuds	Mauve/pale yellow/pale pink flowers	Miniature/32 x 35	20.00	25.00	10.00
Assorted	Pink/maroon/yellow/blue flowers	Miniature/30 x 35	20.00	25.00	10.00
Rosebuds	Pink/maroon/yellow/blue flowers	Miniature/35 x 35	20.00	25.00	10.00
Roses	Pink/maroon/yellow/blue flowers	Miniature/35 x 35	20.00	25.00	10.00
Roses/rosebuds	Mauve/pale yellow/pink flowers	Miniature/32 x 35	20.00	25.00	10.00
Tulips	Yellow/pink/maroon/blue flowers	Miniature/35 x 35	20.00	25.00	10.00
Wild roses	Yellow/pink/maroon/blue flowers	Miniature/32 x 35	20.00	25.00	10.00
Assorted	Blue/yellow/maroon flowers	Small/42 x 45	20.00	25.00	10.00
Pansies	Pink/maroon/yellow/blue flowers	Small/40 x 35	20.00	25.00	10.00
Primroses	Pinl/maroon/yellow/blue flowers	Small/40 x 35	20.00	25.00	10.00
Roses	Pink/maroon/yellow/blue flowers	Small/40 x 45	20.00	25.00	10.00
Stock	Pink/maroon/yellow/blue flowers	Small/40 x 35	20.00	25.00	10.00
Tulips	Pink/maroon/yellow/blue flowers	Small/40 x 35	20.00	25.00	10.00
Wild roses	Purple/yellow/pink/blue flowers	Small/45 x 57	20.00	25.00	10.00
Wild roses	Yellow/blue/pink flowers	Small/42 x 45	20.00	25.00	10.00
Assorted	Pink/yellow/blue flowers	Medium/58 x 45	20.00	25.00	10.00
Rosebuds	Pink/yellow/blue flowers	Medium/58 x 45	20.00	25.00	10.00
Tulips	Pink/yellow/blue flowers	Medium/58 x 47	20.00	25.00	10.00
Wild roses	Pink/yellow/blue flowers	Medium/58 x 45	20.00	25.00	10.00

Shallow Bowls (China), c.1935-1939

Flower	Colourways	Size	U.S. $	Can. $	U.K. £
Pansies/primrose/rose	Pink/mauve/yellow flowers	Small/45 x 35	30.00	35.00	15.00
Primsroses	Pink/maroon/yellow/blue flowers	Small/45 x 35	30.00	35.00	15.00
Roses/rosebuds	Pale yellow/pale pink flowers	Small/45 x 60	30.00	35.00	15.00
Roses/rosebuds	Pale yellow flkowers	Medium/58 x 45	30.00	35.00	15.00

Spherical Bowl (Earthenware), c.1930-c.1935

No Wade sales catalogue number has been found for this shaped bowl

Stock

Wild roses

Wild roses

Backstamp: **A.** Black handwritten "Wade England Stock Elsa"
B. Black handwritten "Wade England"

Flower	Colourways	Size	U.S. $	Can. $	U.K. £
Assorted	Bright yellow/pink/blue/maroon flowers; black bowl	90 x 70	40.00	45.00	20.00
Stock	Bright yellow/pink/blue/maroon flowers; black bowl	90 x 70	40.00	45.00	20.00
Stock	Bright yellow/pink/blue/maroon flowers; yellow bowl	90 x 70	40.00	45.00	20.00
Wild roses	Bright yellow/pink/blue/maroon flowers; yellow bowl	90 x 70	40.00	45.00	20.00
Wild roses	Bright yellow/pink/blue/maroon flowers; black bowl	90 x 70	40.00	45.00	20.00

Stepped Bowl (Earthenware), c.1930-c.1935

This unusual shaped bowl, which at first glance resembles a teapot lid, has a hollowed base with embossed Wade England number 506. No Wade sales catalogue number has been found for this shaped bowl.

The sample shown in the photo is badly damaged and has been repainted.

Backstamp: Embossed "Wade England No. 506" with a black handwritten "Wild Rose J"

Flower	Colourways	Size	U.S. $	Can. $	U.K. £
Wild roses	Blue/mauve/pink/yellow flowers; black bowl	55 x 60	30.00	35.00	15.00

Vulcan Pots (Earthenware), c.1930-c.1935

Wild roses

Backstamp: Black handwritten "Wade England"

Flower	Colourways	Size	U.S. $	Can. $	U.K. £
Pansies	Purple/blue/yellow flowers; black pot	110 x 75	40.00	45.00	20.00
Poppies	Red/purple/yellow flowers; black pot	110 x 75	40.00	45.00	20.00
Tulips	Red/blue/yellow flowers; black pot	110 x 75	40.00	45.00	20.00
Wild roses	Purple/blue/yellow flowers; yellow pot	110 x 75	40.00	45.00	20.00

JUGS

Large-Spout Miniature Jugs

The Wade catalogue number for the large-spout miniature jug is unknown.

Poppies

Roses

Backstamp: A. Black handwritten "Wade England"
B. Black handwritten "Wade Made in England A. Jug"

Flower	Colourways	Size	U.S. $	Can. $	U.K. £
Pansies	Maroon/yellow flowers; yellow jug; green handle	66 x 68	30.00	35.00	15.00
Poppies	Maroon/yellow flowers; yellow jug; green handle	66 x 68	30.00	35.00	15.00
Rosebuds	Pink/yellow flowers; black jug; yellow handle	60 x 68	30.00	35.00	15.00
Roses	Pink/yellow flowers; black jug; yellow handle	66 x 68	30.00	35.00	15.00

Long-Neck Miniature Jugs

*Photograph not available
at press time*

Backstamp: Unknown

Flower	Colourways	Size	U.S. $	Can. $	U.K. £
Wild roses	Dark pink/yellow/blue flowers; black jug	110 X 40	30.00	35.00	15.00

Regency Miniature Jug

This miniature jug has a ribbed body similar to the Wade Regency and Empress design items. The Wade sales catalogue number for this jug is unknown.

Backstamp: Black handwritten "Wade England 9 G. Jug"

Flower	Colourways	Size	U.S. $	Can. $	U.K. £
Roses	Dark pink/yellow flowers; yellow jug; green handle	80 x 35	35.00	40.00	18.00

Roman Jug

The Wade sales catalogue number for this jug is 63.

Backstamp: Black handwritten "Wade 9 England No 63"

Flower	Colourways	Size	U.S. $	Can. $	U.K. £
Roses	Dark pink/yellow flowers; green/brown speckled jug	240 x 195	80.00	90.00	40.00
Roses	Dark pink/yellow flowers; green jug	240 x 195	80.00	90.00	40.00

Short-Necked Miniature Jug

The Wade sales catalogue number for this jug is 31.

Backstamp: **A.** Black handwritten "Wade 2 England"
                 B. Black handwritten "Wade England No. 31 Wild Rose"

Flower	Colourways	Size	U.S. $	Can. $	U.K. £
Poppies	Dark pink/blue flowers; black jug	60 x 35	30.00	35.00	15.00
Tulips	Dark pink/yellow flowers; black jug	60 x 35	30.00	35.00	15.00
Wild roses	Dark pink/yellow/blue flowers; black jug	60 x 35	30.00	35.00	15.00

Sloping-Neck Miniature Jugs

Backstamp: Black handwriten "Wade England"

Flower	Colourways	Size	U.S. $	Can. $	U.K. £
Pansies	Blue/yellow/maroon flowers; black jug; pale yellow handle	65 x 21	30.00	35.00	15.00
Wild roses	Blue/yellow/maroon flowers; black jug; pale yellow handle	80 x 22	30.00	35.00	15.00

Straight-Backed Miniature Jugs

Backstamp: Black handwritten "Wade England"

Flower	Colourways	Size	U.S. $	Can. $	U.K. £
Roses	Pink/yellow flowers; yellow jug; black handle	85 x 25	50.00	55.00	25.00
Roses	Pink/yellow flowers; yellow jug; pale green handle	85 x 25	50.00	55.00	25.00

Wide-Mouth Miniature Jug

Backstamp: Raised "British Made" and black handwritten "Wade England"

Flower	Colourways	Size	U.S. $	Can. $	U.K. £
Wild roses	Pink/yellow flowers; black jug; yellow handle	75 x 50	30.00	35.00	15.00

MENU HOLDERS

Menu Holders (Earthenware), c.1930-c.1935

Although listed in the Wade sales catalogue as menu holders, there is no slot or fixture on these flowers in which to stand a menu. Produced in two sizes the catalogue numbers are as follows: roses, large-12, small-11; water lilies, large-15, small-16.

Rose

Water Lily

Backstamp: **A.** Black handwritten "Wade England N. 12" on roses
B. Black handwritten "Wade England No. 15" on waterlily

Flower	Colourways	Size	U.S. $	Can. $	U.K. £
Water lily	Pink flower; green leaves	Small/unknown	30.00	35.00	15.00
Roses	Deep red flowers; green leaves	Large/55 x 100	30.00	35.00	15.00
Water lily	Pink flower; green leaves	Large/50 x 90	30.00	35.00	15.00
Water lily	Yellow flower; green leaves	Large/50 x 90	30.00	35.00	15.00

MISCELLANEOUS

Angle (Earthenware), c.1930-c.1935

The Angle is believed to be one half of the square which would account for the odd sides as the Wade square is actually a rectangle.

The Angle has been found with the number 65 included in the backstamp, which is the number used for the 'square.'

Backstamp: Black ink stamp "Wade England"

Flower	Colourways	Size	U.S. $	Can. $	U.K. £
Pansies	Yellow/maroon/blue flowers; black angle	125 x 103	60.00	70.00	30.00
Wild roses	Yellow/maroon/pink flowers; brown angle	125 x 103	60.00	70.00	30.00

Brick (Earthenware), c.1930-c.1935

*Photograph not available
at press time*

Backstamp: "Black handwritten "Wade England"

Flower	Colourways	Size	U.S. $	Can. $	U.K. £
Assorted flowers	Yellow/blue/maroon flowers; light green brick	150 x 175	80.00	90.00	40.00

Horseshoe Window Box (Earthenware), c.1930-c.1935

The Wade sales catalogue number for the window box is unknown. "May Window Box" is handwritten on the bottom of the horseshoe.

Roses

Roses, wild roses

Roses, wild roses, speckled window box

Backstamp: Black handwritten "Wade England May Window Box"

Flower	Colourways	Size	U.S. $	Can. $	U.K. £
Roses	Pink/yellow flowers; green/maroon window box	55 x 130	60.00	70.00	30.00
Roses/wild roses	Yellow/pink/blue flowers; grey and green speckled window box	95 x 140	70.00	80.00	35.00
Roses/wild roses	Yellow/pink/blue flowers; green window box	95 x 140	70.00	80.00	35.00

Posy Rings (Earthenware), Catalogue No. 59, c.1930-c.1935

The earthenware posy rings have a pot in the centre in which could be stood a large candle or one of the many flower centres produced by Wade. In contrast the china ware posy rings had a wide open centre.

Wild roses, side view

Wild roses, top view

Backstamp: **A.** Raised "British Made," "Wade England" and "Made in England"
B. Black handwritten "Wade England"
C. Black handwritten "Wade England" with impressed "England"

Flower	Colourways	Size	U.S. $	Can. $	U.K. £
Pansies	Yellow/maroon/blue flowers	60 x 130	70.00	80.00	35.00
Wild rose	Yellow/blue/maroon flowers	60 x 130	70.00	80.00	35.00

Posy Rings (China), Catalogue No. 130, c.1930-c.1935

Backstamp: Black handwritten "4 Wade England May 130 Mixed"

Flower	Colourways	Size	U.S. $	Can. $	U.K. £
Anemone/carnation/dahlia/pansy/poppy	Blue/pink/purple/yellow flowers	65 x 180 diam	80.00	90.00	40.00

Rock Gardens With Gnome (Earthenware), c.1930-c.1935

Produced in two sizes the Gnome rock garden catalogue numbers are: large-3 and small-7. Although not listed as menu holders in the Wade sales catalogue, the Gnome rock garden does have a slot to one side in which a menu / name card could be placed. It is now known the the Gnome rock gardens were produced in the Wade, Ulster pottery.

Rock Garden

Backstamp: Black ink stamp "Wade Made in Ireland"

Name	Colourways	Size	U.S. $	Can. $	U.K. £
Garden Gnome	Red, grey, black and pink Gnome; multicoloured flowers	Small/45 x 65	100.00	115.00	50.00
Garden Gnome	Red, grey, black and pink Gnome; multicoloured flowers	Large/70 x 100	125.00	135.00	60.00

Square Frame (Earthenware), c.1930-c.1935

Although the Wade catalogue calls this flower decoration square it is actually a rectangle as can be seen from the photo of the base. The overlapping flower petals and leaves give the impression from the top that it is a square.

Assorted flowers

Wild roses

Backstamp: Ink stamp "Wade England"

Flower	Colourways	Size	U.S. $	Can. $	U.K. £
Assorted	Green base; blue/pink/yellow flowers; green leaves	125 x 103	70.00	80.00	35.00
Wild roses	Green base; blue/maroon/yellow flowers; green leaves	125 x 103	70.00	80.00	35.00

Triangle (Earthenware), c.1930-c.1935

This triangle, covered with flowers was intended as a table decoration.

Pansies, top view

Pansies, side view

Backstamp: Ink stamp "Wade England F"

Flower	Colourways	Size	U.S. $	Can. $	U.K. £
Pansies	Mauve/purple/yellow flowers	125 x 125 x 125	70.00	80.00	35.00

VASES

Art Deco Flower Vase (Earthenware), c.1930-c.1935

The Wade sales catalogue number for the Art Deco vase is 51. Impressed on the base is the shape number 105, which would suggest that it was originally produced as a vase and later the flowers were added to produce a new item.

Assorted flowers

Backstamp: Black handwritten "Wade England"

Flower	Colourways	Size	U.S. $	Can. $	U.K. £
Assorted	Red/pink/blue/yellow flowers; light grey/blue speckled vase	305 x 250	175.00	200.00	90.00
Assorted	Red/pink/blue/yellow flowers; light grey/pale green vase	325 x 245	175.00	200.00	90.00

Miniature Vase With Handles (Earthenware), c.1930-c.1935

Pansies

Backstamp: Black handwritten "Wade England"

Flower	Colourways	Size	U.S. $	Can. $	U.K. £
Roses/pansies	Purple/yellow/blue flowers; black vase; green handles	80 x 50	30.00	35.00	15.00

Miniature Vase With Handles (China), c.1935-1939

*Photograph not available
at press time*

Backstamp: Black handwritten "Wade England Nina 4"

Flower	Colourways	Size	U.S. $	Can. $	U.K. £
Primula	Purple/yellow/blue flowers; yellow vase; black handles	80 x 50	30.00	35.00	15.00

Saturn Vases (Earthenware), c.1930-c.1935

The Wade sales catalogue numbers for these vases are 60, 61 and 62.

Backstamp: **A.** Embossed "Regs 827224" and black handwritten "Wade England No. 60"
B. Black handwritten "Wade England Saturn"
C. Black ink stamp "Wade England"

Flower	Colourways	Size	U.S. $	Can. $	U.K. £
Primroses	Yellow flowers; pale green ring	Small/130 x 110	70.00	80.00	35.00
Roses	Yellow/pink/blue flowers; cream/green speckled ring	Small/130 x 110	70.00	80.00	35.00
Wild roses	Yellow/maroon/pink/blue flowers; bright yellow ring	Small/130 x 110	70.00	80.00	35.00
Roses	Yellow/maroon/pink/blue flowers; cream/green ring	Medium/145 x 135	80.00	90.00	40.00
Roses/wild roses	Yellow/maroon/pink/blue flowers; cream/green ring	Medium/145 x 135	80.00	90.00	40.00
Roses	Yellow/maroon/blue flowers; green ring	Large/157 x 145	80.00	90.00	40.00
Roses	Yellow/maroon/blue flowers; yellow ring	Large/157 x 145	80.00	90.00	40.00

Small-Waisted Vases (China), c.1935-1939

Backstamp: **A.** Black handwritten "Wade England"
B. Black ink stamp "Wade Made in England"

Flower	Colourways	Size	U.S. $	Can. $	U.K. £
Campanula/primroses/roses	Blue/yellow/pink flowers; white vase; green base; gold band	80 x 40	40.00	45.00	20.00
Carnations/tulips	Pink/yellow/red flowers; black vase	80 x 40	40.00	45.00	20.00
Carnations/tulips	Pink/yellow/red flowers; white vase; gold band	80 x 40	40.00	45.00	20.00
Daisies/violets/tulips	White/violet/red flowers; black vase	80 x 40	40.00	45.00	20.00
Roses/primroses	Yellow/pink/maroon flowers; black vase	80 x 40	40.00	45.00	20.00
Hibiscus	White/yellow flowers; black vase	95 x 80	40.00	45.00	20.00
Oleanders	Dark pink/yellow flowers; black vase	95 x 80	40.00	45.00	20.00
Oleanders	Dark pink/yellow flowers; light green vase	95 x 80	40.00	45.00	20.00
Pansies	Yellow/mauve/dark pink flowers; white/green vase; gold band	85 x 80	40.00	45.00	20.00

Temple Vase (Earthenware), c.1930-c.1935

The Wade catalogue number for the Temple vase is 58.

Backstamp: Unknown

Flower	Colourways	Size	U.S. $	Can. $	U.K. £
Pansies/roses/wild roses	Red/yellow/blue flowers; yellow vase	110 x 95	40.00	45.00	20.00
Wild rose	Red/yellow/blue flowers; black vase	120 x 100	40.00	45.00	20.00
Wild rose	Red/yellow/blue flowers; mottled green/yellow vase	120 x 95	40.00	45.00	20.00

Triangular Vase, Stepped Base (Earthenware), c.1930-c.1935

The Wade sales catalogue number for this triangular vase with stepped base is unknown.

China vase

Backstamp: **A.** Black handwritten "Wade England"
B. Black handwritten "Wade England NINI 4"

Flower	Colourways	Size	U.S. $	Can. $	U.K. £
Assorted	Red/blue/yellow flowers; green vase	130 x 185	100.00	115.00	50.00

Triangular Vase (China), c.1935-1939

Backstamp: Unknown

Flower	Colourways	Size	U.S. $	Can. $	U.K. £
Carnation/roses	Pink/mauve/yellow flowers; pale green vase	Large 125 x 170	125.00	135.00	60.00

MONEY BOXES

Wade has produced many money boxes as part of their giftware line as well as promotional advertising and commissioned money boxes. All known models and colourways produced by the Wade group of potteries are included. Throughout the years, these pieces have been promoted as money boxes, money box, money bank and banks. All pieces will be referred to as money boxes in this section unless information has been found identifying the piece otherwise.

WADE MONEY BOXES

Andy Capp Money Box, 1998

Reg Smythe, the creator of Andy Capp, died of cancer in 1998, as a mark of respect Wade Ceramics donated £1.00 from the sale of the Andy Capp money box model to cancer research. Original cost direct from the Wade Club was £22.00

Backstamp: Printed "Andy Capp ©1998 Mirror Group Newspapers LTD Andy Capp Wade England"

Name	Colourways	Size	U.S. $	Can. $	U.K. £
Andy Capp	Green cap/scarf; black suit/shoes; brown suitcase; grey stool	181	70.00	80.00	35.00

CATS
Cat Money Box, 1998

Cats, seated

The Cat money box was available for sale from the Wade Factory Shop in 1998. The cats were randomly glazed with black spots so many marking and pattern variations exist. The cost of the money box was £10.00.

Backstamp: Embossed "Wade"

Name	Colourways	Size	U.S. $	Can. $	U.K. £
Cat, seated	White; black markings	160	50.00	55.00	25.00

Cat Safe Money Box, 2004

The Cat Safe money box was produced in 2004 and the original cost direct from Wade was £10.00.

Backstamp: Embossed "Wade England"

Name	Colourways	Size	U.S. $	Can. $	U.K. £
Cat Safe	Pale honey	130 x 160	20.00	25.00	10.00

Comic Animal Money Boxes, 1994

In mid summer 1994, Wade introduced a set of four smiling-animal money boxes, produced in all-over, one-colour glazes. The original price direct from the Wade Pottery was £4 each.

Backstamp: Impressed "Wade England"

Name	Colourways	Size	U.S. $	Can. $	U.K. £
Bob the Frog	Green	120	30.00	35.00	15.00
Gertie the Jersey	Orange brown	150	30.00	35.00	15.00
Lucky the Rabbit	Grey	173	30.00	35.00	15.00
Priscilla the Pig	Pink	112	30.00	35.00	15.00

One-of-a-Kind Derivatives

Blue Chintz Pig Money Box, 2000

This multicoloured chintz pig is from the 'Priscilla the Pig' mould. It was a prize at the first West Coast Wade Fair, held in Kalama, Washington in 2000.

Backstamp: Impressed "Wade England"

Date	Event	Colourways	Qantity.	Size	Price
2000	West Coast Wade Fair	Blue; multicoloured flower prints	1	112	Unique

DELIVERY VANS

Festive Van Money Box, 1997

The Festive Van money box was produced from a similar mould to that of the Jim Beam van money boxes. All of the delivery van money boxes produced by Wade are similar but there is size and pattern differences due to the number of delivery vans issued. This model is decorated with Christmas garlands, teddy bears and Christmas presents in the windows. The licence plate reads "Christmas". It was produced in a limited edition of 225. Original price at the November 1997 Extravaganza was £25.00.

Backstamp: Red printed "Wade England"

Name	Colourways	Size	U.S. $	Can. $	U.K. £
Festive Van	Black; multicoloured prints; gold lettering/highlights	140	125.00	150.00	65.00

One Colour Vans Money Box, 1997

The plain one colour Van money box is from the same mould as the 1995 Ringtons Tea Van. Three of the Jim Beam shaped undecorated vans were re-produced by Wade and sold in the Wade shop and at various Wade shows throughout the year. These vans are the same glazes as the Jim Beam van money boxes.

Keenan Antiques put clear stickers on approximately 16 vans (blue and cream colours) and gave them to collectors who spent a certain amount of money with them at the Oconomowoc Wade show in 1997. The sticker reads "Keenan Antiques Est. 1977 (phone number) Oconomowoc Wade Fair".

Backstamp: Unmarked

Name	Colourways	Size	U.S. $	Can. $	U.K. £
Van	Cream	133 x 205	30.00	35.00	15.00
Van	Pale blue	133 x 205	30.00	35.00	15.00
Van	White	133 x 205	30.00	35.00	15.00

One-of-a-Kind Derivatives

Delivery Van, 1998

At the 1998 Alton Towers Fair, raffle tickets were sold for a special colourway edition of the 1997 Van Money Box. Only 29 money boxes in the special colourway were produced. All colourways were the same but each one has a personalized license plate such as "Wade 1" or "Wade 2" up to "Wade 29".

Backstamp: Red printed "Wade England"

Date	Event	Colourways	Quantity	U.S. $	Can. $	U.K. £
1998	Alton Towers	Black, green, red, gold and silver	29		Rare	

Wade Logo Van Money Boxes, 2003

In 2003, a new style Wade Van money box was produced. The cream colourway was produced for the April 13th Wade Fair.

The side of the Van bears the embossed Wade logo, and the license plate reads 255255, which is the telephone number for the Wade Collector's Club.

All of the vans were made available to the Wade shop, with the burgundy and dark green colourways still available in February 2006 at the issue price of £10.50.

Models have been seen with various decals applied to them, Wade did not issue vans decorated with decals,

Backstamp: Impressed "Wade England"

Name	Colourways	Size	U.S. $	Can. $	U.K. £
Wade Logo Van	Burgundy	148 x 200	20.00	25.00	10.00
Wade Logo Van	Cobalt blue	148 x 200	20.00	25.00	10.00
Wade Logo Van	Cream	148 x 200	20.00	25.00	10.00
Wade Logo Van	Dark green	148 x 200	20.00	25.00	10.00

Delivery Van Money Box, 2006

In 2006, Wade introduced two new styles of Delivery Van money boxes, both were entered into their retail line. The two styles were not backstamped, but are embossed with the Wade logo on each side of the van. The grey (1930) Delivery Van has a rear plate with "225-255," while the brown/black van has a front plate with "255-255," the Club's telephone number.

Both vans were available in the United States from Wade retailers at a cost of $15.45.

1930 Grey Delivery Van

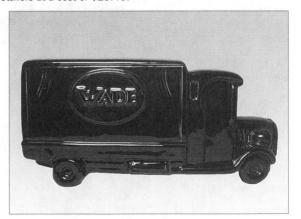

1920 Brown/black Delivery Van

Backstamp: Unmarked

Name	Colourways	Size	U.S. $	Can. $	U.K. £
Delivery Van	Grey	105 x 195	20.00	25.00	10.00
Delivery Van	Brown/black	110 x 215	20.00	25.00	10.00

Disney Money Boxes, 1962

This series comprises a set of five money boxes in the shape of a dog kennel, with an original issue Hat Box figure standing in front of the entrance. The coin slot is in the kennel roof. The issue date for these money boxes was Spring 1962, and they originally sold for 9/11d. Over time, the glue holding the model to the base breaks down, thus the money boxes can be found minus the dog model.

Lady

Lucky

Rolly

Backstamp: Unmarked

Name	Colourways	Size	U.S. $	Can. $	U.K. £
Lady	Beige; blue kennel	95 x 105	150.00	175.00	80.00
Lucky	White; blue kennel	95 x 105	150.00	175.00	80.00
Jock, green coat	Blue-grey; blue kennel	95 x 105	150.00	175.00	80.00
Jock, no coat	Blue-grey; blue kennel	95 x 105	150.00	175.00	80.00
Rolly	White; blue kennel	95 x 105	150.00	175.00	80.00
Scamp	Grey; blue kennel	95 x 105	150.00	175.00	80.00

DOGS
Bengo Money Box, 1965

The Bengo model is based on the popular British television cartoon series called "Bengo and his Puppy Friends." The cartoon series was created by Austrian cartoonist William Timym, a British resident, who signed his cartoons "Tim." William Timym designed the TV Pet model for Wade.

Only one character from the TV Pets series was modelled as a money box. Because the original Bengo model is standing and had no bulk in which to hold coins, it was unsuitable. A new model of a seated Bengo was created with a round body to contain the money. The coin slot is in the dog's back.

Backstamp: Unmarked

Name	Colourways	Size	U.S. $	Can. $	U.K. £
Bengo	Beige; white on face, feet, yellow basket	150 x 140	600.00	675.00	300.00

Kennel and Puppy Money Box, 1987

In 1987, Wade issued a money box based on the earlier 'Disney Kennel' money boxes. Because the original mould was worn, Wade made a new kennel mould. A larger, heavier and less delicate looking mould was produced. The Whinsie Land Puppy was used on the newly modelled kennel money box. The money box was sold in a plain unmarked box.

Backstamp: Unmarked

Name	Colourways	Size	U.S. $	Can. $	U.K. £
Kennel and Puppy	Brown roof; honey walls	95 x 125	70.00	80.00	35.00

Scottie and Westie Dog Money Boxes, 1998 and 2003

The Scottie and Westie dog money boxes were introduced in 1998 and available for sale at the Wade Factory Shop and at various Wade events during the year.

In November 2003, the black Scottie dog money box was reissued into the Wade retail line. In the reissued version, the eyes and nose have been glazed brown. The cost of the reissued money box direct from Wade was £10.00.

Backstamp: Embossed "Wade"

Scottie   Westie

Name	Colourways	Size	U.S. $	Can. $	U.K. £
Scottie	Black	160	50.00	55.00	25.00
Scottie	Black; brown eyes and nose	160	50.00	55.00	25.00
Westie	White	160	50.00	55.00	25.00

Fawn Money Box, First Version, c.1963

Fawn Money Box, First Version c.1963

This figure is different from "Bambi," a *Disney Blow Up*, and has a coin slot in the back. It is believed that a few other *Disney Blow Ups* were remodelled as money boxes. There are unconfirmed reports of a "Lady Money Box," "Jock Money Box" and "Thumper Money Box," but no visual or written evidence has been found. Because of high production costs, only a limited number of the "Fawn Money Box" were made.

Backstamp: A. Black transfer "Made in England"
B. Unmarked

Name	Colourways	Size	U.S. $	Can. $	U.K. £
Fawn	Brown, orange-brown patches	120 x 105	110.00	150.00	75.00

Fawn Money Box, Second Version, 1987

Fawn Money Box, Second Version, 1987

In 1987 Wade issued a money box based on the earlier fawn money box. Because the original mould was worn. Wade made a new mould which produced a larger, heavier and less delicate looking model. The Fawn money box was sold in a plain unmarked box.

Backstamp: A. Black "Wade Made in England"
B. Black "Wade England" on cap that covers hole in base.

Name	Colourways	Size	U.S. $	Can. $	U.K. £
Fawn	Light brown; brown markings	130 x 125	70.00	80.00	35.00

Elephant Money Box, c.1960

As no further evidence of the Elephant Money Box has been found, it is believed that it may have been a prototype and not put into production.

Photograph not available
at press time

Backstamp: Black transfer print "Wade England"

Name	Colourways	Size	Price
Elephant	Dark grey; blue blanket	115	Possibly not put into production

Honey Bear Money Box, 2003

The Honey Bear money box is holding a honey pot. It was available as part of the Wade retail line for 2003-2004. The piece could be bought from the Wade Ceramics mail order shop in October 2004 for £10.00.

Backstamp: Embossed "Wade England"

Name	Colourways	Size	U.S. $	Can. $	U.K. £
Honey Bear	Yellow; orange honey	155	20.00	25.00	10.00

Kellogg's Money Boxes, 2003-2005

Tony the Tiger, Bust

Tony the Tiger Star Saver

Tony the Tiger Grand Prix

Wade produced three Tony the Tiger money boxes under license to Kellogg's. The first money box, 'Tony the Tiger Bust', was issued in 2003, in a limited edition of 500 and cost £35.00. Members of the Wade Club could purchase the money box for a reduced price of £30.00.

The second money box was produced in June 2004 in a limited edition of 2,000 and is of Tony the Tiger as a goal keeper and is called 'Star Saver.' The model was still available from Wade Ceramics in April 2006 at the original issue price of £37.45.

The third money box was released in August 2005 and was called 'Tony the Tiger Grand Prix.' This model features Tony in a blue racing car. The piece is in a limited edition of 500 and cost £35.00.

'Coco the Monkey Bust' was the fourth money box produced under the Kellogg's license. He was produced in a limited edition of 500 in 2005.

Backstamp:
A. Printed "Tony the Tiger™ Kellogg's and all characters are trademarks of Kellog Company ©2003 Kellogg Company" "Limited Edition of 500" with red 'Wade Made in England' Logo
B. Printed "Tony the Tiger Star Saver Limited Edition of 2000 Kellogg's and all characters are trademarks of Kellogg Company ©2004 Kellogg Company" with red 'Wade Made in England' Logo
C. Printed "Tony the Tiger Grand Prix Kellogg's and all characters are trademarks of Kellogg Company © 2005 Kellogg Company" with red "Wade Made in England" Logo.
D. Printed "Coco Moneybox Kellogg's® and all characters are trademarks of Kellogg Company © 2005 Kellogg Company Ltd Edt of 500" eith red "Wade Made in England" Logo

Name	Colourways	Size	U.S. $	Can. $	U.K. £
Coco the Monkey	Unknown	Unknown	70.00	80.00	35.00
Tony the Tiger Bust	Orange, black; white and yellow	127	70.00	80.00	35.00
Tony The Tiger Star Saver	White, grey, orange and black	100 X 135	70.00	80.00	35.00
Tony the Tiger Grand Prix	Orange, black, blue	Unknown	70.00	80.00	35.00

MR. MEN and LITTLE MISS

The Mr. Bump and Mr. Noisy money boxes were produced under the Mr. Man and Little Miss license.

Mr Bump Money Box, 2004

Mr. Bump, riding in a bumper car, was part of the UK Wade retail line, and unavailable outside the UK due to licensing restrictions. The money box was still available from the Wade on-line shop in April 2006, at the original issue price of £19.99.

Backstamp: Printed "Mr. Men and Little Miss ™ & © 2004 Mrs Roger Hargreaves Mr Bump" with black Mr. Men Little Miss characters and red "Wade made in England" logo

Name	Colourways	Size	U.S. $	Can. $	U.K. £
Mr. Bump	Blue; white bandage; white bumper car with yellow/blue /red/white decals	110 x155	40.00	45.00	20.00

Mr. Noisy Money Box 2005

Due to licensing restrictions Mr. Noisy was also only available in the U.K. The money box was available from the Wade on-line shop in April 2006, at the original issue price of £19.99.

Backstamp: Printed " Mr Men & Little Miss ™ & © The Hargreaves Organisation Mr. Noisy" with Mr. Men & Little Miss, and Wade logos

Name	Colourways	Size	U.S. $	Can. $	U.K. £
Mr. Noisy	Red; black mouth; brown shoes; green grass base	130 x 115	40.00	45.00	20.00

Nursery Rhymes Money Boxes, 2004-2005

The first set of large Nursery Rhyme money boxes was produced in February 2004. They were Gingerbread Man, Humpty Dumpty and Old King Cole. Three more Nursery money boxes were added in 2005, they were Old Woman in a Shoe, Puss in Boots, and The Three Bears. All were still available from the Wade on-line shop in April 2006 at £12.50.

Gimgerbread Man

Humpty Dumpty

Old King Cole

Old Woman Who Lived in a Shoe

Puss in Boots

The Three Bears

Backstamp Embossed "Wade England"

Name	Colourways	Size	U.S. $	Can. $	U.K. £
Gingerbread Man	Honey; black eyes	180	20.00	25.00	10.00
Humpty	Honey; black eyes	160	20.00	25.00	10.00
Old King Cole	Honey	112	20.00	25.00	10.00
Old Woman in a Shoe	Honey	180	20.00	25.00	10.00
Puss in Boots	Honey; black eyes & boots	160	20.00	25.00	10.00
The Three Bears	Honey, black eyes	112	20.00	25.00	10.00

One-of-a-Kind Derivatives

Nursery Rhyme Money Boxes, 2003 and 2005

Several Nursery Rhyme money boxes were produced as one-of-a-kind prizes for the Dunstable Wade Shows in 2002 and 2005. Little Miss Muffet has only been seen as a one-of-a-kind and as of 2006 has not been released into the general Wade line.

Photograph not available
at press time

Backstamp: Embossed "Wade England"

Name	Date	Colourways	Size	Price
Humpty Dumpty	2003	Pink head; blue jacket; yellow trousers; grey wall	160	Rare
Little Miss Muffet	2005	Pink dress, blonde hair	160	Rare
Old King Cole	2003	Unknown	160	Rare
Old Woman in a Shoe	2003	Blue dress, brown window frame	160	Rare

Once Upon a Time Money Box, 1998

This money box features a daddy bear sitting in a wing chair reading a book to his son. The money box was produced in a limited edition of 120, with 100 being sold at the Alton Towers Wade Show, and the remaining 20 being sold at the San Antonio Show for $250.00 each.

Backstamp: Decal "Once upon a time.....Limited edition of 120 Wade England 1998"

Name	Colourways	Size	U.S. $	Can. $	U.K. £
Once Upon a Time	Light brown bears; green/dark and light blue/burgundy/white	160 x 120	400.00	450.00	200.00

PIGS

Comical Pig Money Box, 2003

This Comical Pig appears to be scratching at his ribs with his hind foot. The money box was available as a Wade retail line from 2003–2006. The cost from the Wade on-line shop was £9.99 in April 2006.

Backstamp: Embossed "Wade England"

Name	Colourways	Size	U.S. $	Can. $	U.K. £
Scratching Pig	Pink	140 x 165	20.00	25.00	10.00

Paws at the Kerb Money Box, 1955

This money box has a transfer print of a puppy sitting at the curbside, and the words "Paws at the Kerb" on one side, and a print of a Belisha Beacon and the words "Look Right - Look Left - Look Right Again" on the other.

The print was from a winning poster designed by an 11-year-old schoolgirl in a mid-1950s competition to promote British road safety.

The Paws at the Kerb money box is from the same mould as the Smiling Pig money box.

Backstamp: Unmarked

Name	Colourways	Size	U.S. $	Can. $	U.K. £
Paws at the Kerb	White; black transfer prints	127	150.00	175.00	80.00

Pocket Money Pig Family Money Boxes, 2004

Wade's new 'Pocket Money Pig Family' money boxes were introduced as part of the Wade retail line in January of 2004. They are similar in style to the original Wade 1950's 'Smiling Pigs' but are smaller. There are also differences in the feet and ears. They were available in two colourways blue and pink and in three sizes: father, mother and baby pig. The cost of the pigs direct from Wade was small £9.50, medium £10.99, large £14.50.

Backstamp: Decal (WADE MADE IN ENGLAND) logo

Name	Colourways	Size	U.S. $	Can. $	U.K. £
Father Pig	Blue	Large/135 x 170	30.00	35.00	15.00
Father Pig	Pink	Large/135 x 170	30.00	35.00	15.00
Mother Pig	Blue	Medium/130 x 155	25.00	30.00	12.00
Mother Pig	Pink	Medium/130 x 155	25.00	30.00	12.00
Baby Pig	Blue	Small/115 x 130	20.00	25.00	10.00
Baby Pig	Pink	Small/115 x 130	20.00	25.00	10.00

Priscilla the Pig Decorated Money Boxes, 1997

Wade reissued the comic Priscilla the Pig money box at the 1997 Wade Extravaganza in three colourways with various transfer prints on them, many more prints than those listed below can be found. The money boxes were also available from the Wade Shop.

Clown

Cartoon Animal

Hearts and Flowers

Backstamp: Impressed "Wade England"

Name	Colourways	Size	U.S. $	Can. $	U.K. £
Cartoon animals	Blue; multicoloured animals	112	40.00	45.00	20.00
Cartoon animals	Pink; multicoloured animals	112	40.00	45.00	20.00
Cartoon animals	White; multicoloured animals	112	40.00	45.00	20.00
Clowns	Blue; multicoloured clowns	112	40.00	45.00	20.00
Clowns	Pink; multicoloured clowns	112	40.00	45.00	20.00
Clowns	White; multicoloured clowns	112	40.00	45.00	20.00
Flowers	Blue; blue roses gold leaves	112	40.00	45.00	20.00
Flowers	Blue; multicoloured poppies	112	40.00	45.00	20.00
Flowers	Pink; large pink roses	112	40.00	45.00	20.00
Flowers	Pink; small roses	112	40.00	45.00	20.00
Flowers	White; small multicoloured flowers	112	40.00	45.00	20.00
Hearts and flowers	White; green heart, pink flowers	112	40.00	45.00	20.00
Hearts and flowers	Pink; green heart, pink flowers	112	40.00	45.00	20.00
Plain	White; no decoration	112	40.00	45.00	20.00

Smiling Pig Money Boxes, c.1955

The Smiling Pig money boxes have now been found in three sizes, the smallest pig is hardest to find. An unusual pig has been found that has hand painted flowers and the word 'Pennies Make Pounds' on the back. Most of the transfer flower designs, Starburst and Parasols, are seen on Wade Harmony Wares tableware of the 1950s. These money boxes have also been found unmarked.

As these money boxes did not have stoppers, and many had to be broken to remove the coins, they are hard to find.

Spring Flowers, Gold Ears

Green Money Box, large size

Solid Two-Colour Money Box, large

Pale yellow with red roses, large size

"Pennies Make Pounds" Money Box

Starburst Money Box, small size

Backstamp: **A.** Blue or Red printed "Wade England"
B. Unmarked

Large Size

Name	Colourways	Size	U.S. $	Can. $	U.K. £
Galaxy	White; gold inside ears; blue eyes; black stars	127	90.00	100.00	45.00
Pennies Make Pounds	White; multicoloured flowers; black lettering	127	90.00	100.00	45.00
Roses	Pale yellow; brown eyes; red roses; green leaves	127	90.00	100.00	45.00
Solid one colour	Green	127	90.00	100.00	45.00
Solid two colours	Black; red inside ears, eyes, nose; dots around coin slot	127	90.00	100.00	45.00
Spring flowers	White; gold inside ears; blue eyes and flower prints	127	90.00	100.00	45.00
Starburst	White; grey rays; red centre	127	90.00	100.00	45.00
Summer Rose	Yellow; gold inside ears; blue eyes; orange roses	127	90.00	100.00	45.00
Summer Rose	White; gold inside ears; blue eyes; pink roses	127	90.00	100.00	45.00
Summer Rose	White; gold inside ears; blue eyes; yellow roses	127	90.00	100.00	45.00
Violets	White; gold inside ears; blue eyes; violet flowers	127	90.00	100.00	45.00

Smiling Pig Money Boxes (cont.)
Medium size

Name	Colourways	Size	U.S. $	Can. $	U.K. £
Galaxy	Yellow; black eyes and stars	115	90.00	100.00	45.00
Galaxy	White; gold inside ears; blue eyes; black stars	115	90.00	100.00	45.00
Parasols	White; gold inside ears; blue eyes; multicoloured parasols	115	90.00	100.00	45.00
Paws at the Kerb	White; multicoloured prints; black lettering	115	90.00	100.00	45.00
Roses	White; brown eyes; red roses; green leaves	115	90.00	100.00	45.00
Shooting stars	White; blue eyes and nostrils; pink/green/black stars	115	90.00	100.00	45.00
Spring flowers	White; gold inside ears; blue eyes and flowers	115	90.00	100.00	45.00
Starburst	White; grey rays; red centre	115	90.00	100.00	45.00
Summer Rose	Yellow; gold inside ears; blue eyes; orange roses	115	90.00	100.00	45.00
Summer Rose	White; gold inside ears; blue eyes; pink roses	115	90.00	100.00	45.00
Summer Rose	White; gold inside ears; blue eyes; yellow roses	115	90.00	100.00	45.00
Violets	White; gold inside ears; blue eyes; violet flowers	115	90.00	100.00	45.00

Small size

Name	Colourways	Size	U.S. $	Can. $	U.K. £
Starburst	White; grey rays; red centre	90	90.00	100.00	45.00
Violets	White; violet flowers; brown eyes	90	90.00	100.00	45.00
Violets	Yellow; black eyes and stars	90	90.00	100.00	45.00

Pocket Pals Money Boxes, 2006

The Pocket Pal money boxes were issued in March 2006 as part of the Wade retail line. This is a new series and is based on the Pocket Pal whimsie models: Bounce the Rabbit, Specs the Owl and Paddles the Hippo. The cost direct from Wade is £14.50

Backstamp: Decal (WADE MADE IN ENGLAND logo)

Name	Colourways	Size	U.S. $	Can. $	U.K. £
Bounce the Rabbit	White; brown / black eyes; black patches, pink nose	140 x 95	30.00	35.00	15.00
Paddles the Hippo	Pink; blue / black eyes	70 x 110	30.00	35.00	15.00
Specs the Owl	White front; brown back; orange / black eyes; brown beak	120 x 90	30.00	35.00	15.00

TEDDY BEARS

Noel The Christmas Teddy Bear Money Box, 1997

The mould for this teddy bear money box was originally used for the British department store Marks and Spencer's "Edward Bear". The Christmas Extravaganza "Noel" version is in a cream glaze with holly motifs on the soles of the feet. It was produced in a limited edition of 1,500 for the first Wade Christmas Extravaganza held on November 29th, 1997, at Trentham Gardens, Stoke-on-Trent. The Bears were sold on a first-come, first-served basis.

Backstamp: Black printed circular "Christmas Teddy Extravaganza Special 1997 Wade"

Name	Colourways	Size	U.S. $	Can. $	U.K. £
Noel the Christmas Teddy Bear	Cream; black eyes/nose: green/red holly motif on feet	155	50.00	55.00	25.00

Waving Teddy Bear Money Boxes, 1998

The Waving Teddy Bear money box is from the same mould used to produce "Edward Bear" and "Noel the Christmas Teddy Bear." The money box was first produced in a white glaze and later in the same year, blue and pink colourways were produced. Some white money boxes appear to have a blue tint in them.

Blue (left); White (right)

Backstamp: A. White: Red printed "Wade" between two lines
B. Blue and Pink: Black printed circular "Genuine Wade Porcelain"

Name	Colourways	Size	U.S. $	Can. $	U.K. £
Waving Teddy Bear	Blue; black eyes and nose	150	50.00	55.00	25.00
Waving Teddy Bear	Pink; black eyes and nose	150	50.00	55.00	25.00
Waving Teddy Bear	White; black eyes and nose	150	50.00	55.00	25.00

Thomas the Tank Engine Money Boxes, Style One, 1984

Thomas the Tank, based on the storybooks by Reverent Wilbert Awdry and the British television cartoon, was a very short-lived series due to complicated copyright laws. Only two models were produced, "Thomas" and "Percy." Many of these money boxes were unmarked and came in a sleeved box stating they were produced by Wade.

Backstamp: **A.** Decal (Thomas the tank logo) "THOMAS THE TANK ENGINE AND FRIENDS, © KAYE & WARD LTD 1984 © BRITT ALLCROFT LTD 1984 MANUFACTURED BY WADE OF ENGLAND

B. Unmarked

Name	Colourways	Size	U.S. $	Can. $	U.K. £
Thomas the Tank Engine	Blue; red markings	110 x 165	350.00	375.00	175.00
Percy the Small Engine	Green; red markings	110 x 173	350.00	375.00	175.00

Note: For miniature tank engines please see *The Charlton Standard Catalogue of Wade Whimsical Collectables.*

TOADSTOOL COTTAGE MONEY BOXES

Big Ears and Noddy Toadstool Cottage Money Boxes, c.1961

First Version: c.1961; Cream cottage, brown roof with white spots, blue door and windows, yellow chimney and flowers.

Following Wade's policy of using up unsold stock by converting it into better-selling lines (as with *First Whimsies* on candle holders and *Whimtrays*), "Big Ears" and "Noddy" from the *Noddy* set were placed on Toadstool Cottage money boxes, with a coin slot in the back rim of the roof. This series had a very limited production run and is extremely rare. The issue date is unknown, but it was probably soon after the *Noddy* set was finished in 1961. These models originally had black and gold foil labels. The money box can be found without any figurines applied.

Backstamp: **A.** Black and gold foil label "Genuine Wade Porcelain made in England"
B. Unmarked

Name	Colourways	Size	U.S. $	Can. $	U.K. £
Big Ears	Cream/brown/white/blue/yellow	110 x 120	400.00	450.00	200.00
Big Ears	Cream/brown/white/blue/yellow	110 x 120	400.00	450.00	200.00
Big Ears and Noddy	Cream/brown/white/blue/yellow	110 x 120	Rare		
Noddy	Cream/brown/white/blue/yellow	110 x 120	Rare		
Toadstool Cottage	Cream/brown/white/blue/yellow	110 x 120	Rare		

Leprechaun Toadstool Cottage Money Box, 1987

Second Version: 1987; Brown cottage, darker brown roof

In 1987, Wade issued this money box based on the earlier Toadstool Cottage money box. Because the original mould was worn, Wade made a new mould which produced larger, heavier and less delicate looking model than the original. The money box was sold in a plain unmarked box.

Backstamp: Unmarked

Name	Colourways	Size	U.S. $	Can. $	U.K. £
Leprechaun Toadstool Cottage	Browns and green	140 x 155	90.00	100.00	45.00

Wade Collector's Club 10th Anniversary Money Box, 2004

This money box was a mail-in offer in late 2004 to celebrate the Wade Club's 10th Anniversary. The edition size was 483 which was based on the number of orders received by December 31st, 2004. The decals around the sides show all the membership club models for the past ten years. The main decal on the top is of the very first club model, "Burslem", the factory cat. The cost of the money box was £29.95 which included postage and packing.

Backstamp: Printed "10th Anniversary Special" with gold stars and red & black Wade Club Logo

Name	Colourways	Size	U.S. $	Can. $	U.K. £
10th Anniversary	Pearlised; multicoloured decals; gold lettering	90 x 125	50.00	55.00	25.00

COMMISSIONED MONEY BOXES

AMERIWADE

Lucky the Leprechaun Money Box, October 2005

The Lucky the Leprechaun money box was commissioned by Ameriwade. One hundred and forty money boxes produced in three colourways: 100 with blue hats, 25 with red hats and 15 with yellow hats. Fifteen sets of money boxes, one of each colour, were sold for $275.00 per set. These sets contained matching numbered pieces and certificates. The remaining eighty-five blue hat and ten red hat money boxes were randomly packed and sold for $80.00 each. All money boxes were hand-numbered and came with hand-numbered and signed certificates of authenticity.

Backstamp:
- **A.** (Decal) 'Lucky' Limited Edition (#) of 15 ameriwade.com (WADE MADE IN ENGLAND logo)
- **B.** (Decal) 'Lucky' Limited Edition (#) of 25 ameriwade.com (WADE MADE IN ENGLAND logo)
- **C.** (Decal) 'Lucky' Limited Edition (#) of 100 ameriwade.com (WADE MADE IN ENGLAND logo)

Name	Colourways	Size	U.S. $	Can. $	U.K. £
Lucky	Blue hat and suit; blue and green rocky base	165	80.00	130.00	65.00
Lucky	Red hat; blue suit; blue and green rocky base	165	80.00	130.00	65.00
Lucky	Yellow hat; blue suit; blue and green rocky base	165	Rare*		

BARCLAYS BANK

Savings Piggy Money Box, 1998

Produced for a Barclays Bank promotion, this money box is from the same mould as the Priscilla the Pig money box which was produced by Wade Ceramics in 1994 as part of their Wade retail line. The Barclays Savings pig has an applied logo decal on the back. Five thousand of these pigs were produced for the promotion, however no information on how these Pigs were obtained has been found to date.

Backstamp: Impressed "WADE ENGLAND"

Name	Colourways	Size	U.S. $	Can. $	U.K. £
Savings Piggy	Pink; blue and black logo	112	35.00	50.00	25.00

BOOTS THE CHEMIST
Boots Delivery Van Money Box, 1995

Throughout the years, Wade has produced many promotional and giftware items for British department stores houseware departments. A cobalt blue delivery van money box was produced exclusively for the Boots the Chemist. The license plate on the delivery van reads "BOOTS 1".

Backstamp: None

Name	Colourways	Size	U.S. $	Can. $	U.K. £
Delivery Van	Cobalt blue	185 x 210	70.00	80.00	35.00

BRISTOL & WEST BUILDING SOCIETY
Piggy Money Box, 1993–1998

This money box produced in the shape of the 1994 Wade retail Priscilla the Pig , was issued in a limited edition of 1,368. It has the Bristol & West logo on the back, and was produced as a promotional item for the Bristol & West Young Savers programme.

Backstamp: Impressed "WADE ENGLAND"

Name	Colourways	Size	U.S. $	Can. $	U.K. £
Piggy	Pink; blue and white logo	112	50.00	55.00	25.00

BRITANNIA BUILDING SOCIETY
Piggy Money Bank, 1999 and 2002

This money box was produced for Britannia Building Society. The piece is based on their hot air balloon named "Piggles". Two variations of this model exist due to the mould being reworked, and the time between the two editions. Both models contain a gold coin above the "slot" and a red and white Britannia logo decal on the back. The first version pig was produced in 1999 and has painted eyebrows and a small coin slot. The second version, produced in 2002, has no eyebrows and a longer coin slot. There is also a slight difference in the width of coin and the pink colour between the two versions of the money box. One thousand money boxes were produced as part of the promotion. No information has been found as to how the money box was obtained.

First Version, left; Second Version, right

Backstamp: **A.** (Decal) First Version: "Wade Est 1810 England" logo
B. (Decal) Second Version: "WADE" Red print

Name	Colourways	Size	U.S. $	Can. $	U.K. £
First Version	Pink; black eyebrows; red label; white lettering	135	50.00	55.00	25.00
Second Version	Pink; red logo; red label; white lettering	135	50.00	55.00	25.00

C&S COLLECTABLES

Betty Boop Bust Money Box, 2001

The Betty Boop Bust money box was produced in a limited edition of 500. Twenty were produced without the slot or stopper for prizes and promotions and are not classified as a money box. The Wade Betty Boop line is under license from King Features Syndicate, Inc/Fletcher Studios, Inc. The issue price was £49.95.

For more Betty Boop models from C&S Collectables, see *The Charlton Standard Catalogue of Wade Whimsical Collectables*. All Betty Boop models come with a certificate of authenticity.

Backstamp: **A.** (Decal) "500 LIMITED EDITION BETTY BOOP™ Bust Moneybank © 2001KFS/FS"
           B. (Decal) C&S and WADE logos

Name	Colourways	Size	U.S. $	Can. $	U.K. £
Betty Boop Bust	Red, black and gold	115	300.00	350.00	150.00

C&S Miniature Delivery Van Money Box, 2004

The Miniature Delivery Van money box was issued in two colourways: 100 in cream, and 20 in cream with gold and silver highlights. Each piece was issued with a certificate of authenticity. The cream, gold and silver colourway was given as prizes in raffles and competitions.

Backstamp: Impressed "Wade England" the same backstamp was used on the special.

Cream and gold with blue C&S decal

Name	Colourways	Size	U.S. $	Can. $	U.K. £
C&S Mini van	Cream; blue C&S decal; black, red and blue lettering	110 x 180	45.00	50.00	22.00
C&S mini van	Cream; gold lettering; silver headlights, mirrors and hub caps	110 x 180		Rare	

C&S COLLECTABLES (cont.)

Dinosaur Money Boxes

Saurolophus Money Box, 2006

The Saurolophus money box was produced in two colourways: 100 in green and 20 in pearl and gold. The original cost for the green money box was £29.95 which included the shipping costs. The 20 pearl models with gold bases were given as prizes in raffles and competitions held by C&S. Each piece was issued with a certificate of authenticity.

Backstamp: **A.** (Decal) Regular: "Saurolophus Money Bank Limited Edition of 100" (C&S and Wade logos)

B. (Decal) Special: (C&S and Wade Logos)

Name		Colourways	Size	U.S. $	Can. $	U.K. £
Saurolophus	Green		120 x 135	60.00	70.00	30.00
Saurolophus	Pearl, bold base		120 x 135		Rare	

Tyrannosaurus Rex Money Box, 2003

The second money box in the Dinosaur series was issued in October 2003, also in three colourways: 400 in beige, 100 white and 20 in white and gold. Each model was issued with a certificate of authenticity.

The edition of 100 white money boxes was available to collectors during a "phone-in" promotion held October 26th, 2003, at a special price of £27.50.

The 20 models with gold bases were given as prizes in raffles and competitions held by C&S.

The issue price for the beige money box was £29.95.

Backstamp: **A.** Regular: Printed "Tyrannosaurus Rex Money Bank Limited Edition of 400" with red 'Wade' logo and blue 'C&S' logo

B. White special: Printed "Limited Edition of 100 Tyrannosaurus Rex Money Bank" with red 'Wade' logo and blue 'C&S' logo

C. Gold special: Printed gold foil 'Wade'

Name		Colourways	Size	U.S. $	Can. $	U.K. £
Dinosaur T Rex bank	White' brown base		125	100.00	115.00	50.00
Dinosaur T Rex bank	White; gold base		125		Rare	
Tyrannosaurus Rex	Beige; green base		125	70.00	80.00	35.00

C&S COLLECTABLES (cont.)
Vulcanodon Money Box, 2003

C&S Collectables issued their Vulcanodon dinosaur money box at the 2003 Arundel Collectors Meet. It was produced in three colourways: 500 blue, 100 white, and 20 in white and gold. The latter were given as prizes in raffles and competitions held by C&S.

The white colourway money boxes were available to those who attended the Wade Open Day in Arundel July 5th, 2003, the day prior to the Arundel Collectors Meet. Although the white colourway was limited to 100 the backstamp states limited to 500. Each colourway was issued with a certificate of authenticity. The issue price for the blue dinosaur was £29.95.

Backstamp: **A.** Regular and white special: Printed "Dinosaur Money Bank Limited edition of 500" with red 'Wade' and blue 'C&S' logos
      B. Gold special: Printed Gold foil 'Wade'

Vulcanadon (blue)

Name	Colourways	Size	U.S. $	Can. $	U.K. £
Vulcanadon	Blue; brown base	120	70.00	80.00	35.00
Vulcanadon	White; brown base	120	100.00	115.00	50.00
Vulcanadon	White; gold base	120	Rare		

Sam Money Box, 2004

This money box was commissioned by C&S Collectables Direct in a limited edition of 500, with certificate of authenticity, as part of their Mabel Lucie Attwell "Sam and Sarah" series. The piece was produced under the Lucie Attwell, Ltd. license. The cost direct from C&S Collectables was £44.00. A special edition of 20 pieces was produced with a gold bench to be given as prizes in raffles and competitions held by C&S. For more of the Sam and Sarah models from C&S Collectables, see *The Charlton Standard Catalogue of Wade Whimsical Collectables*.

Backstamp: **A.** (Decal) "Ltd Edt 500 © Lucie Attwell Ltd. 2004 Licensed by ©opyrights Group Mabel Lucie Attwell Sam Money Bank" (C&S and Wade Logos)
      B. Gold Special: (Wade and C&S logos)

Sam Money Box, 2004

Name	Colourways	Size	U.S. $	Can. $	U.K. £
Sam	Yellow, white; blue, grey, green, light brown and red	135 x 120	80.00	90.00	40.00

C&S COLLECTABLES (cont.)

Snoopy Mini Money Box, 2000

The Snoopy Mini Money box was produced in a limited edition of 500 pieces under the United Features Syndicate, Inc. license.

The original cost of the money box was £33.00 and was issued with a certificate of authenticity.

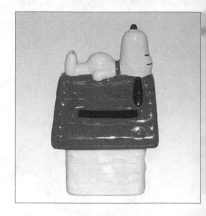

Backstamp: **A.** (Decal) "WADE ENGLAND © UFS INC Modelled by C. Roberts"
B. (Decal) C&S logo adn Peanuts 50th Anniversary logo

Name	Colourways	Size	U.S. $	Can. $	U.K. £
Snoopy Mini Money Box	White, red and black	115	100.00	115.00	50.00

Thomas the Tank Engine Money Box, Style Two, 2001

The Thomas the Tank money box was produced under the Gullane Limited copyright. It was available by mail order. The money box, issued in a limited edition of 500, was accompanied by a certificate of authenticity. The issue price was £39.95.

For more Thomas the Tank models commissioned by C&S Collectables see *The Charlton Standard Catalogue of Wade Whimsical Collectables.*

Backstamp: Printed "Thomas the Tank Engine Money Bank C&S Collectables 500 Limited edition © Gullane (Thomas) Limited 2001 Wade"

Name	Colourways	Size	U.S. $	Can. $	U.K. £
Thomas the Tank	Blue, black, red and red-brown	90 x 90	120.00	140.00	60.00

CADBURY WORLD

Cadabra Chuckle Bean Car Money Box, 2004

The Cadabra car money box was issued in 2004, in a limited edition of 1,000 and features the chuckle bean (chocolate cocoa bean). The money box was available by mail order from Cadbury World at £12.99. The license plate reads "BEAN 2". The glaze can appear purple or blue depending on how thick the glaze was applied and where it was in the kiln.

Backstamp: Embossed "WADE ENGLAND"

Name	Colourways	Size	U.S. $	Can. $	U.K. £
Chuckle Bean Car	Honey bean; cobalt blue	100 x 145	30.00	35.00	15.00

Chomp Money Box, 2004

Cadbury issued a monster money box "Chomp" on August 9th, 2004. Chomp is a carmel monster and is pictured on the Cadbury's "Chomp Chocolate Bar." The money box was produced in a limited edition of 1,000 and was available from Cadbury World by mail order at a cost of £12.99.

Backstamp: Embossed "Wade England"

Name	Colourways	Size	U.S. $	Can. $	U.K. £
Chomp	Honey monster; brown chocolate bar	140	20.00	25.00	10.00

CADBURY WORLD (cont.)

Delivery Van Money Box, 2003

The Cadbury delivery van money box was first issued on August 15th, 2003 in a limited edition of 1,000. It was available by mail order from Cadbury World for £12.99. The license plate reads "CDM 1". The glaze can appear purple or blue depending on how thick the glaze was applied and the model was placed in the kiln.

Backstamp: Impressed "Made for Cadbury World Wade England"

Cobalt Van

Name	Colourways	Size	U.S. $	Can. $	U.K. £
Delivery Van	Cobalt blue	135 x 210	30.00	35.00	15.00

Train and Tenders Car Money Box, 2005

The money box was produced in a limited edition of 1,000 and was available from Cadbury World by mail order for £26.99. The set includes the train, which is a money box and two tenders. Although Wade states that the pieces were only produced in cobalt blue, the glaze can appear purple or blue depending on how thick the glaze was applied, and where the model was placed in the kiln.

Backstamp: Embossed "Wade England"

Name	Colourways	Size	U.S. $	Can. $	U.K. £
Train and Tenders	Cobalt blue	Train 75 x 175; Tenders 40 x 100	50.00	55.00	25.00

CHESHIRE BUILDING SOCIETY

Lucky Black Cat Money Box, 2006

From November 2006, young savers who opened a Black Cat saver account at a Cheshire Building Society branch received a free Lucky Black Cat money box. The front of the money box has a decal in white that reads "MY MONEY".

*Photograph not available
at press time*

Backstamp: Unknown

Name	Colourways		Size	U.S. $	Can. $	U.K. £
Lucky Black Cat	Black		Unknown		Unknown	

DOUGLAS MACMILLAN HOSPICE

Dougie MacTeddy Bear Money Box, 1998

A seated model of a teddy bear was chosen by the Douglas MacMillan Hospice as a fund raiser for their Silver Jubilee. The proceeds from the sale of the money box would be used towards the proposed opening of a daycare centre. Order forms for the money box were included in the May and August issues of the Official Wade Collectors Club Magazine and had to be received by the Hospice before September 30th, 1998. The number of orders determined the number of models to be made. The sale of the money boxes was to commence in October 1998. Original cost was £22.50.

A money box with a gold bow is known to exist.

Backstamp: Embossed "Wade"

Name	Colourways		Size	U.S. $	Can. $	U.K. £
Dougie MacTeddy Bear	Honey bear; platinum bow		155	75.00	85.00	40.00

EDDIE STOBART LTD.

Road Haulage Vehicle Money Box, Twiggy, 1998

Eddie Stobart Ltd. commissioned Wade Ceramics to produce a model of one of their road haulage vehicles.

Eddie Stobart Ltd. give their road haulage vehicles female names. The names are those of members of the Stobart family, lorry drivers wives, famous women, or seriously ill children. The name given to this money box is "Twiggy," who was a famous British model in the 1960s.

The money box was produced in a limited edition of 2,000, and was available to the members of both the Eddie Stobart Club and the Wade Collector's Club.

Backstamp: Printed "Made Exclusively For Eddie Stobart by Wade Ceramics"

Name	Colourways	Size	U.S. $	Can. $	U.K. £
Eddie Stobart Money Box 'Twiggy'	Silver, green, orange and white	115	80.00	110.00	55.00

Steady Eddie Money Box, 2003

The Steady Eddie money box was produced in a limited edition of 2,000 for the Eddie Stobart Children's Collectors Club. The character Steady Eddie is a cartoon in Eddie Stobart children's books and videos. The issue price was £36.00. In April 2006, the Steady Eddie money box was available for sale on the Wade-on-line shop site for £24.99.

Backstamp: (Decal) "STEADY EDDIE DESIGNED AND MADE EXCLUSIVELY BY WADE ENGLAND for EDDIE STOBART LTD"

Name	Colourways	Size	U.S. $	Can. $	U.K. £
Steady Eddie	Green, white, grey, red and yellow	100 x 200	35.00	50.00	25.00

ESSO COMPANY
Tiger Money Box, 1997

One hundred sample models were originally produced for an Esso Petroleum promotion that was not filled. The original date of production is unclear as the models were found in a Wade Ceramics store room during an office move. The money boxes were produced in an unusual biscuit glaze that was in use during the 1970's Wade Anglia Television Survival Animals series. Eighty models of the "Tiger" money box were offered for sale at the Wade Christmas Extravaganza held November 29th, 1997, at a price of £200.00 each. Each piece came boxed with a certificate of authenticity. Twenty models were held over for sale at the 1998 Buffalo, New York, Wade/Jim Beam Collectors Show. At the show, a box of money boxes was dropped and five models were broken (noted in Wade club magazine) leaving 95 models as the edition size.

Backstamp: Printed "Genuine Wade Porcelain"

Name	Colourways	Size	U.S. $	Can. $	U.K. £
Tiger	White; orange; black stripes	190 x 95	300.00	350.00	150.00

HARRODS OF KNIGHTBRIDGE
Doorman Money Box, 1993

Wade produced a number of tableware items for one of the world's most famous department stores - Harrods.

Backstamp: Black transfer "Harrods Knightsbridge"

Name	Colourways	Size	U.S. $	Can. $	U.K. £
Doorman	Green cap and coat; gold buttons and trim	175 x 125	50.00	70.00	35.00

JIM BEAM

Delivery Van Money Box, 1996

The Delivery Van money box was produced in three colourways for the 1996 IAJBBSC 25th Annual Convention: 300 in cream, 300 blue, and 200 white. The white vans were sold to clubs only. The original cost of the vans was $45.00 (U.S.). Unsold vans were given as prizes in raffles. The license plates read "KENTUCKY".

This van is from a similar mould as the 1995 Ringtons Tea Delivery Van money box (see page 317).

Backstamp: Decal:
- **A.** Cream and Blue Vans - "IAJBBSC 26th ANNUAL CONVENTION JULY 6 - 12 1996 SEATTLE, WASHINGTON 1 OF 300 WADE ENGLAND" (IAJBBSC logo)
- **B.** White Van - "IAJBBSC 26th ANNUAL CONVENTION JULY 6 - 12 1996 SEATTLE, WASHINGTON 1 OF 200 WADE ENGLAND" (IAJBBSC logo)

Name	Colourways	Issued	Size	U.S. $	Can. $	U.K. £
Delivery Van	Blue	300	133 x 205	100.00	115.00	50.00
Delivery Van	Cream	300	133 x 205	100.00	115.00	50.00
Delivery Van	White	200	133 x 205	100.00	115.00	50.00

KEY KOLLECTABLES

Fred's Money Box, 2003-2004

This blow-up sized model of Homepride Fred is holding a £1.00 coin and standing next to his favourite tin of Homepride Sweet and Sour Cook in Sauce. The slot for the coins is on the back of the tin. It was offered on a time limited basis, all orders had to be received before January 31st, 2004 when the model would be withdrawn from sale. The edition number of the model depended on the number of orders received by that date. The models were gift boxed and came with a certificate of authenticity. The original cost of the money box was £60.00.

Twenty-five models were produced with a gold coin. A limited number of the gold coin models were sold by Key Kollectables on a first come first served basis for £125.00 each, the others were given as prizes in draws. As with all the Homepride Fred models, they can only be sold to UK addresses due to licensing restrictions.

Backstamp: Printed "Key Kollectables Ltd Fred's Money Box With signed certificate of authenticity This is not a Toy © 2003 & ™ Campbell Grocery Products Ltd Time Limited Edition"

Name	Colourways	Size	U.S. $	Can. $	U.K. £
Fred's Moneybox	Black hat/suit; blue can' brown label; white coin and lettering	190	105.00	140.00	70.00
Fred's Moneybox	Black hat/suit; blue can; brown label; white lettering; gold coin	190		Rare	

KSWADER
Emerald City Money Box, 2005

Emerald City, Dark green and gold colourway

In July 2005, KSWader issued the 6th piece in the Oz by Wade series. The Emerald City money box was issued in a limited edition of 125 at a cost of $55.00. Twenty-five models were produced in a clear glaze for prizes and promotion. For more Oz by Wade models from KSWader, see *The Charlton Standard Catalogue of Wade Whimsical Collectables.*

Backstamp:
A. Green money box: Gold printed "Made in England Emerald City Moneybox Oz by Wade No. 6 Special edition of 25 www.kswader.com with Wade logo
B. White money box: Platinum printed "Made in England Emerald City Moneybox Oz by Wade No. 6 Special Edition of 25 www.kswader.com with Wade logo

Name	Colourways	Size	U.S. $	Can. $	U.K. £
Emerald City	Dark green; gold/platinum windows; gold flags	128	55.00	60.00	28.00
Emerald City	White; gold/platinum windows; gold flags	128		Rare	

MARGARET STRICKLAND
Polacanthus Money Box, 1994

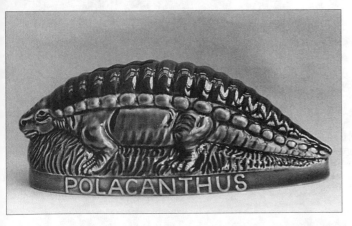

Margaret Strickland, a resident of the Isle of Wight, England, commissioned the Polacanthus Money Box. This model is an artist's impression taken from the skeleton of a Polacanthus dinosaur, whose remains have only been found on the Isle of Wight. The money box was produced in a limited edition of 2,000 with a certificate of authenticity.

Backstamp: Black transfer "Wade" in Isle of Wight outline, numbered

Name	Colourways	Size	U.S. $	Can. $	U.K. £
Polacanthus	Honey and dark brown; green base	79 x 205	100.00	115.00	50.00

MARKS AND SPENCER

Edward Bear Money Box, 1995-1996

This money box was produced for the British department store Marks and Spencer PLC during 1995-1996. He was originally sold filled with milk chocolate coins.

Backstamp: Unmarked

Name	Colourways	Size	U.S. $	Can. $	U.K. £
Edward Bear	Honey brown; black eyes and nose	154	35.00	40.00	18.00

One-of-a-Kind Derivatives

This one-of-a-kind Teddy Bear money box was given as a prize at the Kansas Wade Show.

Backstamp: Unmarked

Date	Event	Colourways	Qty	U.S. $	Can. $	U.K. £
2000	Kansas Wade Show	Honey brown; black eyes and nose	1		Unique	

MARS UK

Milky Way Bar Money Box, c.1980s

Milky Way Bar Money Box, Top View

The Milky Way Bar money box has been thought to be Wade by collectors for many years, but there has never been any firm confirmation from the pottery. Recent information from Wade Ceramics, states that a limited number of samples were produced for Mars and that very few Wade examples of the money box exist.

Backstamp: Unmarked

Name	Colourways	Size	U.S. $	Can. $	U.K. £
Milky Way Bar	Cobalt blue; white lettering and stars; red shooting star	50 x 150		Rare	

MONMOUTHSHIRE BUILDING SOCIETY

Squirrel With Acorn Money Box, 1998

The Monmouthshire Building Society selected this squirrel money box as a promotion to encourage teens under 16 years of age to save (proof of age was required). The money box was given for the opening of an account of £10 or more. Other promotional prizes were available.

The first production run of 2,000 was soon exhausted. Multiple production runs of the money box resulted in colour variations: a tan brown and red brown. Another variation exists with the "Monmouthshire Building Society" decal missing from the acorn.

Backstamp: Embossed "WADE"

Name	Colourways	Size	U.S. $	Can. $	U.K. £
Squirrel with Acorn	Tan brown	145 x 115	60.00	70.00	30.00
Squirrek with Acorn	Red brown	145 x 115	60.00	70.00	30.00

NATIONAL WESTMINSTER BANK

Cousin Wesley, 1998

The National Westminster Bank launched the Children's Bond account in February 1998. When opening an account with an investment of £1,000., for a child under the age of 16 years, the child would receive a model of Cousin Wesley. Five thousand models were produced.

As with the Pig Family fake models of Wesley exist. They were copied from an original mould, however, due to shrinkage during the firing process, they are shorter and lighter in weight. The original Wesley should weigh at least 372 grams. Wade spray paints their models, the fake model was hand painted, and brush strokes are visible.

Another new series of fakes exist where colour, size and weight are very similar making them almost impossible to identify. Wade in the past authenticated their models, but willl no longer.

Backstamp: Unknown

Fake Wesley, left; Wade Wesley, right

Name	Colourways	Size	U.S. $	Can. $	U.K. £
Cousin Wesley	Pink pig; dark blue hat/pants; green shirt	146	250.00	275.00	125.00

Mother Panda and Baby, 1989

This money box was free to children under 7 years who had a World Savers account opened for them. For each account opened the National Westminster Bank donated £1 to the World Wild Fund for Nature.

Backstamp: Raised "Wade England"

Name	Colourways	Size	U.S. $	Can. $	U.K. £
Mother Panda and Baby	Black and white	112	40.00	45.00	20.00

NATIONAL WESTMINSTER BANK (cont.)

Pig Family Money Boxes, 1984-1998

Although the Pig Family models are marked with a Wade England backstamp, they were in fact produced in the County Armagh, Northern Ireland pottery.

A gold colourway (22kt gold glaze) Woody model was presented to each member of the Wade Board of Directors. At the same time 25 similar gold colourway Woody models were given as prizes in a Treasure Hunt competition held by National Westminster Bank *Piggy Press*. In a later competition, a model of Sir Nathaniel Piggy, in a gold suit and blue spotted bow tie, was given as a grand prize.

A large number of the gold Woody piggy money boxes appear for sale, which are not authentic. The fake models are spray-painted gold, including the base. Due to the high cost of gold leaf, the base of the original model was not painted.

There are also unauthorised copies of Maxwell Pig, these models are smaller in size and have a white base, whereas the original has a pink base.

Many white-coated Sir Nathaniel Westminster pigs have been offered for sale as genuine models and rare prototypes since 2004. These pieces were not produced by Wade. There are no records or knowledge of these pieces being produced in this colourways, even as samples.

Models of Woody, with a 'silver nappy pin' are being offered as 'rare.' These smaller models were produced as samples for the National Westminster Bank by a small Staffordshire pottery. They were rejected in favour of the Wade models.

Care should be taken when buying "rare" models of the Pig Family.

Woody, Gold Issue

Woody, Regular issue

Maxwell

The Piggy Family

NATIONAL WESTMINSTER BANK (cont.)

Pig Family Money Boxes, 1984-1998 (cont.)

Backstamp: Embossed "Wade England"

Name	Colourways	Size	U.S. $	Can. $	U.K. £
Woody (baby)	Pink; white nappy; silver/grey safety pin	135	40.00	45.00	20.00
Woody (baby)	Gold (22kt)	135		Rare	
Annabel (girl)	Pink; white blouse; green gym slip; blue bag	175	60.00	70.00	30.00
Maxwell (boy)	Pink; red/white tie; blue trousers	180	90.00	100.00	45.00
Lady Hillary (mother)	Pink; light blue blouse; navy skirt	185	70.00	90.00	35.00
Sir Nathaniel Westminster (father)	Pink; black suit; red bow tie, rose	190	150.00	175.00	75.00
Sir Nathaniel Westminster (father)	Gold; blue spotted bow tie	190		Extremely Rare	

Woody Money Box, 2006

In a NatWest Bank promotion which lasted only eight days, anyone opening a new account between April 6th and 14th, 2006, was entered into a prize draw to win from £100 to £10,000. One hundred and fouteen winner's names were drawn, each receiving a cash prize and an exclusive limited edition golden NatWest Woody pig (which was issued with a certificate of authenticity). The new mould is smaller than the original Woody model.

Photograph not available
at press time

Backstamp: Decal "NatWest 2006" and "Wade" logo

Name	Colourways	Size	U.S. $	Can. $	U.K. £
Woody	Gold (24kt)	Unk.		Extremely Rare	

RANK FILM ORGANISATION
Fried Green Tomatoes Money Box, 1992

This tomato-shaped money box was produced for the Rank Film Organisation of England to promote its film, *Fried Green Tomatoes.* They were produced in a limited edition of 1,000.

Backstamp: Red print "Wade England"

Name	Colourways	Size	U.S. $	Can. $	U.K. £
Fried Green Tomatoes	Pale green tomato; dark green lettering	135 x 155	300.00	375.00	150.00

REDCO FOODS, USA
Dove of Peace Money Box, 2003

In October 2003 Redco Foods, USA (Red Rose Tea) offered a Dove of Peace money box to their collectors. The offer was only available to collectors with a USA mailing address. The money box was available from Redco Foods web site and cost $20.00 US.

Backstamp: Embossed "Wade"

Name	Colourways	Size	U.S. $	Can. $	U.K. £
Dove of Peace	White dove; dark green twig and leaves	115 x 190	70.00	80.00	35.00

RINGTONS TEA LTD.

Delivery Van Money Box, 1995

This van shaped money box was produced for Ringtons in November 1995 and cost £12.99.

Backstamp: Printed "Exclusive Ringtons Delivery Vehicle specially commissioned by Ringtons Limited Produced by Wade England" backstamp includes the Ringtons Tea Logo

Name	Colourways	Size	U.S. $	Can. $	U.K. £
Ringtons Van	Black; yellow and gold crest and lettering	120	70.00	80.00	35.00

SCARBOROUGH BUILDING SOCIETY

Baseball Money Box

The baseball money box has been found with his mouth painted a bright red—the red mouth is not original. The Wade pottery has a long history of difficulties using red glazes. It is believed that the red mouth was added after it left the pottery.

Backstamp: Unmarked

Name	Colourways	Size	U.S. $	Can. $	U.K. £
Baseball	White; blue hat	150	120.00	140.00	60.00

ST. JOHN AMBULANCE BRIGADE
Bertie Badger Money Box, 1989-2002

In 1987 the St. John Ambulance Brigade formed a section for children aged five to ten years, they are known as "Badgers" because of the black and white uniform. A "Bertie Badger" figurine (see *The Charlton Standard Catalogue of Wade Whimsical Collectables*) was produced in a limited edition of 5,000 as a promotional item for the British St. John Ambulance Brigade in late 1989. It was given as a reward to child members of the brigade after they completed three years of service and training.

The Bertie Badger money box was produced as a replica of the children's figurine reward exclusively for the St. John Ambulance Brigade. The money box was first produced in October 2001, at an issue price of £14.95. One thousand money boxes were produced in that year. This is an on-going line and is still available from the St. John Ambulance gift catalogue.

In 2005 the money box was still available from the St. John's Catalogue shop at a reduced price of £12.72.

Backstamp: Embossed "Wade"

Name	Colourways	Size	U.S. $	Can. $	U.K. £
Bertie Badger	Black and white; white coveralls	180	26.00	30.00	13.00

SILENTNIGHT COMPANY
Silentnight Hippo Money Box, 2002

This Hippo money box was produced in a limited edition of 400, and was given free of charge to purchasers of Silentnight beds. The certificate reads "I'm a limited edition Hippo-bank figure, specially commissioned by Silentnight Beds to celebrate our achievement of becoming the most famous beds in the UK. As with all Wade Ceramics creations, I'm a highly collectable piece and am likely to increase in value over the years. So please do take good care of me." The Silentnight Company applied a plastic logo on the plaque. The money box came in a special blue presentation box with the Silentnight logo.

Backstamp: Printed "Created Exclusively for Silentnight Beds by Wade England"

Name	Colourways	Size	U.S. $	Can. $	U.K. £
Hippo	Pink, blue, white, yellow and orange	135 x 85	450.00	500.00	225.00

SMITHS CRISPS

Monster Muncher Money Box, 1987

Smiths Crisps, a potato chip company in the UK, commissioned the Monster Muncher money box from Wade in 1987. The Monster Muncher was widely used in advertising at this time.

Backstamp: Impressed "Wade England"

Name	Colourways	Size	U.S. $	Can. $	U.K. £
Monster Muncher	Bright blue,red, white, green, blue, yellow and pink	170	200.00	225.00	100.00

STROKE ASSOCIATION

Teddy Bear Money Box, 1999

The Stroke Association commissioned Wade to produce a money box as a fund raiser for their work in the prevention, care, treatment and research into the causes of stroke. The fund also supported stroke victims and their families. The teddy bear, seated with his arms down, has a butterfly decal on his chest. The cost of the money box direct from the Stroke Association was £12.00

Backstamp: Printed "Wade The Stroke Association, Caring for Today, Researching for Tomorrow" with logo

Name	Colourways	Size	U.S. $	Can. $	U.K. £
Teddy Bear	Amber Teddy; black eyes/nose/mouth; dark brown paw pads	165	50.00	55.00	25.00

TETLEY GB LTD.
Archie and Gordon Motorcycle Money Box, 2005

Regular Money Box

A money box in the form of a motorcycle and sidecar was produced for Tetley GB in December 2004. Although the backstamp is dated 2004, the money box was not issued until 2005. The Tetley Tea character Gordon is riding the motorcycle with the Brew Gaffer's nephew Archie sitting in the sidecar. The initials CR in the backstamp are those of the designer Cyril Roberts. The original cost when issued was £38.95.

A special colourway, with gold wheel hubs, exhaust and front tyre fork, was produced in a limited edition of 50 for sale at the Dunstable Wade Show, September 2005. They carry the same backstamp as the 2004 issue. The money boxes were sold with a certificate of authenticity.

Backstamp: A. Printed
B. Printed "An original design for Tetley GB by Wade England CR © Tetley GB Ltd 2004"

Gold Special Motorcycle Moneybox

Name	Colourways	Size	U.S. $	Can. $	U.K. £
Motorcycle	Blue, brown, grey, red, white, black and cobalt blue	125 x 155	70.00	80.00	35.00
Motorcycle	Blue, brown, grey, red, white, black, light blue, cobalt blue, gold	125 x 155	140.00	160.00	70.00

TETLEY GB LTD. (cont.)
Brew Gaffer Money Box, Style One, 1992

In Style One the Brew Gaffer is holding the lapels of his overalls. The money box was issued in a limited edition of 1,000 and came with a numbered certificate of authenticity.

Backstamp: Printed "Made Exclusively for Lyons Tetley by Wade"

Brew Gaffer (Style One)

Name	Colourways	Size	U.S. $	Can. $	U.K. £
Style One	Brown, white , red and blue	140	50.00	70.00	25.00

Brew Gaffer Money Box, Style Two, 1999

In Style Two the Brew Gaffer is holding a cup of tea. The original issue price was £17.99

Backstamp: Printed "An Original Design for Tetley GB by Wade England ® Tetley GB Limited 1999"

Brew Gaffer (Style Two)

Name	Colourways	Size	U.S. $	Can. $	U.K. £
Style Two	Brown, blue, red and white	150	30.00	35.00	15.00

TETLEY GB LTD. (cont.)
Brew Gaffer and Nephew Archie Delivery Van Money Box, 1999 and 2002

The Brew Gaffer and Nephew Archie Delivery Van money box is based on the 1994 Gaffer and Nephew Tea Caddy. The coin slot is in the back of the van, and the license plate reads "TEA 1".

In 2002 Wade issued a special gold colourway of the Delivery Van money box for release at the Dunstable Wade Show, September 29, 2002. A certificate of authenticity accompanied the model. The license plate on the gold edition reads "TEA 2".

Backstamp: **A.** Printed "An Original Design for Tetley GB by Wade England © Tetley Co Limited 1999"

B. Printed " An Original Design for Tetley GB by Wade England © Tetley GB Limited 2002"

Name	Colourways	Size	U.S. $	Can. $	U.K. £
Gaffer and Archie	Cobalt blue, white, brown and red	100 x 100	55.00	60.00	28.00
Gaffer and Archie	Cobalt blue, white, brown, red and gold	100 x 100		Rare	

The Flying Teabag Money Box, 2004

This train money box with Tetley Tea character Maurice, was named The Flying Tea Bag by Tetley. The cost direct from Tetley GB was £34.99.

A special limited edition of 100 money boxes, with gold decoration on Maurice's bow tie and the train wheels, was produced for sale at the Dunstable Wade Show, September 26th, 2004. The money boxes were sold with a certificate of authenticity.

Backstamp: Printed "AN ORIGINAL DESIGN FOR TETLEY GB BY WADE ENGLAND CR"

Name	Colourways	Size	U.S. $	Can. $	U.K. £
Flying Teabag	Train: Blue, white lettering; Maurice: brown, white and blue	100 x 242	70.00	80.00	35.00
Flying Teabag	Train: Blue/gold/white; Maurice: Brown/gold/white/blue	100 x 242		Rare	

TETLEY GB LTD. (cont.)

Gaffer Chocks Away Aeroplane Money Box, 2002

This money box depicts the Tetley Brew Gaffer flying his aeroplane. It was modelled by Cyril Roberts. A special limited edition of 50 models was produced with gold propellers and tie, and sold at the April 4th, 2004 Wade Collectors Fair held at the North Stafford Hotel in Stoke-on-Trent, England.

Backstamp: Printed "An Original Design for Tetley GB by Wade England CR © Tetley GB Limited 2002."

Name	Colourways	Size	U.S. $	Can. $	U.K. £
Chocks Away	Blue plane; brown hat; red tie; white coat/lettering	125 x 160	50.00	60.00	25.00
Chocks Away	Brown, gold, white, blue and gold	125 x 160	Rare		

Lyons / Tetley Delivery Van Money Box, 1990

Both vans were produced in 1990, with the Lyons' Coffee delivery van being issued in an edition of 5,000. The license plate for the Lyons' Coffee van reads "COF E1," and for the Tetley's Teas van "TEA 1".

Lyons' Coffee Delivery Van

Tetley's Tea Delivery Van

Backstamp: **A.** White transfer print "Manufactured Exclusively for Lyons Tetley Wade Made in England," impressed "Wade" "Wade Made in England"
B. Impressed "MANUFACTURED EXCLUSIVELY FOR LYONS TETLEY MADE IN ENGLAND"

Name	Colourways	Size	U.S. $	Can. $	U.K. £
Lyons' Coffee Delivery Van	Dark green; gold/white lettering "Lyons' Coffee Est 1904"	140	90.00	120.00	60.00
Tetley's Teas Delivery Van	Dark blue; gold/white lettering "Tetley's Teas Est 1837"	140	90.00	120.00	60.00

TETLEY GB LTD. (cont.)

Morris Minor Car Money Box, 2006

The Morris Minor car features the Tetley Tea folk character the Gaffer. This piece is very unusual as Wade combined this piece with their new holding—Northlight @ Wade. The Gaffer is produced from resin and is applied to the ceramic money box. This license plate is "TETLEY 1" and was issued in May 2006.

A limited edition of 50 special colourway money boxes was produced for the Setpember 24th, 2006 Dunstable Wade show. The car features gold detailing as well as platinum headlights and wheel hub caps. As with the regular issue the Gaffer is produced in resin by Northlight @ Wade. A certificate of authenticity accompanied the piece.

Backstamp: (Printed) "AN ORIGINAL DESIGN FOR TETLEY GB BY WADE ENGLAND CR © Tetly GB Limited 2006

Name	Colourways	Size	U.S. $	Can. $	U.K. £
Morris Minor	Blue car, resin figure	100 x 165	70.00	80.00	35.00
Morris Minor	Blue car, resin figure, gold and platinum details	100 x 165		Rare	

Sydney Holding Tea Bag Money Box, 1999 and 2003

The 1999 issue of Sydney Holding Tea Bag money box was still available from the Wade on-line-shop in April 2006 at the issue price of £17.99.

In 2003, to commemorate the 50th anniversary of the Tetley tea bag, Lyons Tetley commissioned a limited edition of 500 pieces with gold highlights. "Celebrating 50 years of the Tea Bag" in gold lettering was added to the tea bag, and gold highlighting was added to Sydney's shoes. The cost directly from Tetley was £34.99

Backstamp:
A. Printed "Wade England © Tetley GB Limited 1999"
B. Printed "Wade England © Tetley GB Limited 2003"

Name	Colourways	Size	U.S. $	Can. $	U.K. £
Sydney	Brown, white and blue	180	35.00	40.00	18.00
Sydney, 50 Years	Brown, white, blue and gold	180	100.00	115.00	50.00

J. W. Thornton Ltd., Money Boxes, 1984 - 1993

Wade produced five money boxes for J.W. Thornton Ltd. of England, manufacturer of chocolate and toffee: three "Delivery Vans" (1984, 1991 and 1993), a "Pillar Letter Box" (1986) and "Peter the Polar Bear" (1989) .The original price for the delivery vans and the pillar letter box was £3.99 each. The original 1984 delivery van and the 1991 issues have two circular holes in the rear doors.

The original 1984 delivery van was reissued for Christmas 1993 in a lighter brown. It was marked "Wade" on the packaging. The back doors were left solid on this reissue. Printed on the box is "1609 a Wade's Collectable Money Box." The original price from Thornton's was £14.95.

All delivery van money box license plates read "JWT 1".

The Pillar Letter Box had a label on it stating that it originally contained assorted toffees (Devon, liquorice, hazelnut, butter and rum flavour).

Delivery Van, solid door

Backstamp:
A. Impressed "Made Exclusively for J. W. Thornton Ltd MADE IN ENGLAND"

B. Unmarked (Pillar Letter Box, Peter Polar Bear)

Peter the Polar Bear

Pillar Letter Box

Name	Colourways	Size	U.S. $	Can. $	U.K. £
1984 Delivery Van (two holes)	Brown	120	70.00	80.00	35.00
1991 Delivery Van (two holes)	Blue	120	70.00	80.00	35.00
1993 Delivery Van (solid doors)	Light brown	120	60.00	70.00	30.00
1985 Pillar Letter Box	Brown	180	50.00	60.00	25.00
1989 Peter Polar Bear	Off white	160	50.00	60.00	25.00

TEAPOT COLLECTABLES

JOHN WADE TEAPOTS, c.1888-c.1901
KNOWN SHAPES

BRITANNIA SHAPE, c.1901

The teapot gets its name from the shape of the lid finial which resembles the helmet worn by the British figure "Britannia."

Berries and Flowers Decoration

Backstamp: Ink stamp white circular ribbon wreath "Britannia W & Co B" gold: REGd 369349 "1 /1" (pattern No)

Name	Colourways	Size	U.S. $	Can. $	U.K. £
Berries/flowers	Black; grey/green panels; orange berries; gold/white flowers	162	250.00	275.00	120.00

CENTURY SHAPE, c.1888

Garland design

Daffodil design

Wild Violets design

Backstamp: Ink stamp white circular ribbon wreath "Century W & Co B"

Name	Colourways	Size	U.S. $	Can. $	U.K. £
Garland	Black; grey/green panel; green garland; white/pink forget-me-not flowers	165	250.00	275.00	120.00
Daffodil	Light brown; black/green panel; yellow and white flower, grean leaves	165	250.00	275.00	120.00
Wild Violets	Cream and gold; violet flowers; pale green leaves	200	275.00	300.00	130.00

EUREKA SHAPE, c.1895

Forget-Me-Nots Decoration

Backstamp: Ink stamp gold circular ribbon wreath "Eureka W & Co B" Gold regd No "Rd 282788" "V816" (pattern No)

Name	Colourways	Size	U.S. $	Can. $	U.K. £
Teapot	Black; grey/green panel; gold fern leaves; white forget-me-not flowers	159	250.00	275.00	120.00

EXCELSIOR SHAPE, c.1894

Forget-Me-Nots Decoration

Backstamp: Gold ink stamp "Patent locks lid prevents overflow. Regd No '220194' '763'" (pattern no.)

Name	Colourways	Size	U.S. $	Can. $	U.K. £
Forget-Me-Nots	Black, grey/green panles, blue forget-me-not flowers	146	250.00	275.00	120.00
Leaves and Berries	Black; green panel. gold leaves, white berries	146	250.00	275.00	120.00
Lily of the Valley	Black; grey/green panels; gold and white lily of the valley flowers, leaves	146	250.00	275.00	120.00

GADROON SHAPE, c.1900

Backstamp: Ink stamp gold circular ribbon wreath "Gadroon W & Co B"
Gold Regd No "Rd 355036"

Name	Colourways	Size	U.S. $	Can. $	U.K. £
Garland	Black, grey/green panels, light green garland; pink, green, white forget-me-not flowers	171	250.00	275.00	120.00
Ivy	Black; grey/green panels; blue forget-me-not flowers; black/gold ivy leaves	171	270.00	370.00	185.00

Note: The teapot illustrated above is the garland design and is shown with an incorrect lid. Illustrated for pattern only.

GLADSTONE SHAPE, 1899
Forget-Me-Nots Decoration

Backstamp: Ink stamp gold circular ribbon wreath "W & Co B Gladstone'
gold reg No. 315844' "

Name	Colourways	Size	U.S. $	Can. $	U.K. £
Teapot	Black; green panels; blue forget-me-not flowers; orange berries; gold	159	250.00	275.00	120.00

MAFEKING SHAPE, 1900
Forget-Me-Nots Decoration

Backstamp: Ink stamp gold circular ribbon wreath "Mafeking W & Co B" Gold Regd No "Rd 382006

Name	Colourways	Size	U.S. $	Can. $	U.K. £
Teapot	Black; black and gold ivy leaves; grey/green body; pink forget-me-not flowers; white berries	140	250.00	275.00	120.00

QUEEN SHAPE, c.1890
Forget-Me-Nots Decoration

Backstamp: Unmarked

Name	Colourways	Size	U.S. $	Can. $	U.K. £
Teapot	Black; white flowers; gold leaves and highlighting	153	150.00	175.00	75.00

REGINA SHAPE, c.1897

Forget-Me-Nots and Berries Decoration

This teapot was produced to celebrate the Diamond Jubilee of Queen Victoria in 1897.

Backstamp: Unmarked

Name	Colourways	Size	U.S. $	Can. $	U.K. £
Teapot	Black; grey/green panels; blue dots; gold striped leaves; small white flowers	165	350.00	400.00	175.00

UNKNOWN SHAPES, c.1888-1902

Blossom Decoration, c.1890

The John Wade backstamps had the shape name of each teapot included in the wreath shaped backstamp as shown in the 'Eureka' backstamp below. Although none of the teapots listed below have a complete backstamp it is believed from the colours, designs and method of decoration used that they are indeed John Wade designs. Blossom Decoration

Backstamp: Unmarked

Name	Colourways	Size	U.S. $	Can. $	U.K. £
Teapot	Black; grey/green panel; pinky white blossoms; gold veined leaves; white dots	153	250.00	275.00	120.00

Daffodil Decoration, c.1888

The Daffodil teapot is similar in shape to the 'Mafeking' design teapot but there are differences in the body and handle. It has a lock lid.

Backstamp: Unmarked

Name	Colourways	Size	U.S. $	Can. $	U.K. £
Teapot	Black; grey/green panel; gold daffodil flowers, leaves	146	250.00	275.00	120.00

Daisy and Forget-Me-Not Decoration

Backstamp: Unmarked

Name	Colourways	Size	U.S. $	Can. $	U.K. £
Teapot	Black; green panel; dull yellow forget-me-not flowers;, black gold veined leaves; white daisies with yellow centres; gold highlights	170	250.00	275.00	120.00

Fan Decoration

Teapot

Stand for Teapot

Backstamp: Gold "455" or "655"

Name	Colourways	Size	U.S. $	Can. $	U.K. £
Teapot	Black; grey, blue, green panels; gold fan, leaves and flower	155	250.00	275.00	120.00
Stand for Teapot	Black, grey, blue, green and gold	205	150.00	175.00	75.00

Flower Decoration

Backstamp: Unknown

Name	Colourways	Size	U.S. $	Can. $	U.K. £
Teapot	Black; green and dark red panels; white/blue/orange five petal flowers	150	250.00	275.00	120.00
Stand	Black; green and dark red panels; white/blue/orange five petal flowers	Oval / 205	80.00	90.00	40.00

Gold Leaves and Flowers Decoration, c.1888

This teapot has the patented "hook lid."

Backstamp: Unknown

Name	Colourways	Size	U.S. $	Can. $	U.K. £
Teapot	Black; grey and green panels; gold leaves and flowers	165	250.00	275.00	120.00

Gold Loops Decoration

Although this teapot does not have the grey-blue green panels of the other John Wade items listed, it does have the gold loop design seen on the Daffodil teapot and the Fan teapot.

Backstamp: Unknown

Name	Colourways	Size	U.S. $	Can. $	U.K. £
Teapot	Black; gold loops and scallop shells	145	175.00	200.00	85.00

Ivy Leaves Decoration

Style One

The lid on this teapot is referred to as an "automatic lock lid."

Backstamp: Embossed "Wade Patent" on underside of lid, gold handwritten "369" on base

Name	Colourways	Size	U.S. $	Can. $	U.K. £
Teapot	Black; green ivy leaves with yellow veins; gold highlights	153	250.00	275.00	120.00

Ivy Leaves Decoration (cont.)

Style Two

The ivy leaf pattern found on this round-footed teapot is similar to that found on the Excelsior teapot (see page 311).

Backstamp:　None

Name	Colourways	Size	U.S. $	Can. $	U.K. £
Teapot	Black; large green ivy leaves with gold veins; small gold leaves	175	250.00	275.00	120.00

Style Three

The ivy leaf pattern on these square-footed teapots varies from the large to small size, with the smaller size having more gold highlights.

Backstamp:　Unmarked

Name	Colourways	Size	U.S. $	Can. $	U.K. £
Teapot, 6-cup	Black; large green ivy leaves with gold veins; small gold leaves	170	250.00	275.00	120.00
Teapot, 4-cup	Black; large green ivy leaves with gold veins; small gold leaves	145	250.00	275.00	120.00

Leaves and Berries Decoration, c.1899

Backstamp: Gold with registration mark

Name	Colourways	Size	U.S. $	Can. $	U.K. £
Teapot	Black; grey-green panels; gold leaves; orange and white berries	170	250.00	275.00	120.00

Poppies Decoration

Backstamp: Unknown

Name	Colourways	Size	U.S. $	Can. $	U.K. £
Teapot	Black; green panels; red poppies; white lily of the valley; gold leaves	175	250.00	275.00	120.00

Snowdrops Decoration

Backstamp: Gold "978 II"

Name	Colourways	Size	U.S. $	Can. $	U.K. £
Teapot	Black; grey-green panels; white snowdrops and beaded garlands; gold leaves; orange berries	160	250.00	275.00	120.00

TEAPOTS

The teapots listed here are those that were produced as either a single teapot with no matching items, or a teapot with only one or two matching pieces.

BEE SHAPE, 1932-c.1940

Chintz Decoration

Produced during the 1930s and 1940s, this octagonal teapot was first advertised in 1932.

Backstamp: Black ink stamp "Wade Heath England J" (1939-c.1948)

Name	Colourways	Size	U.S. $	Can. $	U.K. £
Teapot, 6-cup	White; blue/pink flowers; grey leaves	159	200.00	250.00	100.00

CANTON SHAPE

Flowers and Gold Leaves Decoration

Flowers and Gold Swirls Decoration

This decagonal (ten sided) shaped teapot was first advertised in 1931.

Backstamp: A. Ink stamp "Wade Heath England" (straight W c.1945-c.1952)
B. Ink stamp "Wadeheath England" with lion (1933-1934)

Name	Colourways	Size	U.S. $	Can. $	U.K. £
Flowers/Leaves	Black; orange/pale blue flowers; gold leaves and highlighting	159	60.00	70.00	30.00
Flowers/Swirls	Black; orange flowers; white spots; gold swirls	159	60.00	70.00	30.00

COMPACTO SHAPE
Style One

The lid of the style one teapot is level with the top and the handle is curved.

Gold Wreath Design

Backstamp: Embossed "Wades Made in England" red ink stamp "Wades Compacto, Teapot" with registration number

Name	Colourways	Size	U.S. $	Can. $	U.K. £
Gold Wreath	Dark green; gold decoration; white beaded garland; pale blue flowers/beads	108	175.00	200.00	90.00

Paisley Decoration

The popular Paisley chintz print was used by many other potteries.

Backstamp: Orange ink stamp "Wade England Compacto"

Name	Colourways	Size	U.S. $	Can. $	U.K. £
Paisley	White; multicoloured paisley design	108	175.00	200.00	90.00

COMPACTO SHAPE (cont.)
Style Two

Style two pieces have raised lids with a loop finial and angled handles and a straight body.

Backstamp: Orange ink stamp "Wades England"

Name	Colourways	Size	U.S. $	Can. $	U.K. £
Hand-painted design	Black; gold edging/trellis decoration; orange flowers	135 x 235	175.00	200.00	90.00
Plum Blossom	Dark blue background; light blue plum blossoms, brown branches	135 x 235	175.00	200.00	90.00

FORTH SHAPE

The Forth shape teapot is very similar in shape to the Selby shape teapot but does not have the bands of raised beads around the neck, it also has a thicker spout. Please note that the teapot shown has the wrong lid. The Forth teapot was first advertised in February 1931.

Paisley Decoration

The popular Paisley chintz decoration was used by many other potteries.

Backstamp: Black ink stamp "Wade Heath England A"

Illustration shows incorrect teapot lid.

Name	Colourways	Size	U.S. $	Can. $	U.K. £
Teapot, 6-cup	Paisley chintz; multicoloured	153	200.00	225.00	100.00

PEKIN SHAPE, 1930
Plum Blossom Decoration

The first advertisement found for the Pekin teapot was January 1930. It was advertised as "Wades famous teapots finest ever Pekin No. 6299".

Backstamp: Orange ink stamp "Wades England" with lion (1927-1933) [Gold pattern No. 6151]

Name	Colourways	Size	U.S. $	Can. $	U.K. £
Teapot, 6-cup	Dark blue; white blossoms; brown branches	159	100.00	115.00	50.00

SELBY SHAPE, 1930

The Selby shape teapot is very similar in shape to the Forth teapot but has two bands of raised beads around the neck which is hidden by the chintz pattern.

This shape was first advertised in *The Pottery and Glass Trades Review* in February 1930.

Paisley Decoration

Backstamp: Orange ink stamp "Wades England" with lion (1927-1933)

Name	Colourways	Size	U.S. $	Can. $	U.K. £
Teapot, 4-cup	Paisley chintz	140	200.00	225.00	100.00

NOVELTY TEAPOTS

Army Tank Teapot, 1937

This unusual Army Tank shaped teapot has a Flaxman Wade Heath backstamp which was in use just prior to World War II.

Backstamp: Ink stamp "Flaxman Wade Heath England" c.1937-1939

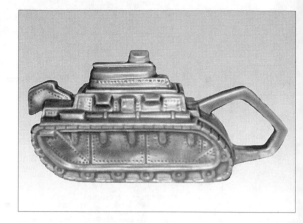

Name	Colourways	Size	U.S. $	Can. $	U.K. £
Army Tank Teapot	Orange	115 x 220	300.00	350.00	150.00

Bird's Nest Teapot, 1940

This embossed teapot has a tree branch and round petalled flowers design. Branches form the handle and spout. The lid is a bird's nest with four chicks, two with their beaks open, two with their beaks closed. A mother bird forms the finial.

An advertisement for the "Bird's Nest" teapot has been found dated September 1940.

Backstamp: Ink stamp "Wade Heath England"

Name	Colourways	Size	U.S. $	Can. $	U.K. £
Bird's Nest Teapot	Cream, brown, green, maroon, yellow and purple	153	125.00	150.00	65.00

Cottage Shape, 1934-1937

The Cottage teapot is shaped as a beamed and thatched cottage with an embossed decoration of small flowers. The windows on this shape are square lattice.

Backstamp: **A.** Black ink stamp :Wadeheath England" with lion
B. Ink stamp "Wade Heath England"

Name	Colourways	Size	U.S. $	Can. $	U.K. £
Teapot	Blue	159	150.00	175.00	75.00
Teapot	Cream cottage, grey beams	159	250.00	275.00	125.00
Teapot	Cream cottage, brown beams	159	250.00	275.00	125.00

Garden Trellis Shape, 1934-c.1945

Garden Trellis Teapot, red-brown beams

Backstamp: **A.** Ink stamp "Wadeheath England"
B. Ink stamp "Wade Heath England A" This backstamp with a capital letter "A" included shows that the teapot was in production during the years 1939-1945

Name	Colourways	Size	U.S. $	Can. $	U.K. £
Teapot, 4-cup	Cream, dark brown, light brown, grey, maroon, yellow and green	146	100.00	115.00	50.00
Teapot, 4-cup	Pale blue, red-brown, light brown, burgundy, blue, yellow and pink	146	100.00	115.00	50.00

Garden Wall Shape, 1935-1937

Backstamp: Ink stamp "Wade Heath England"

Name	Colourways	Size	U.S. $	Can. $	U.K. £
Teapot, 4-cup	Cream, brown, light brown, maroon, yellow and green	146	100.00	115.00	50.00

Genie Shape, 1990-1995

The first of these two Genie teapots was introduced in 1990 and decorated in copper lustre. The second, introduced in 1991, had a yellow background with copper lustre tints.

Backstamp: Printed "The Genie Teapot Made by Wade England" with two lines

Name	Colourways	Size	U.S. $	Can. $	U.K. £
Teapot	Copper lustre, cream, green, black and red	216	100.00	115.00	50.00
Teapot	Yellow, copper lustre; cream, green, black and dark red	216	70.00	80.00	35.00

Golf Bag Teapot

The lid of this teapot is shaped as the top of golf clubs and a golf ball.

Backstamp: Embossed "Wade England"

Name	Colourways	Size	U.S. $	Can. $	U.K. £
Golf Bag teapot	Dark green; white lid	235	50.00	60.00	25.00

Mr. Caddie, 1954-c.1962

When first introduced in mid-1954 the teapot was called the Scottie Teapot because of his tartan hat. The name was changed to Mr. Caddie in November 1954 when a golf bag cream jug and a golf ball sugar bowl were added to boost sales. This shape has also been referred to as "Andy Capp." The teapot was produced with four different coloured tartan hat lids.

Backstamp: **A.**   Gold printed semi-circular "Wade made in England Hand Painted" (1950s)
B.   Black ink circular "Royal Victoria Pottery Wade England" (1950-1960)

Name	Colourways	Size	U.S. $	Can. $	U.K. £
Teapot, 4-cup	Creamy brown hat	146	80.00	90.00	40.00
Teapot, 3-cup		133	80.00	90.00	40.00
Teapot, 4-cup	Light green hat	146	80.00	90.00	40.00
Teapot, 3-cup		133	80.00	90.00	40.00
Teapot, 4-cup	Pale blue hat	146	80.00	90.00	40.00
Teapot, 3-cup		133	80.00	90.00	40.00
Teapot, 4-cup	Pale yellow hat	146	80.00	90.00	40.00
Teapot, 3-cup		133	80.00	90.00	40.00

Old English Castle Shape, 1937-1940

Backstamp: Ink stamp "Wade Heath England" with impressed "Old English Castle" (round W 1937-1940)

Name	Colourways	Size	U.S. $	Can. $	U.K. £
Teapot	Yellow; brown turrets/windows/door; green bushes	130	225.00	250.00	120.00

Two Spout Teapot

The backstamp on this teapot has worn away, but the same gold flower and fern leaves design has been seen on a teapot stand which still carried a 'Wades England' backstamp. Although no information has been found as to why this unusual teapot should have two spouts, it has been suggested that it was a 'Farmers teapot' used to quickly pour cups of tea for a number of workers during a 'Harvest Meal' in the farmyard.

Backstamp: Unmarked, but gold pattern number 4956

Name	Colourways	Size	U.S. $	Can. $	U.K. £
Two-Spout Teapot	Black; gold flowers and leaves; pink flowers	190 x 300	90.00	100.00	45.00

WHIMSICAL FELINES SERIES, 1989-1992

| Cat Fish | Cat Litter | Cat Nap |

Backstamp: Printed "Whimsical Teapots, Feline collection, Designed by Judith Wooton, Wade England"

Cat Fish Design

Name	Colourways	Size	U.S. $	Can. $	U.K. £
Teapot, large	Pale blue goldfish bowl; blue/black marked cat; multicoloured print	130	40.00	45.00	20.00
Teapot, small	Pale blue goldfish bowl; blue/black marked cat; multicoloured print	120	30.00	35.00	15.00

Cat Litter Design

Backstamp: Printed "Whimsical Teapots, Feline collection, Designed by Judith Wooton, Wade England"

Name	Colourways	Size	U.S. $	Can. $	U.K. £
Teapot, large	Grey dustbin; brown and grey cat on lid; multicoloured print of cats	155	40.00	45.00	20.00
Teapot, small	Grey dustbin; brown and grey cat on lid; multicoloured print of cats	140	30.00	35.00	15.00

Cat Nap Design

Backstamp: Printed "Whimsical Teapots, Feline collection, Designed by Judith Wooton, Wade England"

Name	Colourways	Size	U.S. $	Can. $	U.K. £
Teapot, large	White arm chair; yellow/blue/red flowers; black/white cats	165	40.00	45.00	20.00
Teapot, small	White arm chair; yellow/blue/red flowers; black/white cats	150	30.00	35.00	15.00

COMMISSIONED TEAPOTS

BOOTS THE CHEMIST
Barleymow, 1991

Backstamp: **A.** Printed "Wade England" with two lines
B. Printed "Barleymow Designed Exclusively for Boots by Wade"

Name	Colourways	Size	U.S. $	Can. $	U.K. £
Barleymow	White; orange, green, blue and red	165	50.00	60.00	25.00

Dressage, 1992

This novelty teapot, produced for Boots the Chemist, is shaped as a horse with a number 67 rosette on his bridle. A woman in a 1930s riding habit forms the lid.

Backstamp: Printed "Dressage Designed Exclusively by Wade" with two lines and print of teapot

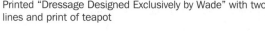

Name	Colourways	Size	U.S. $	Can. $	U.K. £
Dressage	White horse; black hooves; female rider with black hat/riding habit	170	100.00	115.00	50.00

Gymkhana Pony, 1991

This novelty teapot was produced for Boots the Chemist with an original price of £12.99.

Backstamp: Printed "Gymkhana Designed Exclusively for Boots by Judith Wootton Wade" with two lines and print of teapot

Name	Colourways	Size	U.S. $	Can. $	U.K. £
Gymkhana	Grey horse; black hooves; child with black hat, red jacket and white jodhpurs	159	100.00	115.00	50.00

Jungle Fun Elephant Shape, 1990

Backstamp:
A. Printed "Jungle Fun Designed Exclusively for Boots by Wade Ceramics"
B. Embossed "Wade England"
C. Printed "Jungle Fun Wade England"

Name	Colourways	Size	U.S. $	Can. $	U.K. £
Elephant, long spout	White; multicoloured print of jungle animals	200	40.00	45.00	20.00
Elephant, short spout	White; multicoloured print of jungle animals	200	40.00	45.00	20.00

White Rabbit Shape, 1992

Produced in 1992 for Boots the Chemist, this novelty teapot had an original selling price of £12.99.

Backstamp: Printed "White Rabbit Designed Exclusively by Wade" with two lines

Name	Colourways	Size	U.S. $	Can. $	U.K. £
White Rabbit	White; red/white squares; red heart design; blue spout tip	210	70.00	80.00	35.00

GRANADA TELEVISION LTD.

Bet Lynch Teapot, 1999

This novelty teapot portrays the head of 'Bet Lynch' one of the characters in Granada Television's long running television programme 'Coronation Street'. It was produced in November 1999 and available by mail order from Granada Television.

Backstamp: Printed "Official The Street Merchandise, Coronation St. © Granada Television Ltd. 1999 Licensed by GMCP Wade"

Name	Colourways	Size	U.S. $	Can. $	U.K. £
Bet Lynch Teapot	Yellow, pink, blue, red and white	165	60.00	70.00	30.00

Note: A teapot, with a transfer print of the Rover's Return Inn on the front is known. We have no further information on this teapot.

NOVELTIO
Mother Duck Shape, 1936

This unique teapot is shaped as a mother duck, with a duckling on her back forming the lid. Noveltio was a British export company exporting British products, including Wade, to North America during the late 1940s and 1950s.

Backstamp: **A.** Green ink stamp "Wade Heath England" (round W 1937-c.1945)
   B. Green ink stamp "Noveltio made in England" (c.1940-c.1950)

Name	Colourways	Size	U.S. $	Can. $	U.K. £
Mother Duck	Yellow duck; orange beak, feet; green-edged wing feathers	127	375.00	425.00	185.00
Mother Duck	Yellow duck; orange beak, feet; brown and green striped wingsx	127	250.00	275.00	120.00

THE TEA COUNCIL

Decorative Teapots, 1989

In 1989 the Wade Royal Victoria Pottery was commissioned to produce an unknown quantity of decorative teapots for the British based 'Tea Council', an independent body which is dedicated to promoting tea, and who represent the world's major tea producing and tea exporting countries.

The teapots were produced in a two-cup size and decorated with multicoloured prints of flowers, the lid has applied porcelain flowers on the top. The flower petals are easily chipped.

Pansies

Roses

Violets

Backstamp: Printed "The Tea Council Collection Designed Exclusively by Wade Royal Victoria Pottery 1989 England"

Flower	Colourways	Size	U.S. $	Can. $	U.K. £
Buttercup	White; yellow flowers; green leaves	115	50.00	60.00	25.00
Daffodils	White; yellow flowers; green leaves	115	50.00	60.00	25.00
Pansies	White; blue and pink flowers; green leaves	115	50.00	60.00	25.00
Primroses	White; yellow flowers; green leaves	115	50.00	60.00	25.00
Roses	White; pink and white flowers; green leaves	115	50.00	60.00	25.00
Violets	White; violet flowers; green leaves	115	50.00	60.00	25.00

TETLEY TEA FOLK

Lyons Tetley changed their name to Tetley GB Limited in early 1996. Tetley GB Limited transferred the sales of all their collectable items to the Wade Ceramics On-Line-Shop in 2005.

For Tetley Tea Money Boxes, see Money Box Section, pages 303-307.

Brew Gaffer and Sydney Cruet
Style One, 1990-1992

The first Brew Gaffer and Sydney cruet set was produced in 1990 and discontinued in 1992.

Backstamp: Printed "Wade England"

Name	Colourways	Size	U.S. $	Can. $	U.K. £
Brew Gaffer salt	Light brown, white, blue, red, and black	90	40.00	45.00	20.00
Sydney pepper	Light brown, white, blue and black	100	40.00	45.00	20.00

Style Two, 1996

Name	Colourways	Size	U.S. $	Can. $	U.K. £
Brew Gaffer pepper	Dark brown, white, blue, red, and black	83	40.00	45.00	20.00
Sydney salt	Light brown, white, blue and black	102	40.00	45.00	20.00

Brew Gaffer and Sydney: Eggcups, Jugs and Mugs, 1999-2006

The eye decals can be found looking up or down on similar items.

Brew Gaffer Eggcup, Eyes Up

Brew Gaffer Milk Jug, Eyes Up

Sydney Head Eggcup, Eyes Up

Backstamp: **A.** Printed "Wade England © Tetley GB Limited 1999"
B. Printed "An Original Design for Tetley GB by Wade England © Tetley GB Limited 1999"

Name	Colourways	Size	U.S. $	Can. $	U.K. £
Brew Gaffer eggcup, eyes down	Dark brown hat; white shirt; red tie	50	20.00	25.00	10.00
Brew Gaffer eggcup, eyes up	Brown hat; white shirt; red tie	50	20.00	25.00	10.00
Brew Gaffer milk jug, eyes down	Brown hat; white overall; red tie; blue dungarees	90	30.00	35.00	15.00
Brew Gaffer milk jug, eyes up	Brown hat; white overall; red tie; blue dungarees	90	30.00	35.00	15.00
Brew Gaffer mug eyes, down	Brown hat; white shirt; red tie	100	20.00	25.00	10.00
Brew Gaffer mug, eyes up	Brown hat; white shirt; red tie	100	20.00	25.00	10.00
Sydney eggcup, eyes down	Brown hat; white overall; blue dungarees	65	20.00	25.00	10.00
Sydney eggcup, eyes up	Brown hat; white overall; blue dungarees	65	20.00	25.00	10.00

Brew Gaffer and Sydney Derivatives

Eggcups and Mug, 2003

A limited edition of fifty Gaffer and Sydney eggcups and Gaffer mugs were issued in 2003, and sold at the North Staffordshire Hotel Wade Show, April 3rd. They were issued with a certificate of authenticity. The issue price was £35.00 for the two eggcupsa, and £20.00 for the mug.

Gaffer Eggcup   Gaffer Mug   Sydney Egg Cup

Backstamp: Printed "Wade England © Tetley GB Limited 1999"

Name	Colourways	Size	U.S. $	Can. $	U.K. £
Gaffer eggcup	Blue hat; white shirt; red tie	50	40.00	45.00	20.00
Gaffer mug	Blue hat; white shirt; red tie	100	50.00	60.00	25.00
Sydney eggcup	Blue hat; white shirt; red tie	65	40.00	45.00	20.00

Containers, 1989-1999

Four Tetley Tea Folk containers were issued between 1989 and 1999. The first was the Brew Gaffer cookie jar in 1993. It was reissued in 1996, the only difference being a slight blue shading of the eye glasses. In 1998 the Brew Gaffer tea caddy was issued, followed in 1999 with the sugar bowl. The sugar bowl can be found without the 'Sugar' decal.

Brew Gaffer cookie jar

Brew Gaffer tea caddy

Brew Gaffer sugar bowl with decal

Brew Gaffer sugar bowl without decal

Backstamp:
  A. Printed ""An Original Design for Lyons Tetley by Wade England"
  B. Printed ""An Original Design for Tetley GB By Wade England © Tetley GB Ltd 1998"
  C. Printed ""An Original Design for Tetley GB By Wade England © Tetley GB Ltd 1999"
  D. Printed ""Wade England © Tetley GB Limited 1999"

Name	Colourways	Size	U.S. $	Can. $	U.K. £
Brew Gaffer cookie jar	Dark brown hat; dark blue jar; white lettering	215	90.00	100.00	45.00
Brew Gaffer sugar bowl with decal	Dark brown hat; dark blue bowl; white lettering	120	30.00	35.00	15.00
Brew Gaffer sugar bowl no decal	Dark brown hat; dark blue bowl; white lettering	120	30.00	35.00	15.00
Brew Gaffer tea caddy	Dark brown hat; dark blue pot; white lettering	190	50.00	55.00	25.00
Sydney storage Jar	Dark brown hat; dark blue jar	250	60.00	70.00	30.00

Tea Caddy, 1994-1995

Lyons Tetley and Esso Petrol stations in Britain joined forces in a promotion that lasted from September 1994 to February 1995. Purchasers of £6.00 worth of Esso petrol were given a Tiger token, 200 tokens were needed to obtain the "Gaffer and Nephew" van-shaped tea caddy. The caddy has moulded figures of the Tetley Tea Brew Gaffer with his nephew Archie sitting beside him. The top of the van lifts off for access to the tea. Due to the large quantity of tokens required, and the short period of this promotion, this tea caddy is considered hard to find. The licence plate on the tea caddy van is "Tea 1".

Backstamp: Printed "An Original Design for Lyons Tetley by Wade England"

Name	Colourways	Size	U.S. $	Can. $	U.K. £
Tea Caddy	Cobalt blue, white, brown, red and pale blue	137	150.00	175.00	75.00

Teapots, 1990-1996

The Sydney teapot was the first to be issued in 1990 and was followed by the Brew Gaffer teapot in 1996. The Brew Gaffer and Sydney decal teapot and toast rack were issued in the latter half of 1996.

The Sydney teapot has a 'teabag' lid with a full figure Sydney lying on top as the finial. There is a rope ladder decal on the back of the teapot which makes it appear that Sydney has climbed up onto the teapot lid.

Brew Gaffer Teapot

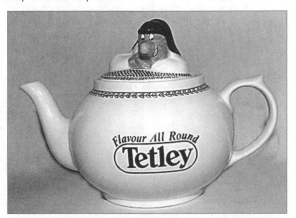
Sydney Teapot

Toast Rack; Brew Gaffer and Sydney Teapot

Two-Cup Teapot

Backstamp:
  A. Sydney Teapot 1990; Printed "Made Exclusively for Lyons Tetley by Wade"
  B. Gaffer & Sydney Decal Teapot 1996; Printed "An Original design for Lyons Tetley by Wade England"
  C. Gaffer Teapot 1996; Printed ""An Original Design for Tetley GB by Wade England © Tetley GB Limited 1996"

Name	Colourways	Size	U.S. $	Can. $	U.K. £
Brew Gaffer, 2-cup teapot	Brew Gaffer Lid: Brown hat; bluish glasses - Pot: Dark blue	140	40.00	45.00	20.00
Brew Gaffer/Sydney teapot	Dark blue teapot; multicoloured print	127	40.00	45.00	20.00
Sydney teapot	Brown cap, slippers; white overall - Pot: White; brown/black rope	135	40.00	45.00	20.00
Brew Gaffer toast rack	Dark blue; multicoloured print	70	20.00	25.00	10.00
Two-cup teapot	Dark blue teapot, white with blue lettering "Tetley"	120	20.00	25.00	10.00

Wall Clocks, 2003

To commemorate the 50th anniversary of their teabag, Lyons Tetley commissioned three flat-backed teapot-shaped wall clocks. The wording on the clocks read "Celebrating 50 Years of the Tetley Tea Bag."

The white colourway with gold lettering clock was issued in a limited edition of 500, with 50 clocks being sent to Tetley U.S.A. and 15 to Tetley Canada. The issue price was £29.99.

The "white colourway with gold centre panel and lettering" clock was a special edition, number and issue price unknown.

A special edition of 50 clocks in a cobalt blue colourway with gold lettering was sold at the Wade Dunstable Show, September 28, 2003 and came with a certificate of authenticity.

| "50 Years" Commemorative Clock | Gold "Centre Panel" Clock | Wade Dunstable Show Edition |

Backstamp: Gold printed "Wade England © Tetley GB Limited 2003"

Name	Colourways	Issued	Size	U.S. $	Can. $	U.K. £
Wall clock	Cobalt blue; gold edging, lettering and numerals	50	165 x 255	110.00	150.00	75.00
Wall clock	White; gold edging and lettering; black numerals	500	165 x 255	45.00	60.00	30.00
Wall clock	White; gold panel and lettering; black numerals	Unk.	165 x 255	75.00	100.00	50.00

WADE IRELAND

BACKSTAMPS

Some backstamps, especially the embossed types, were incorporated in the mould, and when worn moulds were replaced, the backstamps were not always changed. This resulted in old backstamps being used at the same time as the current one. Some backstamps are found with the letters *A, B, C, E, F, G* or *P* usually incorporated in the centre, under or beside a shamrock leaf. They are the potters mark.

Impressed and Embossed Backstamps

The Ulster Ware tankards, produced from the early 1950s to the 1980s, all have a variety of impressed or embossed "Wade Ireland" marks. It is difficult to place an accurate date on the early Irish porcelain tankards, as no accurate records were kept. When moulds became worn they were replaced, and sometimes a new backstamp was added.

Impressed, c.1952-c.1980

Impressed, c.1952-c.1962

WADE IRELAND ANIMALS AND BIRDS

Donkey with Baskets, 1965, 1970-1980

The models of a small donkey with large baskets (panniers) on each side were produced by Wade Ireland for a short time in 1965. It is believed these models may have been reissued during the late 1970s–1980 with the original backstamp. Some models have been found with the names of Irish towns hand painted on the baskets.

Donkey with Baskets · · · · Donkey with Baskets 'Alexford'

Backstamp: **A.** Ink stamp "Wade Ireland"
              B. Ink stamp "Made in Ireland"

Name	Colourways	Size	U.S. $	Can. $	U.K. £
Donkey with Baskets	Grey/blue/green	95	70.00	80.00	35.00
Donkey with Baskets 'Axelford'	Grey/blue/green	95	70.00	80.00	35.00

Duck, c.1954-1960s

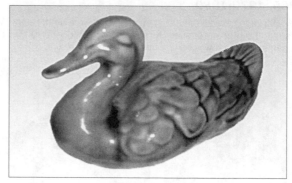

Duck

Backstamp: Ink stamp "Irish Porcelain Made in Ireland" with shamrock leaf

Name	Colourways	Size	U.S. $	Can. $	U.K. £
Duck	Grey, blue and brown	105 x 173	110.00	150.00	75.00

Duck Derivative

Duck Posy Bowl

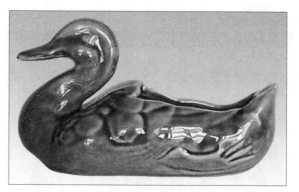

Duck Posy Bowl

Backstamp: **A.** Impressed "Irish Porcelain Made in Ireland" with a shamrock leaf
B. Black ink stamp "Irish Porcelain Made in Ireland" with a shamrock leaf
C. Unmarked

Name	Colourways	Size	U.S. $	Can. $	U.K. £
Duck Posy Bowl	Grey, blue and green	105 x 173	90.00	100.00	45.00
Duck Posy Bowl	Grey, blue and brown	105 x 173	90.00	100.00	45.00
Duck Posy Bowl	Grey and blue	105 x 173	90.00	100.00	45.00

Flying Birds

Set One: Swifts, 1960-1961

Following the production of the *Flying Birds* series in the George Wade Pottery, these models were made by Wade (Ulster) Ltd. As with the George Wade production, two sets were made. In this case, however, the numbers of the sets were reversed. Set One was now the "Swifts;" Set Two was the "Swallows."

The original price for three "Swifts" was 6/11d.

Set One: Swifts

Set Two: Swallows

Backstamp: Unmarked

Name	Colourways	Size	U.S. $	Can. $	U.K. £
Swift	Blue head, wings	86 x 76	40.00	45.00	20.00
Swift	Yellow head, wings	86 x 76	40.00	45.00	20.00
—	Boxed set (3)	—	100.00	115.00	50.00

Set Two: Swallows, 1960-1961

On the front of the original box was printed, "Flying Birds Made in Ireland by Wade Co. Armagh, The Mourne Range of Porcelain Miniatures." "The Mourne Range of Wade Porcelain Miniatures" is on the end of the box and inside is "No. 2 The Mourne Range of Porcelain Miniatures, Made in Ireland by Wade Co. Armagh." The original price for a box of three "Swallows" was 5/11d per boxed set.

Backstamp: Unmarked

Name	Colourways	Size	U.S. $	Can. $	U.K. £
Swallow	Beige wings, tail	65 x 68	20.00	25.00	12.00
Swallow	Blue wings, tail	65 x 68	20.00	25.00	12.00
Swallow	Green wings, tail	65 x 68	20.00	25.00	12.00
Swallow	Grey wings, tail	65 x 68	20.00	25.00	12.00
Swallow	Yellow wings, tail	65 x 68	20.00	25.00	12.00
—	Boxed set (3)	—	100.00	115.00	50.00

Wildlife Animals, 1978

The original name of this series is unknown, it was produced by Wade Ireland in 1978. Although the set was said to be of seven wild animals, it is known that only a few samples of a lion was produced but not put into production.

In 1997 the mould for the Koala was used by Wade, England, to produce a show special for the UK Fairs Dunstable Show. Although there is very little difference in the glaze colours, the UK Fair Koala can be distinguished by its backstamp.

Chimpanzee

Koala

Polar Bear

Elephant

Rhinoceros

Backstamp: **A:** Red and gold label "Wade Ireland"
B. Unmarked

Name	Colourways	Size	U.S. $	Can. $	U.K. £
Chimpanzee	Black and grey; brown eyes; off white face; grey/green base	115	900.00	1,000.00	450.00
Elephant	Grey streaked body; small off white tusks	90	900.00	1,000.00	450.00
Koala	Light brown, grey nose, brown tree stump, green leaves	115	900.00	1,000.00	450.00
Koala	Brown; dark brown nose/tree stump; dark green leaves	115	900.00	1,000.00	450.00
Polar Bear	White, black nose	140	900.00	1,000.00	450.00
Rhinoceros	Grey brown streaks	70 x 170	900.00	1,000.00	450.00
Walrus	Mottled brown/black; white tusks	85	900.00	1,000.00	450.00

COMMISSIONED WADE IRELAND

Not many commissioned items were produced by Wade Ireland. The earliest known piece was produced for Pex Nylons, c.1952.

A. S. COOPER

Egg Coddlers, 1968

In 1968 a large china store in Bermuda, A. S. Cooper, imported a number of Wade Ireland products which included the single and double size egg coddlers (shape Nos. I.P. 631 and I.P. 632), the backstamps on the coddlers bore the store name.

The coddlers have a single row of impressed shamrocks around the rim. A label attached to the coddler by a cord reads 'Wade Ireland Ltd a Genuine Irish Porcelain Creation by Wade (Ireland) Ltd', also included were directions on how to coddle an egg. These coddlers can be found with two backstamps.

Double Coddler

Single Coddler

Backstamp: **A.** Black Ink stamp 'Made in Ireland AS. Cooper' (c.1968)
B. Impressed 'Made in Ireland AS. Cooper' (c.1968)

Name	Colourways	Size	U.S. $	Can. $	U.K. £
Coddler Double	Blue, grey and green	101	30.00	35.00	15.00
Coddler Single	Blue, grey and green	70	20.00	25.00	10.00

BALLYFREE FARMS

Breakfast Set, 1974-1975

Wade Ireland produced the following breakfast items for Ballyfree Farms, Glenealy, County Wicklow. They were designed by Kilkenny Design Workshop. Six of the breakfast set items were produced in 1974, and because the promotion was so successful three more items were added to the set in 1975.

Ballyfree Farms sold brown eggs, Scotch eggs and "Take 'n Bake Turkeys". Tokens were collected from the egg boxes and when the appropriate number were collected they could be exchanged at the nearest Ballyfree Farms Collection Centre.

Item	Date	No. of Tokens Required
Cereal Bowl	(1974)	28 tokens
Egg Coddler	(1975)	45 tokens
Egg Cup, double	(1974)	20 tokens
Egg Cup, single	(1974)	20 tokens
Milk Jug	(1974)	60 tokens
Mug	(1974)	30 tokens
Mug, large	(1975)	45 tokens
Plate	(1974)	20 tokens
Salt and Pepper set	(1975)	55 tokens

Egg Coddler

Double Egg Cup

Milk Jug

Backstamp: Impressed "Ballyfree Farms Wade Irish Porcelain Made in Ireland" with Chicken on Nest logo

Name	Colourways	Size	U.S. $	Can. $	U.K. £
Cereal Bowl	Treacle	Unknown	20.00	25.00	10.00
Egg Coddler single	Treacle	70	30.00	35.00	15.00
Egg Cup, double	Treacle	Unknown	30.00	35.00	15.00
Egg Cup, single	Treacle	Unknown	10.00	12.00	5.00
Milk Jug	Treacle	Unknown	40.00	45.00	20.00
Mug	Treacle	Unknown	20.00	25.00	10.00
Mug , large	Treacle	Unknown	30.00	35.00	15.00
Plate	Treacle	Unknown	20.00	25.00	10.00
Salt and Pepper set	Treacle	Unknown	20.00	25.00	10.00

COLIBRI
Ashtray and Cigarette Lighter, c.1965-1970s
Raindrop Design

The raindrop design was mostly used on Irish Wade tableware. The ashtray was also advertised as a tea strainer bowl.

Ashtray

Lighter

Backstamp: Embossed "Colibri made in U.K."

Name	Colourways	Size	U.S. $	Can. $	U.K. £
Ashtray	Blue, grey and green	55	16.00	20.00	8.00
Lighter	Blue, grey and green	75	20.00	25.00	12.00

Cigarette Lighter, c.1965
Beard Pullers Design

Although this cigarette lighter is in the beautiful Celtic porcelain Beard Pullers design it was never part of the Celtic Porcelain Range and was a special commission for 'Colibri' who manufacture cigarette lighters. The backstamp is unusual because it states "Irish Porcelain Made in U.K."

Backstamp: Embossed "Colibri Irish Porcelain Made in U.K."

Name	Colourways	Size	U.S. $	Can. $	U.K. £
Celtic Beard Pullers Lighter	Blue, grey and green	80	90.00	100.00	45.00
Celtic Beard Pullers Lighter	Brown and grey	80	90.00	100.00	45.00

DAVIDSON & CO. LTD.

Sirocco Engineering Works
Ashtray, c.1970s

This advertising ashtray was produced for Davidson & Co. Ltd., Sirocco Engineering Works, Belfast, N. Ireland. They manufactured 'Sirocco' ventilation system fans, some of which were installed on the 'Titanic'.

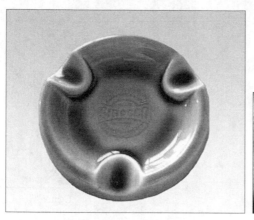

Backstamp: Black ink stamp "Irish Porcelain Wade Co Armagh"

Name	Colourways	Size	U.S. $	Can. $	U.K. £
Ashtray	Blue, gold logo	25 x 100	80.00	90.00	40.00

GRAY FINE ARTS OF BELFAST
Pin Tray, c.1980
Shape I.P.612

The pintray is from the same mould as used for the butter pats and Leprechaun trays.

Backstamp: Embossed "Made in Ireland Irish Porcelain Wade eire tir a dheata IP619" with shamrock and crown in the centre.

Name	Colourways	Size	U.S. $	Can. $	U.K. £
Pintray Horse Head	Greenish brown; multicoloured print	73	30.00	35.00	15.00

Plaques, c.1988-c.1990

Wade Ireland produced a large assortment of picture plaques for Gray Fine Arts of Belfast, Northern Ireland. The porcelain plaques all have photographs of paintings by famous Irish Artists J. C. Gray and E. McEwen on the front. Produced in four shapes, circular, oval, rectangular and square, with a choice of Banded or Irish Knot rims. The plaques were produced with an applied ring for hanging, a foot on the back for standing, a slotted stand to stand the plaque in and as a circular pintray (Shape I.P. 619). These plaques are more often found with no labels.

Circular

Oxylis

Primrose

Backstamp:
A. Yellow paper label "One in a series of Paintings By Irish Artist James Gray All Copyrights Reserved Manufactured by Gray Fine Arts.Belfast.Ireland"
B. Gold paper label "One of a series of paintings by Irish artist James C. Gray All Copyrights Reserved Manufactured by Gray Fine Arts Belfast. Ireland" with "Gray Fine Art Belfast" logo
C. Paper insert in box with painting title & story of painting
D. Embossed "Made in Ireland Irish Porcelain Wade eire tire a dheante IP619" with shamrock and crown in the center (on pintray only)

Name	Colourways	Size	U.S. $	Can. $	U.K. £
Blaze (Horse Head)	Grey green plaque; multicoloured print	72	25.00	30.00	12.00
Oxylis (Flowers)	Grey green plaque; multicoloured print	72	25.00	30.00	12.00
Primrose (Flowers)	Grey green plaque; multicoloured print	72	25.00	30.00	12.00

Oval

Camillia

Christmas Rose

Daffodils

Sunrise

Winter Morning

Name	Colourways	Size	U.S. $	Can. $	U.K. £
Camellia (flowers)	Grey green plaque; multicoloured print	105 x 85	40.00	45.00	20.00
Christmas Rose (flowers)	Grey green plaque; multicoloured print	105 x 85	40.00	45.00	20.00
Daffodils (flowers)	Grey green plaque; multicoloured print	105 x 85	40.00	45.00	20.00
Nice Morning (blacksmith)	Grey green plaque; multicoloured print	105 x 85	40.00	45.00	20.00
Primrose (flowers)	Blue-grey; yellow flowers	105 x 85	40.00	45.00	20.00
Primula (flowers)	Blue-grey; yellow flowers	105 x 85	40.00	45.00	20.00
Red Clover (flowers)	Blue-grey; pink flowers	105 x 85	40.00	45.00	20.00
Rose (flowers)	Blue-grey; white flowers	105 x 85	40.00	45.00	20.00
Sunrise (ducks flying)	Grey green plaque; multicoloured print	105 x 85	40.00	45.00	20.00
Title unknown (springer spaniel / pheasant)	Grey green plaque; multicoloured print	105 x 85	40.00	45.00	20.00
Winter Morning (springer spaniel / pheasant)	Grey green plaque; multicoloured print	105 x 85	40.00	45.00	20.00

Rectangular

Red Clover

Thoughts and Surprise

Name	Colourways	Size	U.S. $	Can. $	U.K. £
Autumn Morning (trees and leaves)	Grey green plaque; multicoloured print	110 x 90	70.00	80.00	35.00
Camellia (flowers)	Grey green plaque; multicoloured print	110 x 90	50.00	55.00	25.00
Christmas Rose (flowers)	Grey green plaque; multicoloured print	110 x 90	50.00	55.00	25.00
Lipizzaner Mare (white horse)	Grey green plaque; multicoloured print	110 x 90	70.00	80.00	35.00
Mandarin (ducks)	Grey green plaque; multicoloured print	110 x 90	70.00	80.00	35.00
Mare and Foal, walking	Grey green plaque; multicoloured print	110 x 90	70.00	80.00	35.00
Nice Morning (blacksmith)	Grey green plaque; multicoloured print	110 x 90	70.00	80.00	35.00
Oxylis (flowers)	Grey green plaque; multicoloured print	110 x 90	70.00	80.00	35.00
Red Clover (flowers)	Blue-grey; pink flowers	110 x 90	30.00	35.00	15.00
Spring Morning (spaniel and pigeon)	Grey green plaque; multicoloured print	110 x 90	70.00	80.00	35.00
Springer and Woodchuck	Grey green plaque; multicoloured print	110 x 90	70.00	80.00	35.00
Surprise (Irish setter and pheasant)	Grey green plaque; multicoloured print	110 x 90	70.00	80.00	35.00
The Cobbler (old man)	Grey green plaque; multicoloured print	110 x 90	70.00	80.00	35.00
The Farrier (blacksmith)	Grey green plaque; multicoloured print	110 x 90	70.00	80.00	35.00
Thoughts (Lady looking out of window)	Grey green plaque; multicoloured print	110 x 90	70.00	80.00	35.00
Up and Away (pheasant flying)	Grey green plaque; multicoloured print	110 x 90	40.00	45.00	20.00
Winter Morning (spaniel / woodchuck)	Grey green plaque; multicoloured print	110 x 90	70.00	80.00	35.00
Title Unknown (couple in cart)	Grey green plaque; multicoloured print	110 x 90	70.00	80.00	35.00
Title Unknown (couple in field)	Grey green plaque; multicoloured print	110 x 90	70.00	80.00	35.00
Title Unknown (huntsman / hounds)	Grey green plaque; multicoloured print	110 x 90	70.00	80.00	35.00
Title Unknown (plough horse and dog)	Grey green plaque; multicoloured print	110 x 90	70.00	80.00	35.00
Title Unknown (reaper)	Grey green plaque; multicoloured print	110 x 90	70.00	80.00	35.00

Self-Standing

These self-standing plaques have a triangular foot on the back. Some can be found with the original labels attached. The Old Chimney Corner Inn is situated in County Antrim, Northern Ireland. The plaque was a complimentary gift to visitors to the Inn.

Backstamp: Gold label printed "From the chimney corner with compliments"

Name	Colourways	Size	U.S. $	Can. $	U.K. £
The Old Chimney Corner Inn	Blue grey frame; gold edging; multicoloured print	Square/102	70.00	75.00	35.00

Square, Large

Name	Colourways	Size	U.S. $	Can. $	U.K. £
Away	Grey green plaque; multicoloured print	98 x 98	70.00	80.00	35.00
Blaze (horse's head)	Grey green plaque; multicoloured print	98 x 98	70.00	80.00	35.00
Dog Rose (flowers)	Grey green plaque; multicoloured print	98 x 98	70.00	80.00	35.00
In The Open (golden retriever and pheasant)	Grey green plaque; multicoloured print	98 x 98	70.00	80.00	35.00
Mare and Foal	Grey green plaque; multicoloured print	98 x 98	70.00	80.00	35.00
Nice Morning (blacksmith)	Grey green plaque; multicoloured print	98 x 98	70.00	80.00	35.00
Primrose (flowers)	Grey green plaque; multicoloured print	98 x 98	70.00	80.00	35.00
Rock Rose (flowers)	Blue-grey; yellow flower	98 x 98	70.00	80.00	35.00
Spring Morning (springer spaniel and pigeon)	Grey green plaque; multicoloured print	98 x 98	70.00	80.00	35.00
Springer and Woodchuck	Grey green plaque; multicoloured print	98 x 98	70.00	80.00	35.00
Stepping Out (horse)	Grey green plaque; multicoloured print	98 x 98	70.00	80.00	35.00
Sunrise (ducks flying)	Grey green plaque; multicoloured print	98 x 98	70.00	80.00	35.00
Sunset (tree and mountains)	Grey green plaque; multicoloured print	98 x 98	40.00	45.00	20.00
Surprise (Irish setter and pheasant)	Grey green plaque; multicoloured print	98 x 98	70.00	80.00	35.00
Title Unknown (Giants Causeway portrush bush)	Grey green plaque; multicoloured print	98 x 98	40.00	45.00	20.00

Square, Small

Blaze	Oxylis	Primrose

Name	Colourways	Size	U.S. $	Can. $	U.K. £
Blaze (horse's head)	Grey green plaque; multicoloured print	66 x 66	25.00	30.00	12.00
Oxylis (flowers)	Grey green plaque; multicoloured print	66 x 66	25.00	30.00	12.00
Primrose (flowers)	Grey green plaque; multicoloured print	66 x 66	25.00	30.00	12.00

Wall Hanging

The O'Connell Street, Dublin plaque is in an unusual honey glaze.

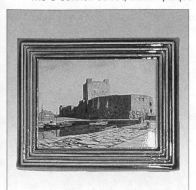

Carrickfergus Castle

Belfast Cathedral

Irish Cottage

Backstamp: Gold foil or Yellow paper label "One in a Series of Paintings by Irish Artists James C. Gray, All Copyrights Reserved, Manufactured by Gray Fine Arts. Belfast, Ireland" with "Gray Fine Art Belfast" logo

Name	Colourways	Size	U.S. $	Can. $	U.K. £
Carrickfergus Castle	Grey green plaque; multicoloured print	110 x 90	40.00	45.00	20.00
Belfast Cathedral	Grey green plaque; multicoloured print	110 x 90	40.00	45.00	20.00
O'Connel Street	Honey plaque; multicoloured print	110 x 90	40.00	45.00	20.00
Irish Cottage	Grey green plaque; multicoloured print	110 x 90	40.00	45.00	20.00
Lagan Towpath	Grey green plaque; multicoloured print	110 x 90	40.00	45.00	20.00
River Scene	Grey green plaque; multicoloured print	110 x 90	40.00	45.00	20.00

HARRODS OF KNIGHTSBRIDGE

Caviar Pots, c.1970

These caviar pots with prints of 'Sturgeon' swimming round them were produced in large quantities by Wade Ireland for Harrods of Knightsbridge and also for W.G. White of London, England. They have been found in three sizes.

*Photograph not available
at press time*

Backstamp: Impressed 'Wade Porcelain Co. Armagh' (1970s) (Harrods)

Name	Colourways	Size	U.S. $	Can. $	U.K. £
Pot, 4oz	White pot; black lettering	95	50.00	55.00	25.00

PEX NYLONS

Fairy and Candle Holder, c.1952

One of the first promotional models produced by Wade (Ulster Ltd) was in the early 1950s for Pex Nylons. It was a model of a fairy sitting in a pink water lily, and was also produced as a candle holder, although only a very limited number of the candle holders exist. The models were issued with Wade foil labels; however, they are often seen unmarked because the labels have fallen off.

In the late 1950s, the surplus fairy models were sent to the George Wade Pottery, with the intention of using them in a water babies series. But because of high production costs, the series was never issued.

Backstamp: A. Black and gold foil label "Made in Ireland by Wade County Armagh"
 B. Unmarked

Name	Colourways	Size	U.S. $	Can. $	U.K. £
Fairy	Blue wings; blue, pink and yellow flowers	55 x 35	400.00	450.00	200.00
Fairy	Pink wings; blue, pink and yellow flowers	55 x 35	400.00	450.00	200.00
Fairy	Yellow wings; blue, pink and yellow flowers	55 x 35	400.00	450.00	200.00
Flower Candle Holder	Pink; green	25 x 75	Rare		

POTTER & MOORE

Advertising Plaque, c.1970s

Potter & Moore of Lavender House, Mitcham, London, England, are producers of ladies perfumeries and cosmetics. The design on this plaque is the hallmark of Potter & Moore, and has been used in various forms since the 1920s. The design is of a lady riding a horse, the baskets/panniers contain lavender.

 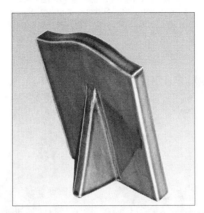

Backstamp: Unmarked

Name	Colourways	Size	U.S. $	Can. $	U.K. £
Plaque	Brownish green; honey horse; grey green; pink clothed rider	135		Rare	

R.H.M. FOODS OF ENGLAND

Bisto Kids, 1977

The *Bisto Kids* salt and pepper cruets were actually produced in the Wade Ireland pottery, but because they were intended for the British market they were marked 'Wade Staffordshire' on their bases. They were produced in November and December 1977 for Rank, Hovis, & McDougall Foods Co. (RHM) of England and were based on a pair of well-known animated characters in advertisements for Bisto Gravy Powder on British television. To receive the Bisto Kids, one had to mail in two tokens from the packet tops, plus a cheque for £1.95.

They were available from November 1977 to January 1978.

Backstamp: Brown transfer "© RHM Foods Ltd & Applied Creativity Wade Staffordshire"

Name	Colourways	Size	U.S. $	Can. $	U.K. £
Bisto Boy	Red hat; blue braces and trousers; grey jacket	110 x 58	100.00	115.00	50.00
Bisto Girl	Yellow hair and blouse; brown hat	115 x 48	100.00	115.00	50.00

SAMUEL MCGREDY NURSERIES

Ashtray, Cigarette Box and Tankard, 1962-1970
Paddy McGredy Rose Design

Samuel McGredy Nurseries in Portadown, Co. Armagh, was famous for growing and selling roses. The McGredy family emigrated to New Zealand in the mid 1970s, there they started another business growing roses. The Paddy McGredy rose, was bred in 1962, and was named after Samuel's sister 'Paddy'. The tankard is inscribed on the back "Paddy McGredy, Florabunda. Raised by Sam McGredy From Spartan x Tzigane. Awarded Gold Medal National Rose Society, Award of Merit Royal Horticultural Society."

Ashtray

Cigarette / Candy Box

Half Pint Tankard

Backstamp: Unknown

Name	Colourways	Shape / Size	U.S. $	Can. $	U.K. £
Ashtray	Olive green/grey; multicoloured print	I.P.622/146	20.00	25.00	10.00
Cigarette / Candy Box	Grey/blue/green; multicoloured print	I.P.92/127	60.00	70.00	30.00
Tankard, half pint	Grey/blue/green; multicoloured print	I.P.1/105	30.00	35.00	15.00

SOLOMON'S MINES
Egg Coddler, c.1984

Solomon's Mines are a chain of retail stores located in Nassau, Bahamas. The first store, a tobacconist shop was opened by two brothers named Solomon in 1908. In 1983 three new stores were opened and named Solomon's Mines. The egg coddler was commissioned sometime between 1983-1986.

Backstamp: Impressed 'Solomon's Mines Bahamas' Found on egg coddlers commissioned by the 'Solomon's Mines stores in Bahamas (c.1983)

Name	Colourways	Size	U.S. $	Can. $	U.K. £
Egg Coddler	Blue, grey and green	70	10.00	12.00	5.00

W.G. WHITE
Caviar Pots, 1972-1977 and 1980s

These caviar pots of sturgeon swimming were produced in large quantities for W.G. White of London, England. They have been found in three sizes.

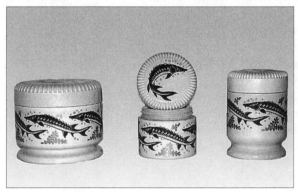

Backstamp:
- **A.** Hand written '2' (on W.G. White Caviar Pot 1980s)
- **B.** Impressed 'Wade Porcelain Co. Armagh' with Hand written '4 W.G. White London' (1970s)
- **C.** Impressed '4 W.G. White London' (1980s)
- **D.** Impressed 'Wade Porcelain Co. Armagh' with Hand written '8 W.G. White London' (1970s)

Name	Colourways	Size	U.S. $	Can. $	U.K. £
Pot, 8oz	Stone coloured pot, purple / gold fish; gold seaweed	88 x 101	40.00	45.00	20.00
Pot, 4oz	Stone coloured pot, purple / gold fish; gold seaweed	101 x 70	40.00	45.00	20.00
Pot, 4oz	Stone coloured pot, purple / pink fish; gold seaweed	101 x 70	40.00	45.00	20.00
Pot, 2oz	Stone coloured pot, purple / gold fish; gold seaweed	63 x 63	40.00	45.00	20.00

DECORATIVE AND TABLEWARE

BOXES

Candy / Cigarette Boxes, c.1955

These boxes have been advertised as both cigarette boxes and as candy boxes. One gift pack comprised a cigarette box, tankard and ashtray, another a cigarette box and ashtray. When they were sold as candy boxes, they were sold singly. All had embossed shamrocks around the box and on the lid with a transfer print in the centre, though one box with no decoration on the lid has been found. The box with the "Sailing Ship and Whale" design has a verse inside the lid, which extols the virtues of drinking 'Guinness'.

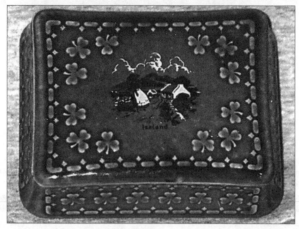

Backstamp: Impressed "Irish Porcelain" over a small shamrock with "Made in Ireland by Wade of Co. Armagh" underneath

Shape No.: I.P.92

Name	Colourways	Size	U.S. $	Can. $	U.K. £
Fox hunter, hat on head	Grey/blue/green; multicoloured print	I.P.92/127 x 101	50.00	55.00	25.00
Fox hunter, hat in hand	Grey/blue/green; multicoloured print	I.P.92/127 x 101	50.00	55.00	25.00
Hunter firing rifle	Grey/blue/green; multicoloured print	I.P.92/127 x 101	50.00	55.00	25.00
Irish colleen carrying peat	Grey/blue/green; multicoloured print	I.P.92/127 x 101	50.00	55.00	25.00
Irish kitchen	Grey/blue/green; multicoloured print	I.P.92/127 x 101	50.00	55.00	25.00
Plain	Grey/blue/green	I.P.92/127 x 101	30.00	35.00	15.00
Sailing Ship / whales	Grey/blue/green; multicoloured print	I.P.92/127 x 101	90.00	100.00	45.00
Stag's head	Grey/blue/green; multicoloured print	I.P.92/127 x 101	50.00	55.00	25.00
Stag's head	Amber; multicoloured print	I.P.92/127 x 101	50.00	55.00	25.00
The Giant Finn MacCoul	Grey/blue/green; multicoloured print	I.P.92/127 x 101	50.00	55.00	25.00

CANDLE HOLDERS AND CANDLESTICKS

Candle-holder Ashtray, c.1960s

This unusual ashtray has a round candle holder in the centre.

Backstamp: Embossed Circular 'Irish Porcelain Made in Ireland Z' around a central shamrock (early 1950s)

Name	Colourways	Size	U.S. $	Can. $	U.K. £
Candle-holder ashtray	Blue and grey	52 x 155	20.00	25.00	10.00

Crosses and Raised Dots Knurled Candlesticks, 1988

A limited number of candle holders were produced by Wade Ireland. There are three rows of raised knurls and an etched design of crosses on these candlesticks.

Backstamp: Unknown

Name	Colourways	Size	U.S. $	Can. $	U.K. £
Candlesticks	Blue and grey	Unk.	40.00	45.00	20.00

Horse's Head Candle Holder, c.1988

A small number of candle holders with a portrait of a horse's head in the centre was produced by Wade Ireland. There are indentations for four candles, one in each corner. The corners are decorated with shamrock leaves.

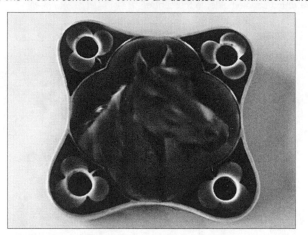

Backstamp: Unmarked

Name	Colourways	Size	U.S. $	Can. $	U.K. £
Candle holder	Chestnut brown, beige and grey	23 x 95	20.00	25.00	10.00

DISHES

Pearlstone Geode Dishes, c.1963-1964

These dishes resembling a cut and polished 'Geode' were produced at approximately the same time as the Pearlstone Wall plaques. They can be found in two sizes and with a different number of white 'crystals' in the centre, some have four to six crystals, others have none. New information and photographs have been found that show a 'Geode' dish sitting in the recess of a pearlstone plaque and sold as an ashtray.

| Pearlstone, six white crystals | Pearlstone, four white crystals | Pearlstone, no crystals |

Backstamp: Black ink stamp "Made in Ireland by Wade County Armagh"

Name	Colourways	Size	U.S. $	Can. $	U.K. £
Pearlstone	Stone rim; white/yellow bands; shiny brown centre; six white crystals	150	35.00	40.00	17.00
Pearlstone	Stone rim; white/yellow bands; shiny brown centre; four white crystals	150	35.00	40.00	17.00
Pearlstone	Stone rim; white/brown bands; bright yellow centre; no crystals	137	35.00	40.00	17.00
Pearlstone	Stone rim; white/brown bands; bright yellow centre; five crystals	137	35.00	40.00	17.00

Royal Victoria Hospital, Belfast, Candy Dish, 1953

Photo not available
at press time

Name	Colourways	Size	U.S. $	Can. $	U.K. £
Royal Victoria Hospital Belfast 1953	Pale blue; gold coat of arms and lettering	120	20.00	25.00	10.00

Pin Tray
Tudor Rose, c.1957
Shape #I.P.625

Wade Ireland first produced this pretty pin tray shaped as a 'Tudor' rose in the mid-1950s.

Backstamp: A. Impressed 'Irish Porcelain (slanted over Shamrock) Wade Co Armagh' in straight line (mid 1950s)
B. Embossed 'Wade IP/625' printed 'Made in Ireland' (c.1960s)

Name	Colourways	Size	U.S. $	Can. $	U.K. £
Tudor Rose Tray / Dish	Blue grey	34 x 85	40.00	45.00	20.00

Table Lighters, c.1958-c.1980
Shape #I.P.95

Some of the table lighters are set in the tops of Irish Porcelain models which were originally sold as souvenirs such as the Irish Cooking Pot and the Killarney Urn Posy Bowls. The decoration on the porcelain is an impressed band of shamrocks and knurls.

The Posy Bowl, Miniature Tankard and 'Stemmed' lighters are Irish Wade shapes which have not been previously recorded. The stemmed lighter has a model of the First Whimsie Crocodile attached to the base.

Irish Cooking Pot

Killarney Urn

Miniature Tankard

Posy Bowl

Stemmed

Backstamp **A:** Impressed Irish Porcelain Made in Ireland curved over a shamrock
B: Circular embossed "Irish Porcelain Made in Ireland"

Name	Colourways	Size	U.S. $	Can. $	U.K. £
Irish cooking pot table lighter	Grey and blue	85	25.00	30.00	12.00
Killarney urn table lighter	Grey and blue	100	25.00	30.00	12.00
Miniature tankard table lighter	Grey and blue	100	25.00	30.00	12.00
Posy bowl table lighter	Grey and blue	60	25.00	30.00	12.00
Stemmed table lighter	Grey and blue; greenish brown crocodile	100	40.00	45.00	20.00

CELTIC PORCELAIN SERIES, 1965

The designs of writhing snakes (Serpents) and longhaired and bearded men (Beard Pullers) on these items were based on illustrations made by medieval monks in an Irish manuscript entitled, *The Book of Kells*. The snakes represents those banished from Ireland by St. Patrick, the Beard Pullers represent merchants thrown out of the Temple by Jesus. Only one piece, the Lidded Jar has been found in the Beard Pullers design, all other pieces in the Celtic Porcelain series have been found with the Serpents design.

The small urn has a flat lid while the large urn has a domed lid. James Borsey designed the set.

Shape No	Item	Design
C.K. 1	Jar	Serpent
C.K. 2	Dish	Serpent
C.K. 3	Urn, large	Serpent
C.K. 4	Jar	Beard Pullers/Serpent
C.K. 5	Urn, small	Serpent
C.K. 6	Bowl, lidded	Serpent

Jar

Dish

Urn, small

Backstamp: Embossed "Celtic Porcelain by Wade Ireland" in an Irish knot wreath

Name	Design	Colourways	Size	U.S. $	Can. $	U.K. £
Bowl	Serpent	Mottled blue-grey	50	70.00	80.00	35.00
Dish	Serpent	Mottled blue-grey	50	60.00	70.00	30.00
Jar	Serpent	Mottled blue-grey	50	60.00	70.00	30.00
Jar	Beard Pullers	Blue/green	114	100.00	115.00	50.00
Urn, large	Serpent	Mottled blue-grey	293	150.00	175.00	75.00
Urn, small	Serpent	Greenish brown	146	125.00	150.00	65.00

Mourne Series, 1971-1976

The Mourne items were produced with a design of an impressed rose, lily, daisy or sunflowers, except for the preserve jar, which is decorated with blackberries. They are completely different in colour and style from previously produced Wade Ireland products. The vase Shape C.345 has been found in an unusual honey glaze.

Shape No.	Item	Shape No.	Item	Shape No.	Item	Shape No.	Item
C.345	Vase	C.349	Footed bowl/dish	C.353	Preserve jar	C.357	Sugar bowl
C.346	Vase	C.350	Vase	C.354	Dish, square	C.358	Salt pot
C.347	Vase	C.351	Tankard, pint	C.355	Butter dish w/lid	C.359	Pepper pot
C.348	Candy box	C.352	Tankard, ½ pint	C.356	Milk jug	C.360	Bowl, oval

 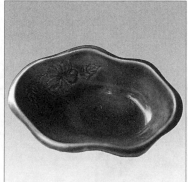 

Backstamp: **A.** Embossed circular "Made in Ireland Porcelain Wade eire tir a dheanta" around a shamrock and W crown design

B Transfer printed black circular 'Made in Ireland Wade eire tir A dheanta' . Found on honey Vase (1976)

Name	Colourways	Size	U.S. $	Can. $	U.K. £
Candy box	Green-brown; orange flower	348/50 x 127	80.00	90.00	40.00
Bowl/dish, footed	Browny green; orange flowers	349/185	50.00	60.00	25.00
Bowl/dish, oval	Green-brown; orange flower	360/130	50.00	60.00	25.00
Butter dish with lid	Browny green; orange rose	355/57 x 95	60.00	70.00	30.00
Dish, square	Green-brown; orange rose	354/135	50.00	60.00	25.00
Milk jug	Green brown; orange rose	356/108	60.00	70.00	30.00
Pepper pot	Grey green; yellow rose	359/75	30.00	35.00	15.00
Preserve jar	Mottled green/ brown lid; orange blackberries	353/95	100.00	115.00	50.00
Preserve jar	Mottled honey brown; orange blackberries	353/95	100.00	115.00	50.00
Salt pot	Grey green; yellow rose	358/75	30.00	35.00	15.00
Sugar bowl	Green brown; orange rose	357/76	70.00	80.00	35.00
Tankard, 1/2 pint	Green-brown; orange flower	351/100 x 127	80.00	90.00	40.00
Tankard, 1/2 pint	Green-brown; yellow flower	351/100 x 127	80.00	90.00	40.00
Tankard, pint	Green-brown; orange flower	352/124	80.00	90.00	40.00
Vase, C.345	Grey/green; orange sunflower	345/95	80.00	90.00	40.00
Vase, C.345	Honey; orange sunflower	345/95	80.00	90.00	40.00
Vase, C.346	Grey/green; yellow flower	346/100	80.00	90.00	40.00
Vase, C.347	Grey/green; orange rose	347/190	80.00	90.00	40.00
Vase, C.350	Grey/green; orange flower	350/170	80.00	90.00	40.00
Vase, C.350	Grey/brown	350/170	80.00	90.00	40.00

Shamrock Series, c.1982-1986

This unusual range of white items has a green shamrock leaf design. The shape of the teapot, coffee-pot, creamer, and sugar bowl is the same as the Raindrop tea set but without the embossed design. The pint tankard has two rows of knurls around the base. The decanter is the same shape as the Poteen jug but without the embossed design. It was originally sold as a boxed set with two Irish coffee goblets/mugs.

Shape No.	Item	Shape No.	Item
S.R. 01	Tankard, ½ pint	S.R. 12	Candlestick
S.R. 02	Tankard, pint	S.R. 13	Decanter (Potten jug)
S.R. 03/5	Bell	S.R. 014/5	Goblet
S.R. 06	Coffeepot, cream jug, sugar bowl	S.R. 15	Irish Coffee Goblet, single
S.R. 07	Salt and pepper pot	S.R. 16	Irish Coffee Goblets, gift pack of two
S.R. 08	Tea / Coffee cup	S.R. 17	Ashtray
S.R. 09	Vase (bud)	S.R. 18	Ashtray
S.R. 10	Vase (round)	S.R. 19	Urn
S.R. 11	Vase (Oval)	S.R. 20	Cooking pot

Backstamp: Green circular transfer print "Made in Ireland Porcelain Wade Eire tir a dheanta" around a shamrock and W crown design

Name	Colourways	Size	U.S. $	Can. $	U.K. £
Ashtray	White; gold rim; green print	177	20.00	25.00	10.00
Ashtray	White; green print	152	20.00	25.00	10.00
Bell	White; green print	146	60.00	70.00	30.00
Candlestick	White; gold rim; green prints	101	20.00	25.00	10.00
Coffee pot	White; green print	159	70.00	80.00	35.00
Cooking pot	White; green print	60	40.00	45.00	20.00
Creamer and sugar bowl	White; green print	83/62	70.00	80.00	35.00
Decanter	White; green print	200	70.00	80.00	35.00
Goblet	White; green print	115	50.00	55.00	25.00
Irish coffee mug / goblet	White; gold lettering; green shamrocks	127	12.00	15.00	6.00
Salt and pepper pots	White; green print	63	30.00	35.00	15.00
Tankard, half pint	White; gold bands; green shamrocks	105	30.00	35.00	15.00
Tankard, pint	White; green bands; shamrocks	155	30.00	35.00	15.00
Tea / coffee cup	White; green print	63	30.00	35.00	15.00
Teapot	White; green print	120	70.00	80.00	35.00
Urn	White; green print	202	40.00	45.00	20.00
Vase, bud	White; green print	220	50.00	55.00	30.00
Vase, oval	White; green print	115	50.00	55.00	25.00
Vase, round	White; green print	Unknown	50.00	55.00	30.00

WADE IRELAND FIGURINES

THE BABY, 1986

This charming model is very hard to find, it is one of the last models produced in the Wade Ireland Pottery. The Shape number, modeller and production number are unknown.

Backstamp: **A.** Printed "Wade Ireland The Baby 1986"
             B. Printed "Irish Porcelain Figures Made in Ireland" in Irish knot wreath; embossed "2"

Name	Colourways	Size	U.S. $	Can. $	U.K. £
The Baby	Light brown hair; blue suit; white collar and cuffs	110	900.00	1,000.00	450.00
The Baby	Blonde hair; pale blue suit	110	900.00	1,000.00	450.00

IRISH CHARACTER FIGURES

SOLID MODELS

First Issue, Small Size, 1977-1986

The overall colour of these models is honey, with varying shades of mottled grey-blue, grey-brown, etc., making the colour description difficult. Only the major colour variation has been noted.

The backstamp used was an ink stamped "Made in Ireland" which over time wears away. These models were issued in a see-through box.

Shape No.	Name	Shape No.	Name
S. 16	Danny Boy	S. 22	Not assigned
S. 17	Molly Malone	S. 23	Not assigned
S. 18	Kathleen	S. 24	Rose of Tralee
S. 19	Mother MacCree	S. 25	Eileen Oge
S. 20	Phil the Fluter	S. 26	Paddy Reilly
S. 21	Paddy Maginty		

Eileen Oge

Kathleen

Molly Malone

Paddy Maginty

Paddy Reilly

Rose of Tralee

Backstamp: **A.** Ink stamp "Made in Ireland"
B. Unmarked

IRISH CHARACTER FIGURES (cont.)

Name	Colourways	Size	U.S. $	Can. $	U.K. £
Danny Boy	Grey green coat/hat/bag; pink vest/trousers; black shoes	95	40.00	45.00	20.00
Danny Boy	Brown hat/jacket; honey vest/trousers; dark brown bag/shoes	95	40.00	45.00	20.00
Eileen Oge	Mottled black brown shawl; bright blue hem on skirt	95	40.00	45.00	20.00
Eileen Oge	Mottled black brown shawl; grey blue hem on skirt	95	40.00	45.00	20.00
Kathleen	Grey blue headscarf; mottled brown shawl	88	40.00	45.00	20.00
Molly Malone	Mottled grey headscarf/skirt; pink blouse	88	40.00	45.00	20.00
Molly Malone	Dark blue-grey headscarf/skirt; pale pink blouse	88	40.00	45.00	20.00
Mother MacCree	Mottled brown cloak/vest; brown shoes	70	40.00	45.00	20.00
Mother MacCree	All over honey; brown shoes; green stool	70	40.00	45.00	20.00
Mother MacCree	Varying shades of honey; brown shoes; green stool	70	40.00	45.00	20.00
Paddy Maginty	Mottled grey hat, coat/shoes; pink vest; grey brown leaves	90	40.00	45.00	20.00
Paddy Maginty	Mottled grey hat, coat/shoes; pink vest; green leaves	90	40.00	45.00	20.00
Paddy Reilly	Dark grey brown hat/coat; dark blue grey vest; red brown dog	95	40.00	45.00	20.00
Paddy Reilly	Dark blue grey vest; red brown dog; dark brown shoes	95	40.00	45.00	20.00
Phil the Fluter	Grey blue vest; red brown shoes	85	40.00	45.00	20.00
Rose of Tralee	Light grey blue hat/arm bands/hem; pink flower	100	40.00	45.00	20.00

Irish Character Figures Derivatives

Solid Models on Plinth, 1977–1986

Some of the Irish Character models have been found attached to 'Genuine Connemara Marble' bases, there are many variations in shape and size of the marble base. As there is no way of seeing the backstamp an overall price is given for these models.

| Danny Boy | Eileen Oge | Rose of Tralee |

Name	Colourways	Size	U.S. $	Can. $	U.K. £
Danny Boy	Honey; brown hat/coat/bag; black shoes; light grey marble	105	50.00	55.00	25.00
Eileen Oge	Pale honey; mottled black-brown shawl; blue hem; dark grey marble	115	50.00	55.00	25.00
Kathleen	Grey blue headscarf; honey shawl	98	50.00	55.00	25.00
Paddy Maginty	Honey-brown figure; greenish brown stand	95	100.00	110.00	50.00
Paddy Reilly	Light brown hat/coat; pink waistcoat; honey trousers; light grey marble	105	50.00	55.00	25.00
Phil the Fluter	Honey-brown figure; greenish brown stand	95	100.00	110.00	50.00
Rose of Tralee	Honey; light grey blue hat/arm bands/hem; light grey marble	120	50.00	55.00	25.00

SOLID MODELS

Second Issue, Small Size, 1991

In 1991 the Irish Character figures were reissued and now carried the Seagoe Ceramics backstamp.

As with the first issue the overall colour is a dark honey glaze with varying shades of mottled grey-blues and grey-browns. Only the major colour differences have been noted in the colourways description: for example the dog on the model Paddy Reilly is red-brown in the first issue, and tan in the second.

Mother MacCree

Kathleen

Molly Malone

Paddy Maginty

Paddy Reilly

Phil the Fluter

Backstamp:
- **A.** Circular ink stamp "Seagoe Ceramics Wade '91 Ireland"
- **B.** Black ink stamp "Wade 91"
- **C.** Unmarked

Name	Colourways	Size	U.S. $	Can. $	U.K. £
Danny Boy	Dark honey hat/coat/bag; grey blue neck scarf; honey vest/trousers	95	50.00	60.00	25.00
Danny Boy	Dark blue grey coat; dark brown bag; honey vest; black shoes	95	50.00	60.00	25.00
Eileen Oge	Mottled brown and black shawl; grey blue hem on skirt; black shoes	95	50.00	60.00	25.00
Kathleen	Dark grey blue headscarf; mottled brown shawl	88	50.00	60.00	25.00
Molly Malone	Blue grey scarf and skirt; yellow vest	88	50.00	60.00	25.00
Mother MacCree	Blue grey vest; black shoes	70	50.00	60.00	25.00
Paddy Maginty	Light olive hat and coat; honey vest; brown shoes; green leaves	90	50.00	60.00	25.00
Paddy Reilly	Grey brown hat and coat; blue grey vest; honey trousers; tan dog	95	50.00	60.00	25.00
Phil the Fluter	Grey blue vest; brown shoes	85	50.00	60.00	25.00
Rose of Tralee	Dark grey blue hat, arm bands and hem; yellow or honey flower	100	50.00	60.00	25.00

IRISH PORCELAIN FIGURES

HOLLOW MODELS
First Issue, Large Size, 1962

Although Phoebe Stabler had been credited as the modeller of these large figures, it is now known that they were in fact modelled by Raymond Piper, a well-known Ulster artist. He named the three models "Himself," "Herself" and "Felicity." They were based on people known by the modeller. "Himself" is based on Harry McMullan, well known at that time for his storytelling in Belfast pubs. "Herself" is based on Mary Kelly, an 87 year old, who had fallen on hard times and resided in a Catholic shelter for homeless women. "Felicity" was the daughter of Major and Mrs. Straker Carryer.

A disiagreement arose between Raymond Piper and Wade over the glaze colours for these three models. Because of this Mr. Piper declined to model any other figures for Wade.

Felicity

Herself

Himself

Backstamp:
A. Printed "Irish Porcelain Figures" in Irish knot wreath with hand written "Felicity"
B. Printed "Irish Porcelain Figures" in Irish knot wreath with "Herself modelled by Raymond Piper"
C. Printed "Irish Porcelain Figures" in Irish knot wreath with "Himself modelled by Raymond Piper"

Name	Colourways	Size	U.S. $	Can. $	U.K. £
Felicity	Grey hair, blue dress, white sewing; mottled green and white base	Unk.		Rare	
Herself	White hair/collar; grey eyes/shawl; bright blue vest; light brown shoes	225	800.00	900.00	400.00
Herself	White hair/collar; grey eyes/shawl; turquoise vest; light brown shoes	225	800.00	900.00	400.00
Himself	Dark grey hat; grey eyes; white scarf; grey-blue suit; light brown shoes	220	800.00	900.00	400.00
Himslef	Dark grey het; grey eyes; white scarf, pale blue suit; light brown shoes	220	800.00	900.00	400.00

HOLLOW MODELS
Second Issue, Large Size, c.1963

For the second issue the models were assigned new shape numbers, given new names and different colourways.

Shape No.	Name
C. 507	Dan Murphy
C. 508	Mother MacCree
C. 509	Eileen Oge

Dan Murphy · Eileen Oge · Mother MacCree

Backstamp: Printed "Irish Porcelain Figures Made in Ireland" in Irish knot wreath

Name	Colourways	Size	U.S. $	Can. $	U.K. £
Dan Murphy	Dark green speckled brown hat; grey eyes/suit; black shoes	220	700.00	800.00	350.00
Dan Murphy	Green speckled brown hat; grey eyes; light grey suit; black shoes	220	700.00	800.00	350.00
Dan Murphy	Dark grey hat; grey eyes; grey-blue suit, black shoes	220	700.00	800.00	350.00
Eileen Oge	Blue-grey hair; bright blue dress; white sewing	225	700.00	800.00	350.00
Mother MacCree	White hair; mottled beige/grey shawl; grey collar; blue vest	225	700.00	800.00	350.00
Mother MacCree	White hair; mottled blue/grey shawl, white collar, blue vest	225	700.00	800.00	350.00

HOLLOW MODELS
Third Issue, Large Size, 1991

In 1990 the Wade Ireland Pottery was renamed Seagoe Ceramics Ltd. The 1991 issue of Irish Porcelain Figures carries the addition of Seagoe Ceramics to the backstamp.

Dan Murphy

Eileen Oge

Mother MacCree

Backstamp: Printed "Irish Porcelain Figures Made in Ireland" in Irish knot wreath with "Seagoe Ceramics" underneath

Name	Colourways	Size	U.S. $	Can. $	U.K. £
Dan Murphy	Dar brown hat; black eyes and shoes; grey suit; olive green stool	220	500.00	575.00	250.00
Dan Murphy	Red brown hat; black eyes and shoes; mottled beige grey suit	220	500.00	575.00	250.00
Eileen Oge	Dark grey hair; blue dress; white sewing; mottled dark green base	225	500.00	575.00	250.00
Eileen Oge	Light grey hair; pale blue dress; white sewing; olive green base	225	500.00	575.00	250.00
Mother MacCree	White hair; black eyes/shoes; light grey shawl; light blue vest/skirt	225	500.00	575.00	250.00
Mother MacCree	White hair; black eyes/shoes; mottled beige grey shawl; grey vest/skirt	225	500.00	575.00	250.00

IRISH PORCELAIN SONG FIGURES

HOLLOW MODELS

First Issue, Small Size, 1963

William K. Harper, who worked for Wade, England, (1953-1962) was asked to model eight figures for the new smaller size Irish Procelain Song figures.

Shape No.	Name	Shape No.	Name
C. 500	Phil the Fluter	C. 504	Irish Emigrant
C. 501	Widda Cafferty	C. 505	Star of Co. Down
C. 502	Little Mickey Mullligan	C. 506	Molly Malone
C. 503	Little Crooked Paddy	C. 510	Bard of Armagh

| Bard of Armagh | Molly Malone | Mickey Mulligan |

Backstamp: Black printed "Modelled by William Harper Irish Porcelain Made in Ireland" with year '63 and name of model

Name	Colourways	Size	U.S. $	Can. $	U.K. £
Bard of Armagh	Beige brown coat; dark brown shoes/harp; grey vest/trousers	125	300.00	350.00	150.00
Irish Emigrant	Light brown suit/hat; blue tie; dark brown hair/belt/shoes	155	300.00	350.00	150.00
Irish Emigrant	Light brown suit/hat; brown tie; dark brown hair/belt/shoes	155	300.00	350.00	150.00
Irish Emigrant	Light brown suit/hat; green tie; brown hair/belt/shoes	155	300.00	350.00	150.00
Little Crooked Paddy	Grey suit and hat; black shoes; light brown stick	135	300.00	350.00	150.00
Little Mickey Mulligan	Black hair; brown suit/tie/shoes; dark grey hat/blanket;	150	300.00	350.00	150.00
Little Mickey Mulligan	Dark grey hair; brown tie/shoes; grey coat/hat; beige trousers	150	300.00	350.00	150.00
Molly Malone	Black hair; dark grey shawl; blue dress; beige brown barrow	150	300.00	350.00	150.00
Phil the Fluter	White hair; grey vest/jacket; blue trousers; brown flute/shoes	160	300.00	350.00	150.00
Star of Co Down	Dark brown hair; grey dress; chickens' have yellow eyes/combs	160	300.00	350.00	150.00
Star of Co Down	Light brown hair; light grey dress; chickens' have yellow eyes	160	300.00	350.00	150.00
Widda Cafferty	Light grey hair/shawl/stockings; pale blue dress	160	300.00	350.00	150.00
Widda Cafferty	Grey hair/ stockings; dark grey shawl; pale blue dress	160	300.00	350.00	150.00
Widda Cafferty	Light grey hair/stocking; grey shawl; pale blue dress;	160	300.00	350.00	150.00

HOLLOW MODELS
Second Issue, Small Size, 1980

Minor colour variations appear on the 1980 issue. The date is no longer included in the backstamp.

Bard of Armagh

The Irish Emigrant

Little Crooked Paddy

Mickey Mulligan

Phil the Fluter

Widda Cafferty

Backstamp: **A.** Black printed "Modelled by William Harper Irish Porcelain Made in Ireland" with name of model
B. Black Printed "Irish Porcelain Made in Ireland" (Widda Cafferty)

Name	Colourways	Size	U.S. $	Can. $	U.K. £
Bard of Armagh	Light brown coat; dark brown shoes/harp; grey trousers	125	250.00	300.00	125.00
Bard of Armagh	Light grey coat; dark brown harp; blue grey vest/trousers	125	250.00	300.00	125.00
Irish Emigrant	Grey-brown coat/hat; green tie; red-brown hair/belt	155	250.00	300.00	125.00
Little Crooked Paddy	Grey suit/hat; black shoes; dark brown stick	135	250.00	300.00	125.00
Little Crooked Paddy	Grey hat; blue-grey suit; black shoes; dark brown stick	135	250.00	300.00	125.00
Little Mickey Mulligan	Black hair; white pink streaked tie; brown suit; dark grey hat	150	250.00	300.00	125.00
Molly Malone	Black hair; grey shawl/barrow; blue dress; blue-grey mussels	150	250.00	300.00	125.00
Phil the Fluter	White hair; grey vest/jacket; blue trousers; dark brown flute	160	250.00	300.00	125.00
Star of Co Down	Light brown hair; light grey dress; white chicken	160	250.00	300.00	125.00
Widda Cafferty	Light grey hair/shawl/stockings; pale blue dress; white apron	160	250.00	300.00	125.00
Widda Cafferty	Grey hair/stockings; pale blue dress; mottled dark grey shawl	160	250.00	300.00	125.00

HOLLOW MODELS

Third Issue, Small Size, 1991

Although it is believed all eight models in this series were reissued in a new colourway in 1991, only six have been found to date. They carry the Seagoe Ceramics backstamp.

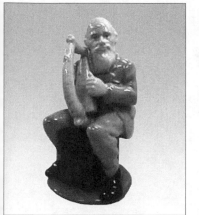

Bard of Armagh

Irish Emigrant

Little Mickey Mulligan

Molly Malone

Phil the Fluter

Star of Co Down

Backstamp: Black printed "Modelled by William Harper Irish Porcelain Seagoe Ceramics Made in Ireland" with name of model

Name	Colourways	Size	U.S. $	Can. $	U.K. £
Bard of Armagh	Light brown suit; yellow harp; black shoes; dark brown stool	125	200.00	225.00	100.00
Irish Emigrant	Beige suit and hat; yellow tie; red brown belt; dark brown shoes	155	200.00	225.00	100.00
Little Crooked Paddy	Unknown	135	200.00	225.00	100.00
Little Mickey Mulligan	Charcoal grey hair, hat and blanket; fawn suit; yellow tie	150	200.00	225.00	100.00
Molly Malone	Black hair; mottled grey black shawl; blue dress; grey barrow	150	200.00	225.00	100.00
Phil the Fluter	White hair; grey waistcoat; blue trousers; silver flute	160	200.00	225.00	100.00
Star of Co Down	Fawn hair; off white apron; grey dress; brown chickens	160	200.00	225.00	100.00
Widda Cafferty	Unknown	160	200.00	225.00	100.00

Pixie and Toad, c.1965

This hard to find model of a pixie and toad was produced by Wade Ireland in the mid-1960s, but was designed and modelled at the George Wade pottery in England. The modeller is unknown. Eileen Moore, head of the costing department at Wade Ireland at that time, remembers a number of production problems with this model, and that fewer than 500 pieces were produced.

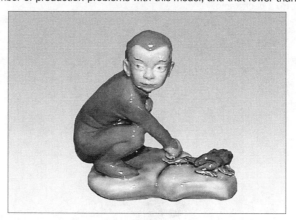

Backstamp: B. Printed "Irish Porcelain Figures Made in Ireland"

Name	Colourways	Size	U.S. $	Can. $	U.K. £
Pixie and Toad	Blue grey suit; olive green toad; mottled green base	150	1,400.00	1,600.00	700.00

Pogo, 1959

"Pogo" is based on a 1940s possum character created by Walt Kelly and featured in American children's books, newspapers and comics. This model of Pogo holding his hat in his lap with a bluebird in a nest on his head, was modelled by William Harper, who worked for the George Wade Pottery during the 1950s.

Backstamp: Black ink stamp "Pogo Copyright, Walt Kelly, Made in Ireland 1959"

Name	Colourways	Size	U.S. $	Can. $	U.K. £
Pogo	Grey; blue jacket; blue and pink bird	85 x 30	500.00	575.00	250.00

WADE IRELAND WHIMSIES

BALLY-WHIM IRISH VILLAGE, 1984-1987

Due to the success of the *English Whimsey-on-Why* models, Wade Ireland introduced a set of eight Irish village houses. When the Wade Ireland pottery ceased production of giftware in August 1987, only one *Bally-Whim Irish Village* set had been issued. Each model is marked in a hollow under the base. The model number is printed on the side.

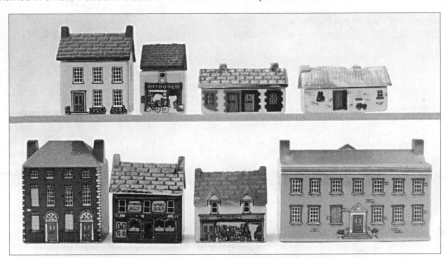

Backstamp: Embossed "Wade Ireland"

Name	No.	Colourways	Size	U.S. $	Can. $	U.K. £
Undertaker's House	1	Beige; brown roof, door	50 x 38	30.00	35.00	15.00
Moore's Post Office	2	Cream; brown roof	38 x 25	30.00	35.00	15.00
Barney Flynn's Cottage	3	Grey roof; red windows, door	28 x 45	30.00	35.00	15.00
Kate's Cottage	4	Yellow-brown roof	23 x 45	30.00	35.00	15.00
The Dentist's House	5	Dark brown; grey roof; red door	50 x 45	30.00	35.00	15.00
Mick Murphy's Bar	6	Green and grey	35 x 38	30.00	35.00	15.00
W. Ryan's Hardware Store	7	Yellow and brown roof	35 x 38	30.00	35.00	15.00
Bally-Whim House	8	Grey; blue roof; honey door	40 x 82	30.00	35.00	15.00

"TINKER'S NOOK"

The George Wade Whimsey-on-Why model "Tinker's Nook" has been reported with a Wade Ireland backstamp, this would suggest that some Whimsey-on-Why moulds were given to the Irish pottery to produce.

Backstamp:
Embossed 'Wade Ireland'

Name	Colourways	Size	U.S. $	Can. $	U.K. £
Tinker's Nook	Red-brown roof; yellow and white windows	38 x 22	30.00	35.00	15.00

LEPRECHAUNS AND PIXIES, 1956-1986

BABY PIXIE, c.1978-1980s

The *Baby Pixie* models can be found free standing, on a circular pin tray or on a shamrock leaf dish.

Backstamp: Black ink stamp "Made in Ireland"

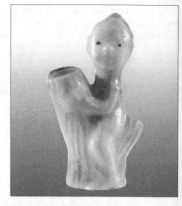

Name	Colourways	Size	U.S. $	Can. $	U.K. £
Baby Pixie	Blue suit, cap, boots	35 x 10	25.00	30.00	12.00

Baby Pixie Derivative

The shamrock leaf dish has been found with a 1950s backstamp on the base, which suggests they were probably old stock reissued with pixies on them to create new products.

Backstamp: **A.** Embossed "Made in Ireland, Porcelain Wade, Eire Tir-Adheanta"
        B. Impressed "Irish Porcelain Made in Ireland Co. Armagh"
        C: Impressed "Irish Porcelain Made in Ireland"
        D. Impressed "Irish Porcelain Made in Ireland by Wade Co. Armagh"

Baby Pixie on Shamrock Leaf Dish

Name	Colourways	Size	U.S. $	Can. $	U.K. £
Baby Pixie Pin Tray	Blue suit; blue-green tray	40 x 75	30.00	35.00	15.00
Baby Pixie Shamrock Leaf Dish	Blue suit; blue-grey dish	40 x 75	30.00	35.00	15.00
Baby Pixie Shamrock Leaf Dish	Blue suit; brown dish	40 x 75	30.00	35.00	15.00

LARGE LEPRECHAUNS, 1974-1985
Shape S11

Although it appears that these models were in production for over ten years, the multicoloured models are rarely seen. See also Toadstool Cottage Money Box, page 278.

Backstamp: Unmarked, but most models can be found with Wade's characteristic ribbed base.

Name	Colourways	Size	U.S. $	Can. $	U.K. £
Leprechaun	Bright blue all over	70 x 30	40.00	45.00	20.00
Leprechaun	Brown all over	70 x 30	40.00	45.00	20.00
Leprechaun	Green hat; dark brown jacket; beige trousers	70 x 30	40.00	45.00	20.00
Leprechaun	Grey-green	70 x 30	40.00	45.00	20.00
Leprechaun	Turquoise blue	70 x 30	40.00	45.00	20.00
Leprechaun	Yellow hat; green jacket; beige trousers	70 x 30	40.00	45.00	20.00

Large Leprechaun Derivatives

Large Leprechaun on Marble Bases, 1974-1985

The model mounted on a square block of Connemara marble is the original 1974 model. It was intended for the tourist trade. The model is also found on a circular resin base, which was made to simulate Connemara marble.

Large Leprechaun on Connemara Marble Base

Large Leprechaun on Simulated Marble Base

Large Leprechaun on Pin Tray

Backstamp:
A. Gold label "Real Connemara Marble Made in Ireland"
B. Gold label "Lucky Irish Leprechaun Made in Ireland"
C. None

Name	Colourways	Size	U.S. $	Can. $	U.K. £
Leprechaun	Dark grey-green; gold label, square base	90 x 55	100.00	115.00	50.00
Leprechaun	Dark grey green; mottled grey circular resin base	85	50.00	55.00	25.00
Leprechaun	Dark grey-green leprechaun and pin tray	75 x 110	50.00	55.00	25.00

LARRY AND LESTER, THE LEPRECHAUN TWINS, 1974-1985
Shape S.22

These models are identical except for the colouring.

Backstamp: Black ink stamp "Made in Ireland"

Name	Colourways	Size	U.S. $	Can. $	U.K. £
Larry	Green hat; purple jacket; brown leggings	100 x 60	90.00	100.00	45.00
Lester	Yellow hat; green jacket; red leggings	100 x 60	90.00	100.00	45.00

Larry and Lester Derivatives

Bookends, 1974-1985

The leprechaun twins were added to a heavy porcelain, L-shaped base to form a pair of bookends.

Backstamp: Purple ink stamp "Made in Ireland"

Name	Colourways	Size	U.S. $	Can. $	U.K. £
Bookends	Larry on one base; Lester on the other; dark green bookends	115 x 75	250.00	275.00	125.00

LEPRECHAUN ON TOADSTOOL WITH CROCK O'GOLD, c.1975

This model is of a smiling leprechaun sitting on top of a toadstool with his hands resting on top of a crock o'gold.

Backstamp: Black ink stamp "Made in Ireland"

Name	Colourways	Size	U.S. $	Can. $	U.K. £
Leprechaun	Grey and brown	125	60.00	70.00	30.00
Leprechaun	Grey and brown leprechaun; grey blue toadstool	125	60.00	70.00	30.00

LUCKY FAIRY FOLK

The *Lucky Fairy Folk*, produced by Wade (Ulster) Ltd., is a set of three models, sitting on the backs of a rabbit and a pig and on top of an acorn. Each figure was sold separately in a cylindrical-shaped acetate packet, with a multicoloured string handle. On the end of the string was a black foil label, which read "Made in Ireland by Wade Co. Armagh" in gold lettering. The models themselves are not marked, so once removed from the packet, there is no indication of which pottery they were from.

First Version: Brown Faces, 1956-1960s

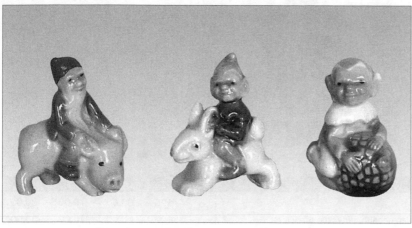

Leprechaun on Pig, Pixie on Rabbit, Pixie on Acorn

Original Packaging

Backstamp: Black and gold foil label "Made in Ireland by Wade Co. Armagh" in gold lettering on packet; models are unmarked

Name	Colourways	Size	U.S. $	Can. $	U.K. £
Leprechaun on Pig	Dark green hat, grey coat, blue trousers	45 x 35	60.00	65.00	30.00
Leprechaun on Pig	Orange hat, blue coat, grey trousers	45 x 35	60.00	65.00	30.00
Leprechaun on Pig	Red hat, blue coat, grey trousers, white boots	45 x 35	60.00	65.00	30.00
Leprechaun on Pig	Red hat, blue coat/boots, grey trousers	45 x 35	60.00	65.00	30.00
Pixie on Acorn	Blue hat/boots; grey coat, white trousers	40 x 30	70.00	80.00	35.00
Pixie on Acorn	Dark green hat; grey coat, white trousers	40 x 30	70.00	80.00	35.00
Pixie on Acorn	Orange hat, grey coat, white trousers, blue boots	40 x 30	70.00	80.00	35.00
Pixie on Acorn	Red hat, grey coat, white trousers, blue boots	40 x 30	70.00	80.00	35.00
Pixie on Acorn	Dark yellow hat, grey coat, white trousers, blue boots	40 x 30	70.00	80.00	35.00
Pixie on Acorn	White hat/trousers; grey coat, blue boots	40 x 30	70.00	80.00	35.00
Pixie on Rabbit	Dark green hat, blue coat, grey trousers, blue boots	40 x 32	100.00	115.00	50.00
Pixie on Rabbit	Red hat, blue coat, grey trousers, blue boots	40 x 32	100.00	115.00	50.00
Pixie on Rabbit	Dark yellow hat, blue coat, grey trousers , blue boots	40 x 32	100.00	115.00	50.00

Lucky Fairy Folk First Version Derivatives

Pixie on Acorn Butter Dish, 1960s

Backstamp: Embossed "Wade England"

Name	Colourways	Size	U.S. $	Can. $	U.K. £
Pixie/Butter Dish	Green hat; yellow dish	65 x 80	50.00	55.00	25.00
Pixie/Butter Dish	Yellow hat, dish	65 x 80	50.00	55.00	25.00
Pixie/Butter Dish	Red hat; yellow dish	65 x 80	50.00	55.00	25.00
Pixie/Butter Dish	Blue hat; yellow dish	65 x 80	50.00	55.00	25.00

Pixie on Rabbit Whimtray Pin Tray, 1960s

Backstamp: Unknown

Name	Colourways	Size	U.S. $	Can. $	U.K. £
Pixie on Rabbit Whimtray	Pixie: Yellow, blue and grey; white rabbit; yellow tray	60 x 75	50.00	55.00	25.00

Second Version: Leprechaun on a Pig 1980-1986

On the first version "Leprechaun on Pig" the colour of the face is beige-brown and the snout and toes of the pig are grey; on the second issue the leprechaun's face is flesh coloured and the snout and toes of the pig changed to beige.

Backstamp: Unmarked

Name	Colourways	Size	U.S. $	Can. $	U.K. £
Leprechaun on Pig	Dark green, flesh, white and grey; Pig: light beige snout/toes	45 x 35	50.00	55.00	25.00
Leprechaun on Pig	Orange, flesh, blue and grey; Pig: light beige snout/toes	45 x 35	50.00	55.00	25.00
Leprechaun on Pig	Red, flesh, blue, white and grey; Pig : light beige snout/toes	45 x 35	50.00	55.00	25.00
Leprechaun on Pig	Yellow, flesh, blue, white and grey; Pig: light beige snout/toes	45 x 35	50.00	55.00	25.00

LUCKY LEPRECHAUNS, 1956-1986

This set of three *Lucky Leprechauns* was first issued in 1956 by Wade (Ulster) Ltd. When the models were originally shipped to retailers, they were packaged in decorative display boxes of 24 models, with hat colours of white, yellow, orange, red, maroon, blue or green. Also included was a porcelain shamrock leaf to use as a price display, see page 404. On it was was printed "Lucky Leprechauns Made in Ireland By Wade Co. Armagh 1/11d each." Many of these shamrock plaques have survived and are sought by collectors. The *Lucky Leprechauns* set was reissued in the mid-1960s and again in the 1980s.

First Version: Brown Faces, Paper Foil Label, 1956-1959

Originally the models each had a black and gold foil label on the base. The label is easily washed off and if it is missing it is difficult to tell which version the figure comes from. As a general guide, the 1956-1959 models have brown faces, whereas the faces of later figures are flesh coloured.

Backstamp: **A.** Black and gold foil label "Made in Ireland by Wade Co. Armagh"
             B. Unmarked

Name	Colourways	Size	U.S. $	Can. $	U.K. £
Cobbler	Dark green hat; grey coat, boots; blue trousers	37 x 30	30.00	35.00	15.00
Cobbler	Maroon hat; grey coat, boots; blue trousers	37 x 30	30.00	35.00	15.00
Cobbler	Orange hat; grey coat, boots; blue trousers	37 x 30	30.00	35.00	15.00
Cobbler	Red hat; grey coat, boots; blue trousers	37 x 30	30.00	35.00	15.00
Cobbler	White hat; grey coat, boots; blue trousers	37 x 30	30.00	35.00	15.00
Crock O'Gold	Maroon hat; blue coat; grey trousers; brown boots	34 x 25	30.00	35.00	15.00
Crock O'Gold	Orange hat; blue coat; grey trousers; brown boots	34 x 25	30.00	35.00	15.00
Crock O'Gold	Red hat; blue coat; grey trousers; brown boots	34 x 25	30.00	35.00	15.00
Crock O'Gold	Dark yellow hat; blue coat; grey trousers; brown boots	34 x 25	30.00	35.00	15.00
Crock O'Gold	Yellow hat; green coat; grey trousers; brown boots	34 x 25	30.00	35.00	15.00
Tailor	Blue hat; white coat; blue trousers; grey boot	38 x 19	30.00	35.00	15.00
Tailor	Dark green hat; white coat; blue trousers; grey boot	38 x 19	30.00	35.00	15.00
Tailor	Red hat; white coat; blue trousers; grey boot	38 x 19	30.00	35.00	15.00

Lucky Leprechauns First Version Derivatives

Oak Leaf Dish 1957-1959

The George Wade Pottery's 1957 oak leaf dish was issued with the 1956-1959 "Leprechaun Crock O'Gold" to produce this particular dish. The original selling price was 2/11d.

Backstamp: Embossed "Shamrock Pottery Made in Ireland"

Name	Colourways	Size	U.S. $	Can. $	U.K. £
Crock O'Gold	Maroon hat; blue jacket; brown boots; green leaf	40 x 100	30.00	35.00	15.00
Crock O'Gold	Orange hat; blue jacket; brown boots; green leaf	40 x 100	30.00	35.00	15.00
Crock O'Gold	Yellow hat; blue jacket; brown boots; green leaf	40 x 100	30.00	35.00	15.00
Crock O'Gold	Yellow hat; green jacket; white/brown boots; green leaf	40 x 100	30.00	35.00	15.00
Tailor	Blue hat; grey jacket/shoes; blue trousers; green leaf	40 x 100	30.00	35.00	15.00

Pintrays, 1956-1959

The *Lucky Leprechauns* models used on these pin trays were issued by Wade (Ulster) Ltd. from 1956 to 1959. The pin tray in which the Lucky Leprechaun sits was originally produced as a "pin tray" (plain) and as a "butter pat" (with transfer printed decorations) see *The Charlton Standard Catalogue of Wade Decorative Ware, Vol. 2* and *The Charlton Standard Catalogue of Wade Tableware, Vol. 3*. There are two styles of pin trays: one with a recessed centre (Irish Wade Shape I.P.619), and an early 1950s backstamp, the second with a flat centre, and 1971-1976 backstamps. The first version *Lucky Leprechauns* are found only on recessed trays.

There are no price differentials between the recessed and flat centre trays or between Version One, Two or Three Leprechauns.

Colour: Blue-green trays
Backstamp: Embossed Circular "Irish Porcelain Made in Ireland" around a central shamrock with letter T (early 1950s)

Pintrays (cont)

Name	Colourways	Size	U.S. $	Can. $	U.K. £
Cobbler	Dark green hat; grey coat, boots; blue trousers	45 x 75	20.00	25.00	10.00
Cobbler	Orange hat; grey coat, boots; blue trousers	45 x 75	20.00	25.00	10.00
Cobbler	Maroon hat; grey coat, boots; blue trousers	45 x 75	20.00	25.00	10.00
Cobbler	White hat; grey coat, boots; blue trousers	45 x 75	20.00	25.00	10.00
Crock O'Gold	Maroon hat; blue coat; grey trousers; brown boots	45 x 75	20.00	25.00	10.00
Crock O'Gold	Orange hat; blue coat; grey trousers; brown boots	45 x 75	20.00	25.00	10.00
Crock O'Gold	Dark yellow hat; blue coat; grey trousers; brown boots	45 x 75	20.00	25.00	10.00
Tailor	Blue hat; white coat; blue trousers; grey boot	45 x 75	20.00	25.00	10.00
Tailor	Dark green hat; white coat; blue trousers; grey boot	45 x 75	20.00	25.00	10.00
Tailor	Maroon hat; white coat; blue trousers; grey boot	45 x 75	20.00	25.00	10.00

Stone Plinth Souvenir Crock O'Gold Leprechaun, 1957-1959

This Crock o Gold, first version Lucky Leprechaun, with a brown face, is mounted on a thick stone plinth. The plinth has a green and silver shamrock-shaped enamel plaque on the front that reads "Giants Causeway." This model was not produced by Wade in this form. The porcelain models were purchased by individual companies who applied them to the stone plinths. They were produced in this form for the tourist trade.

Backstamp: Unmarked

Name	Colourways	Size	U.S. $	Can. $	U.K. £
Crock O'Gold	Bright yellow hat; blue jacket; grey trousers; brown boots	65 x 52	35.00	40.00	18.00

Second Version: Flesh Coloured Faces, Without Backstamps, 1960s

This boxed set of three *Lucky Leprechauns* had no labels and were unmarked. Once removed from their box, there is no indication of the year of issue or of the maker. The reissued models have flesh-coloured faces, which distinguish them from the original 1956-1959 version.

Backstamp: Unmarked

Name	Colourways	Size	U.S. $	Can. $	U.K. £
Cobbler	Green hat; light grey coat, boots; pale blue trousers	38 x 31	20.00	25.00	10.00
Cobbler	Orange hat; light grey coat, boots; pale blue trousers	38 x 31	20.00	25.00	10.00
Cobbler	Red hat; light grey coat, boots; pale blue trousers	38 x 31	20.00	25.00	10.00
Cobbler	Yellow hat; light grey coat, boots; pale blue boots	38 x 31	20.00	25.00	10.00
Crock O'Gold	Blue hat; pale blue grey coat; light grey trousers; brown boots	34 x 26	20.00	25.00	10.00
Crock O'Gold	Green hat; pale blue grey coat; light grey trousers; brown boots	34 x 26	20.00	25.00	10.00
Crock O'Gold	Red hat; pale blue grey coat; light grey trousers; brown boots	34 x 26	20.00	25.00	10.00
Crock O'Gold	Yellow hat; pale blue grey coat; light grey trousers; brown boots	34 x 26	20.00	25.00	10.00
Tailor	Pale blue hat, trousers; white coat; grey boot	39 x 20	20.00	25.00	10.00
Tailor	Green hat; white coat; pale blue trousers; grey boot	39 x 20	20.00	25.00	10.00
Tailor	Red hat; white coat; pale blue trousers; grey boot	39 x 20	20.00	25.00	10.00
Tailor	Yellow hat; white coat; pale blue trousers; grey boot	39 x 20	20.00	25.00	10.00
—	Boxed set	—	70.00	80.00	35.00

Lucky Leprechaun Second Version Derivatives

Butter Dish, 1970s

The George Wade butter dish was first produced from 1955 to 1959, with a model of a squirrel, rabbit or the 1956 *Hat Box* "Jock" on the back rim. In the 1970s, the dish was combined with surplus Irish Wade, *Lucky Leprechauns* to produce novelty butter dishes.

Backstamp: Embossed "Wade England"

Name	Colourways	Size	U.S. $	Can. $	U.K. £
Cobbler	Blue hat; yellow dish	65 x 80	30.00	35.00	15.00
Cobbler	Green hat; yellow dish	65 x 80	30.00	35.00	15.00
Tailor	Blue hat; yellow dish	65 x 80	30.00	35.00	15.00
Tailor	Green hat; yellow dish	65 x 80	30.00	35.00	15.00
Tailor	Red hat; yellow dish	65 x 80	30.00	35.00	15.00

Marble Plinths, c.1975-1985

These models were taken from the reissued 1974-1985 *Lucky Leprechauns* set and mounted on a block of Connemara marble. The marble plinths can be found in a variety of shapes: circular, rectangular and square, and the thickness and length can vary. They were intended for the tourist trade.

Lucky Leprechauns on Marble Plinths

Backstamp: **A.** Gold foil label "Lucky Irish Leprechauns, Made in Ireland"
B. Unmarked

Name	Colourways	Size	U.S. $	Can. $	U.K. £
Cobbler	Green hat; light brown stool; beige shoe	58 x 52	30.00	35.00	15.00
Crock O'Gold	Blue hat; yellow coins; grey jacket, trousers	58 x 52	30.00	35.00	15.00
Crock O'Gold	Red hat; yellow coins; blue jacket, grey trousers	43 x 48	30.00	35.00	15.00
Crock O'Gold	Red hat; yellow coins; grey blue jacket, trousers	58 x 52	30.00	35.00	15.00
Crock O'Gold	Yellow hat, coins; grey jacket, trousers	58 x 52	30.00	35.00	15.00
Tailor	Blue hat; grey trousers, shoes	58 x 52	30.00	35.00	15.00
Tailor	Yellow hat; grey trousers, shoes	58 x 52	30.00	35.00	15.00

Pin Trays

The second version of the *Lucky Leprechauns* are found on both styles of trays, recessed and flat centre.

Colour: Blue-green trays
Backstamp: Embossed Circular "Irish Porcelain Made in Ireland" around a central shamrock with letter T (early 1950s)

Name	Colourways	Size	U.S. $	Can. $	U.K. £
Cobbler	Dark green hat; grey coat, boots; blue trousers	45 x 75	20.00	25.00	10.00
Cobbler	Maroon hat; grey coat, boots; blue trousers	45 x 75	20.00	25.00	10.00
Cobbler	Orange hat; grey coat, boots; blue trousers	45 x 75	20.00	25.00	10.00
Cobbler	White hat; grey coat, boots; blue trousers	45 x 75	20.00	25.00	10.00
Crock O'Gold	Dark yellow hat; blue coat; grey trousers; brown boots	45 x 75	20.00	25.00	10.00
Crock O'Gold	Maroon hat; blue coat; grey trousers; brown boots	45 x 75	20.00	25.00	10.00
Crock O'Gold	Orange hat; blue coat; grey trousers; brown boots	45 x 75	20.00	25.00	10.00
Tailor	Blue hat; white coat; blue trousers; grey boot	45 x 75	20.00	25.00	10.00
Tailor	Dark green hat; white coat; blue trousers; grey boot	45 x 75	20.00	25.00	10.00
Tailor	Maroon hat; white coat; blue trousers; grey boot	45 x 75	20.00	25.00	10.00

Third Version: Flesh Coloured Faces, With Backstamp, 1971-1976

The third version of the Lucky Leprechauns was issued as a set of three in a cardboard box with a cellophane face. Each model had a black ink stamped backstamp, but as with all ink stamps time and washing of the model removes the ink stamp.

Backtamp: **A.** Small black ink stamp "Made in Ireland"
B. Large black ink stamp "Made in Ireland"

Name	Colourways	Size	U.S. $	Can. $	U.K. £
Cobbler	Red hat; grey coat, boots; pale blue trousers	38 x 31	20.00	25.00	10.00
Cobbler	White hat; dark grey coat, boots; dark blue trousers	38 x 31	20.00	25.00	10.00
Crock O'Gold	Blue hat; blue coat; light grey trousers; brown boots	34 x 26	20.00	25.00	10.00
Crock O'Gold	Green hat; blue coat; light grey trousers; brown boots	34 x 26	20.00	25.00	10.00
Crock O'Gold	Red hat; blue coat; light grey trousers; brown boots	34 x 26	20.00	25.00	10.00
Crock O'Gold	Yellow hat; blue coat; light grey trousers; brown boots	34 x 26	20.00	25.00	10.00
Tailor	Blue hat and trousers; white coat; grey boot	39 x 20	20.00	25.00	10.00
Tailor	Yellow hat; white coat; blue trousers; grey boot	39 x 20	20.00	25.00	10.00
—	Boxed set	—	70.00	80.00	35.00

Lucky Leprechauns Third Version Derivatives

Pin Trays, 1980s

Backstamp: Embossed circular "Made in Ireland Irish Porcelain Wade Eire Tir A Dheanta" IP 619 with shamrock and crown in centre

Name	Colourways	Size	U.S. $	Can. $	U.K. £
Cobbler	Green hat; light grey coat, boots; pale blue trousers	45 x 75	20.00	25.00	10.00
Cobbler	Orange hat; light grey coat, boots; pale blue trousers	45 x 75	20.00	25.00	10.00
Cobbler	Red hat; light grey coat, boots; pale blue trousers	45 x 75	20.00	25.00	10.00
Cobbler	Yellow hat; light grey coat, boots; pale blue trousers	45 x 75	20.00	25.00	10.00
Crock O'Gold	Blue hat; pale blue grey coat; light grey trousers; brown boots	45 x 75	20.00	25.00	10.00
Crock O'Gold	Green hat; pale blue grey coat; light grey trousers; brown boots	45 x 75	20.00	25.00	10.00
Crock O'Gold	Red hat; pale blue grey coat; light grey trousers; brown boots	45 x 75	20.00	25.00	10.00
Crock O'Gold	Yellow hat; pale blue grey coat; light grey trousers; brown boots	45 x 75	20.00	25.00	10.00
Tailor	Pale blue hat, trousers; white coat; grey boot	45 x 75	20.00	25.00	10.00
Tailor	Green hat; white coat; pale blue trousers; grey boot	45 x 75	20.00	25.00	10.00
Tailor	Red hat; white coat; pale blue trousers; grey boot	45 x 75	20.00	25.00	10.00
Tailor	Yellow hat; white coat; pale blue trousers; grey boot	45 x 75	20.00	25.00	10.00

Lucky Leprechaun Shamrock Plaque, 1956-1959

This was originally a display plaque for the Lucky Leprechaun models and would have been distributed to the retailer for display with the models and not intended for sale.

Backstamp: None

Name	Colourways	Size	U.S. $	Can. $	U.K. £
Lucky Leprechaun Plaque	White and green; black lettering	100 x 48	140.00	160.00	70.00

SHAMROCK POTTERY SERIES, 1956-1984

In 1956 Wade Ireland introduced a small series of models known as the *Shamrock Pottery Series.* It consisted of the "Irish Comical Pig," "The Pink Elephant," "Shamrock Cottage," "Pixie Dish" and the "Donkey and Cart Posy Bowl." The last three models were reissued between 1977 and the early 1980s.

Irish Comical Pig, 1956-1961

The *Irish Comical Pig*, made by Wade (Ulster) Ltd., is found in several different combinations of back patterns, nose, ear and tail colours. The original selling price was 2/6d each. The places of interest named on the back of some models are in black lettering.

Backstamp: Green transfer print "Shamrock Pottery Made in Ireland"

Name	Colourways	Size	U.S. $	Can. $	U.K. £
Daisy Pattern	Green and orange daisy; green nostrils; yellow tail	45 x 65	50.00	55.00	25.00
Daisy Pattern	Green and orange daisy; green nostrils and tail	45 x 65	50.00	55.00	25.00
Daisy Pattern	Green and orange daisy; orange nostrils; yellow tail	45 x 65	50.00	55.00	25.00
Daisy Pattern	Green and orange daisy; yellow nostrils; orange tail	45 x 65	50.00	55.00	25.00
Daisy Pattern	Green and orange daisy; yellow nostrils and tail	45 x 65	50.00	55.00	25.00
Loop Pattern	Orange loops; green stars, lines; brown eyes, green nostrils, tail	45 x 65	50.00	55.00	25.00
Shamrocks	Black pig; green shamrocks	45 x 65	50.00	55.00	25.00
Shamrocks	White; green nostrils, tail, shamrocks	45 x 65	50.00	55.00	25.00

Town Names

Name	Colourways	Size	U.S. $	Can. $	U.K. £
Canterbury	Green nostrils, tail; black lettering	45 x 65	50.00	55.00	25.00
Eastbourne	Green nostrils; yellow tail; black lettering	45 x 65	50.00	55.00	25.00
Henley on Thames	Green nostrils; yellow tail; black lettering	45 x 65	50.00	55.00	25.00
Holy Island	Black pig; gold decal Holy Island	45 x 65	50.00	55.00	25.00
Hunstanton	Green nostrils; yellow tail; black lettering	45 x 65	50.00	55.00	25.00
Isle of Wight	Green nostrils; yellow tail; black lettering	45 x 65	50.00	55.00	25.00
Llandudno	Green nostrils; yellow tail; black lettering	45 x 65	50.00	55.00	25.00
Old Smithy Godshill	Green nostrils, tail; black lettering	45 x 65	50.00	55.00	25.00
Penmaenmawr	Green nostrils yellow tail; black lettering	45 x 65	50.00	55.00	25.00
Stratford-Upon-Avon	Green nostrils, tail; black lettering	45 x 65	50.00	55.00	25.00
Stratford-Upon-Avon	Green nostrils; yellow tail; black lettering	45 x 65	50.00	55.00	25.00
Windermere	Green nostrils; yellow tail; black lettering	45 x 65	50.00	55.00	25.00
York	Green nostrils; yellow tail; black lettering	45 x 65	50.00	55.00	25.00

Pink Elephant, 1956-1961

The *Pink Elephant,* made by Wade (Ulster) Ltd., is found with several different slogans on its back associated with the consumption of too much alcohol. Others can be found with the names of places of interest, and towns. Originally, these models sold for 2/6d each.

Backstamp: Green transfer print "Shamrock Pottery Made in Ireland"

Slogans

Name	Slogan	Colourways	Size	U.S. $	Can. $	U.K. £
Elephant	None	Pale pink	40 x 80	60.00	70.00	30.00
Elephant	"Never Again"	Pink; green nostrils, tail	40 x 80	60.00	70.00	30.00
Elephant	"Never Again"	Pink; orange nostrils, tail	40 x 80	60.00	70.00	30.00
Elephant	"Never Mix Em"	Pink; green nostrils, tail	40 x 80	60.00	70.00	30.00
Elephant	"Oh! My Head"	Pink; green nostrils, tail	40 x 80	60.00	70.00	30.00
Elephant	"Stick to Water"	Pink; green nostrils, tail	40 x 80	60.00	70.00	30.00

Places and Town Names

Name	Town	Colourways	Size	U.S. $	Can. $	U.K. £
Elephant	Bournemouth	Pink; orange nostrils, tail	40 x 80	60.00	70.00	30.00
Elephant	Devils Bridge	Pink; green nostrils, tail	40 x 80	60.00	70.00	30.00
Elephant	Henley on Thames	Pink; green nostrils, tail	40 x 80	60.00	70.00	30.00
Elephant	Isle of Wight	Pink; orange nostrils, tail	40 x 80	60.00	70.00	30.00
Elephant	Old Smithy, Godshill	Pink; green nostrils, tail	40 x 80	60.00	70.00	30.00
Elephant	Ramsgate	Pink; orange nostrils, tail	40 x 80	60.00	70.00	30.00
Elephant	Salisbury	Pink; green nostrils, tail	40 x 80	60.00	70.00	30.00

Shamrock Cottage, 1956-1984

The Shamrock Cottage was a slip cast, hollow model of an Irish cottage, produced by Wade (Ulster) Ltd. It was sold in a box decorated with a shamrock design and labelled "Shamrock Pottery" and "Ireland's own Pottery." The original selling price was 2/6d.

First Version: Light Brown Peat, Green Base, 1956-1961

Backstamp: Impressed "Shamrock Pottery Made in Ireland"

Name	Colourways	Size	U.S. $	Can. $	U.K. £
Shamrock Cottage	Yellow roof; blue doors, windows; light brown peat; green base	45 x 40	40.00	45.00	20.00

Second Version: Dark Brown Peat, Mottled Green Base, Early 1970s-1979

The reissued *Shamrock Cottage* is the same as the 1956-1961 model, except that the colour of the base is a mottled green and white and the peat pile at the back of the cottage is a darker shade of brown. It has also been found with names of places of interest in England and Ireland printed in black letters on the front rim of the base. Donaghadee is a small fishing village 20 miles outside Belfast, it is a popular holiday town famous for 'Grace Neill's Bar' which is the oldest pub in Ireland.

A cottage exists with a gold foil label "Aberyswyth" on the roof.

Plain Cottage

Bourton-on-the-Water

Backstamp: Impressed "Shamrock Pottery Made in Ireland"

Name	Colourways	Size	U.S. $	Can. $	U.K. £
Bally Castle	Yellow, dark blue, dark brown, mottled green, white and black	45 x 40	40.00	45.00	20.00
Belfast	Yellow, dark blue, dark brown, mottled green, white and black	45 x 40	40.00	45.00	20.00
Bourton-on-the-Water	Yellow, dark blue, dark brown, mottled green, white and black	45 x 40	40.00	45.00	20.00
Cliftonville	Yellow, dark blue, dark brown, mottled green, white and black	45 x 40	40.00	45.00	20.00
Conway	Yellow, dark blue, dark brown, mottled green, white and black	45 x 40	40.00	45.00	20.00
Donaghadee	Yellow, dark blue, dark brown, mottled green, white and black	45 x 40	40.00	45.00	20.00
Giants Causeway	Yellow, blue, dark brown, mottled green, white and black	45 x 40	40.00	45.00	20.00
Guernsey	Yellow, dark blue, dark brown, mottled green, white and black	45 x 40	40.00	45.00	20.00
Hawkshead	Yellow, dark blue, dark brown, mottled green, white and black	45 x 40	40.00	45.00	20.00
Isle of Wight	Yellow, dark blue, dark brown, mottled green, white and black	45 x 40	40.00	45.00	20.00
Jersey	Yellow, dark blue, dark brown, mottled green, white and black	45 x 40	40.00	45.00	20.00
Omagh	Yellow, dark blue, dark brown, mottled green, white and black	45 x 40	40.00	45.00	20.00
Plain (no name)	Yellow, dark blue, dark brown, mottled green and white	45 x 40	40.00	45.00	20.00
Plain (Aberystwyth)	Yellow, blue, light brown, white, gold label "Aberystwyth"	45 x 40	40.00	45.00	20.00
Shanklin	Yellow, dark blue, dark brown, mottled green, white and black	45 x 40	40.00	45.00	20.00
Windermere	Yellow, blue, dark brown, mottled green, white and black	45 x 40	40.00	45.00	20.00

Shamrock Cottage Second Version Derivatives

Shamrock Cottage on Simulated Marble Base

This *Shamrock Cottage* is glued onto a simulated resin Connemara marble base. Also attached to the base is a miniature tankard with a Guinness label on the front. The miniature tankard is not a known Wade mould.

Backstamp: None

Name	Colourways	Size	U.S. $	Can. $	U.K. £
Cottage/Tankard	Yellow, blue, mottled green, white, and mottled brown	20 x 145	50.00	55.00	25.00

Shamrock Cottage on Simulated Marble Base

This *Shamrock Cottage* is glued onto a simulated resin Connemara marble base. Attached to the base is a gold coloured piece of metal, the top of which is missing the original model, an unknown building or figure.

Backstamp: None

Name	Colourways	Size	U.S. $	Can. $	U.K. £
Cottage	Yellow, blue, green, white and mottled olive green	55 x 50	50.00	60.00	25.00

Third Version: Light Brown Peat, White Base c.1977-Early 1980s

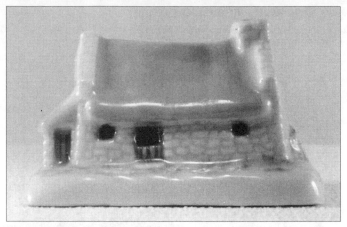

Backstamp: Impressed "Shamrock Pottery Made in Ireland"

Name	Colourways	Size	U.S. $	Can. $	U.K. £
Shamrock Cottage	Yellow roof; dark blue doors; dark brown peat; white base	45 x 40	40.00	45.00	20.00

Shamrock Cottage Third Version Derivatives

Shamrock Cottage and Tailor on a Map of Ireland, Mid 1950s-1979

This model has recently been found with a Shamrock Pottery backstamp, and a brown-faced Leprechaun which would suggest that it was originally produced in the mid 1950s and was reissued in the 1970s, with a later backstamp. The reissued "Tailor" and the reissued *Shamrock Cottage* (1974-1985) were combined by Wade Ireland and placed on a porcelain outline of the map of Ireland to form this unusual and sought-after souvenir model. It was discontinued in 1979.

Backstamp: **A.** Embossed "Shamrock Pottery Made in Ireland by Wade of Armagh"
B. Embossed "Made in Ireland"

Name	Colourways	Size	U.S. $	Can. $	U.K. £
Cottage and Tailor	Blue hat; grey trousers, shoes; grey-green map base	65 x 140	125.00	150.00	65.00
Cottage and Tailor	Yellow hat; grey trousers, shoes; grey-green map base	65 x 140	125.00	150.00	65.00
Cottage and Tailor	Blue hat, trousers; grey shoes; grey-green map base	65 x 140	125.00	150.00	65.00

Shamrock Cottage and Pin Tray on Simulated Marble Plinth, 1970s

In the late 1970s a Shamrock Cottage and a Pin Tray, with a duck hunter print, were combined and mounted on a rectangular imitation marble base. A gold foil label on the front of the base reads "A Present from Ireland"

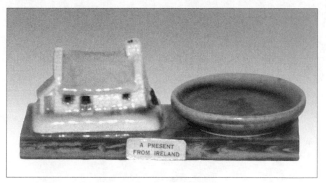

Backstamp: Unknown

Name	Colourways	Size	U.S. $	Can. $	U.K. £
Cottage and Pintray	Yellow, blue, mottled green white, blue-grey and dark brown	48 x 80	60.00	70.00	30.00

Shamrock Cottage Third Version Derivatives (Cont.)

Shamrock Cottage on Simulated Marble Plinth with Lucky Leprechaun 1970s

In the late 1970s the "Cobbler," "Crock O'Gold" and "Tailor" and the Shamrock Cottage were combined and mounted on rectangular simulated marble bases.

Backstamp: Unknown

Name	Colourways	Size	U.S. $	Can. $	U.K. £
Cottage and Cobbler	Beige, white, yellow, blue and dark brown	48 x 80	50.00	60.00	25.00
Cottage and Crock O' Gold	Yellow, blue and dark brown	44 x 80	50.00	60.00	25.00
Cottage and Tailor	Yellow, grey, blue and dark brown	49 x 80	50.00	60.00	25.00

Whimsie Whimtrays, c.1985

In the mid-1980s, Wade Ireland produced *Whimtrays*, but as the original mould used for the George Wade Whimtray was worn, a new one was designed. The plinth on which the figure sits is not gently rounded, as was that of the original George Wade model. Instead, it bends much farther out into the dish, making it easy to distinguish the two styles of trays. The colour of the blue trays may vary slightly in the shading. The following models have been found attached to the Irish tray.

First Whimsies	Englsih Whimsies
Cockatoo	Duck
Husky	Fawn
King Penguin	Trout
Polar Bear Cub	

Duck

Trout

Backstamp: Embossed "Made in Ireland, Irish Porcelain, Wade 'Eire tir a dheanta'" in a circle around a crown and shamrock

Name	Colourways	Size	U.S. $	Can. $	U.K. £
Cockatoo	Yellow crest; black tray	50 x 77	30.00	35.00	15.00
Duck	Blue and brown; blue tray	50 x 77	12.00	15.00	6.00
Duck	Blue and brown; green tray	50 x 77	12.00	15.00	6.00
Fawn	Brown; black tray	50 x 77	12.00	15.00	6.00
Fawn	Brown; green tray	50 x 77	12.00	15.00	6.00
Husky	Fawn and white; blue tray	50 x 77	30.00	35.00	15.00
Husky	Fawn and white; green tray	50 x 77	30.00	35.00	15.00
King Penguin	Black and white; black tray	50 x 77	15.00	20.00	6.00
King Penguin	Black and white; green tray	45 x 77	30.00	35.00	15.00
Polar Bear Cub	White; black tray	40 x 77	30.00	35.00	15.00
Polar Bear Cub	White; green tray	40 x 77	30.00	35.00	15.00
Trout	Brown; black tray	50 x 77	12.00	15.00	6.00
Trout	Brown; blue tray	50 x 77	12.00	15.00	6.00
Trout	Brown; green tray	50 x 77	12.00	15.00	6.00

IRISH WADE WALL PLAQUES

Display Plaques, c.1960

The Irish Porcelain plaque, produced c.1960, was meant to be displayed with Wade Ireland figures.

Backstamp: Unmarked

Name	Colourways	Size	U.S. $	Can. $	U.K. £
Irish Porcelain plaque	Green/grey	135 x 98	40.00	45.00	20.00

Irish Scenes, c.1960

This series of square wall plaques, produced by Wade Ireland, have an embossed design of Irish knots around the rim and a multicoloured print of an Irish scene in the centre.

Backstamp: **A.** Black ink stamp "Irish Porcelain Wade County Armag" with a shamrock leaf
B. Unmarked

Name	Colourways	Size	U.S. $	Can. $	U.K. £
City Hall, Belfast	White; multicoloured print	72	20.00	25.00	10.00
Colleen and Cottage	Grey-green; multicoloured print	75	20.00	25.00	10.00
Colleen and Cottage	White; multicoloured print	72	20.00	25.00	10.00
Giants Causeway	Grey-green; multicoloured print	72	20.00	25.00	10.00
Giants Causeway	White; multicoloured print	72	20.00	25.00	10.00
Ireland	White; multicoloured print	72	20.00	25.00	10.00
Irish fisherman	Grey-green; multicoloured print	72	20.00	25.00	10.00
Irish fisherman	White; multicoloured print	72	20.00	25.00	10.00
Irish jaunting car	Grey-green; multicoloured print	75	20.00	25.00	10.00
Irish jaunting car	White; multicoloured print	72	20.00	25.00	10.00

Pearlstone Wall Plaques, 1963-1964

These plaques were originally designed in 1958-1959 by the Hagen-Renaker Pottery in San Dimas, California, but because of production problems they were soon discontinued.

Sir George Wade's daughter Iris was the art director at Wade Ireland. She left Wade ireland in 1966 to start a new life in the U.S.A. with her huband Straker Carryer. Together they formed Carryer Craft of California. It was in California that Iris met Jim Renaker, and together they agreed to send the wall plaque moulds to Wade Ireland for a trial period.

As with Hagen-Renaker, Wade Ireland had problems producing the plaques. Most would crack during the cooling down period after firing and production was soon discontinued. The original Hagen-Renaker names are given in the listing.

Two styles of backs are found on these plaques. One has large irregular hollows in the back for setting into a stone fireplace or wall by filling with cement. It also has holes into which wire or cord could be strung for hanging, if preferred. Other plaques with Patio Ware labels have a flat back with a large hole on the top horizontal edge for hanging on a wall hook and small holes on the vertical edges for hanging with wire.

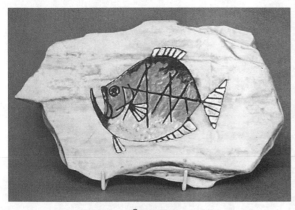

Snapper

Barracuda and Pompano fish

Stallion, running

Stallions, running side-by-side

Backstamp: **A.** Black ink stamp "Made in Ireland by Wade Co Armagh," hollowed back
B. Black ink stamp "Made in Ireland by Wade Co Armagh" and a gold foil label shaped like a sombrero with "Patio Ware Irish Procelain by Wade Co Armagh" flat back
C. Unmarked

Pearlstone Wall Plaques (cont.)

Stallions running, facing right

Stallions running, facing left

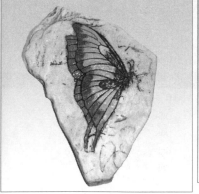

Butterfly, facing right

Butterfly, facing left

Siamese Cats

Name	Colourways	Size	U.S. $	Can. $	U.K. £
Bison	Stone; brown bison	185 x 300			
Bufferfly, facing right	Stone; orange; green; yellow; brown butterfly	210 x 340			
Butterfly, facing left	Stone; blues and yellow; brown butterfly	Unknown			
Barracuda	Creamy beige; turquoise fish	180 x 300			
Barracude	Dark grey; turquoise/white fish	180 x 300			
Pompano	Beige' white/orange/grey fish with red spots	185 x 300		All are	
Snapper	Beige; red/white/black fish	205 x 425		considered	
Snapper	Beige; pink/green/black/white fish	205 x 425		rare	
Siamese Cats	Stone; chocolate brown/cream cats; blue eyes	400 x 290			
Stallion, running facing right	Beige/cream; green stallion; yellow mane, tail	310 x 400			
Stallion, running facing right	Beige/cream; turquoise stallion; white mane, tail	310 x 400			
Stallions, running, facing left	Beige/cream; green stallions; white manes, tails	150 x 325			
Stallions, running, facing right	Beige/cream; green stallions; white manes, tails	150 x 325			
Stallions, running side-by-side	Beige/cream; green stallions; white manes, tails	195 x 290			

Pearlstone Plaque Derivatives

Ashtrays c.1962-1963

The wall plaques were adapted to form decorative table ashtrays by forming a recess in the plaque.

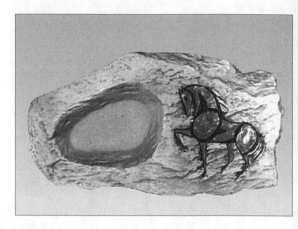

Name	Colourways	Size	U.S. $	Can. $	U.K. £
Pearlstone Ashtray, large	Beige stone plaque; pale blue stallion running	Unk.			
Pearlstone Ashtray, small	Beige stone plaque; green stallion front foot raised	Unk.		All are	
Pearlstone Ashtray, small	Beige stone plaque; pale blue stallion front foot raised	Unk.		considered	
Pearlstone Ashtray, small	Beige stone plaque; purple stallion front foot raised	Unk.		rare	
Pearlstone Ashtray, small	Beige stone plaque; yellow stallion front foot raised	Unk.			

WOOD DESIGN PLAQUES

These plaques which were made to appear like carved wood, were produced at the same time as the pearlstone plaques. They have a contemporary design of glass bottles and jars.

Backstamp: **A.** Black ink stamp "Made in Ireland by Wade Co Armagh"
B. Black ink stamp "Made in Ireland by Wade Co Armagh" and a gold foil label shaped like a sombrero with "Patio Ware Irish Porcelain by Wade Co Armagh"

Name	Colourways	Size	U.S. $	Can. $	U.K. £
Bottles and Jars	Brown; red, green, blue and orange jars	415 x 255	200.00	225.00	100.00

VICTORIAN LADIES CAMEO PORTRAIT PLAQUES

A number of oval Victorian ladies cameo portraits were produced by Wade Ireland, possibly at the same time as the Gray Fine Art plaques. The plaques can be found in two sizes, they can have a plain or plaited rim, have a pierced hole for hanging or, have a ring for hanging glued to the back, others have a slotted porcelain stand for the plaque to sit in.

Some plaques were used on the lids of trinket boxes and set into unglazed pottery frames. The boxes and frames were not produced by Wade.

Variations in design can be found as with the "Longhaired Lady" who has been found with and without a 'cross and chain necklace'. Most variations however are in colour and size.

Backstamp: Unmarked

Name	Colourways	Size	U.S. $	Can. $	U.K. £
Cowboy hat	Brown, hat; blue dress	65	30.00	35.00	15.00
Hair band	Green background, dress	65	30.00	35.00	15.00
Long Pearl necklace, shawl	Brown; blue-grey dress	65	30.00	35.00	15.00
Short Pearl necklace, folded hands	Green; grey dress	65	30.00	35.00	15.00
White Wig	Brownish green; white wig	65	30.00	35.00	15.00
Cowboy hat	Brown, hat; green dress	85	30.00	35.00	15.00
Cowboy hat	Grey; brown hat and dress	85	30.00	35.00	15.00
Hair band	Green background, dress	85	30.00	35.00	15.00
Hair in bun	Beige; green dress	85	30.00	35.00	15.00
Hair in bun	Green-brown; blue-grey dress	85	30.00	35.00	15.00
Hat white frill round face	Grey; grey hat; brown shawl	85	30.00	35.00	15.00
Hat with white band	Green; blue-grey coat dress	85	30.00	35.00	15.00
Holding flowers	Green; blue-grey dress; yellow flowers	85	30.00	35.00	15.00
Holding flowers	Blue-grey background, dress; yellow flowers	85	30.00	35.00	15.00
Holding flowers	Blue-grey; brown dress; yellow flowers	85	30.00	35.00	15.00
Knotted collar	Green; blue-grey dress	85	30.00	35.00	15.00
Pearl and cross necklace	Brown; dark grey-blue dress	85	30.00	35.00	15.00
Lace shawl on head	Grey; white head shawl	85	30.00	35.00	15.00
Long hair, cross and chain necklace	Grey-brown; blue-grey dress	85	30.00	35.00	15.00
Long hair, no cross and chain necklace	Blue-grey; blue-grey dress	85	30.00	35.00	15.00

VICTORIAN LADIES CAMEO PORTRAIT PLAQUES (cont.)

Name	Colourways	Size	U.S. $	Can. $	U.K. £
Long pearl necklace, frilled collar	Browny green; blue-grey dress	85	30.00	40.00	15.00
Long pearl necklace, no collar	Brown; blue-grey dress	85	30.00	40.00	15.00
Ostrich feathers, facing left	Green-brown; blue-grey dress	85	30.00	40.00	15.00
Shawl, buttoned blouse	Green; blue-grey shawl	85	30.00	40.00	15.00
Short pearl necklace, facing left	Grey; brown hair; flesh-coloured lady	85	30.00	40.00	15.00
Short pearl necklace, facing left	Brown; sepia lady	85	30.00	40.00	15.00

Cameo Frame

These plaques are set into an unglazed pottery or plaster frame which were not produced by Wade.

Backstamp: Unmarked

Name	Colourways	Size	U.S. $	Can. $	U.K. £
Hairband	Off white; gold, grey, brown and blue grey	125	20.00	25.00	10.00
Hairband and necklace	Grey, Cream and brown	65	20.00	25.00	10.00
Long pearl necklace	Olive green, white, dark grey, pearl and grey blue	100 x 80	20.00	25.00	10.00

Plaque Stand

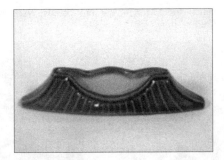

Backstamp: Unmarked

Name	Colourways	Size	U.S. $	Can. $	U.K. £
Plaque stand	Grey, blue and green	20 x 105	10.00	12.00	5.00

Portrait Brooch

Photograph not available
at press time

Backstamp: Unmarked

Name	Colourways	Size	U.S. $	Can. $	U.K. £
Cameo Brooch	Grey, green and white	70 x 50	20.00	25.00	10.00

Pottery / Plaster Frames

This ornate framed wall plaque has an olive green rim with a white border around the cameo portrait. There are two holes in the back of the plaque to hang onto nails.

Photograph not available
at press time

Backstamp: Unmarked

Name	Colourways	Size	U.S. $	Can. $	U.K. £
Wall plaque	Olive green rim; white border; dark grey background; long pearl necklace; grey blue dress	100 x 80	50.00	70.00	25.00

Trinket Boxes

These small trinket boxes have a cameo portrait plaque set into the lids. Wade Ireland produced the plaques but not the boxes, they were produced by a Staffordshire pottery.

Backstamp: **A.** Incised 'FM'

B. Incised script "English Porcelain FM"

Name	Colourways	Size	U.S. $	Can. $	U.K. £
Cross and Chain Necklace	Dark green; blue-grey lid	Oblong/35 x 80	70.00	80.00	35.00
Pearl Necklace	Light grey; blue-grey lid	Oblong/35 x 80	70.00	80.00	35.00
Holding Flowers	Light green; portrait lid	Oval/unknown	70.00	80.00	35.00
Holding Flowers	Mottled green/ brown; blue grey portrait	Rectangular/unknown	70.00	80.00	35.00
Cross and Chain	Dark green; blue-grey lid	Round/35 x 80	70.00	80.00	35.00
Holding Flowers	Light grey; off-white lid	Round/35 x 80	70.00	80.00	35.00

WALL DECORATIONS

The earliest plaques and wall decorations were made by Wade Heath in the 1930s, followed by Gothic Ware wall pockets and by wall masks. Beginning in the 1950s, transfer prints were commonly used to decorate plaques.

WALL MASKS

Face Masks c.1938-c.1948

These wall masks have been found in three glaze types — cellulose, matt and high gloss. The masks all have cellulose glazed backs, with a backstamp from the late 1930s. This suggests the cellulose glaze was used first, then the unsold masks were reglazed in a matt or high gloss glaze at a later date.

Dyllis   Frolic

Pan   Sonia

Backstamp: Black ink stamp "Wade Figures," a red leaping deer over "Made in England" and the model name hand-written in black

Name	Colourways	Size	U.S. $	Can. $	U.K. £
Dyllis	Black hair; cream face; pink flowers; cellulose glaze	180 x 95	275.00	300.00	140.00
Dyllis	Black hair; cream face; pink flowers; high gloss glaze	180 x 95	300.00	325.00	150.00
Frolic	Green; matt glaze	180 x 160	275.00	300.00	140.00
Frolic	Pale yellow; high gloss glaze	180 x 160	300.00	325.00	150.00
Pan	Cream; matt glaze	180 x 115	275.00	300.00	140.00
Pan	Green; matt glaze	180 x 115	300.00	325.00	150.00
Sonia	Black hair; flesh-coloured face; pink flowers; cellulose glaze	220 x 110	275.00	300.00	140.00
Sonia	Black hair; flesh-coloured face; pink flowers; high gloss glaze	220 x 110	300.00	325.00	150.00

WALL PLAQUES

Exotic Fish, 1958-1959

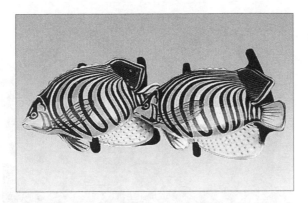

Backstamp: Embossed "Wade Porcelain Made in England"

Name	Colourways	Size	U.S. $	Can. $	U.K. £
Exotic Fish	Blue head; white and orange body; pink tail	65 x 95			
Exotic Fish	Green head; green and pink body; yellow tail	65 x 95			
Exotic Fish	Green head; white and pink body; yellow tail	65 x 95		All all	
Exotic Fish	Green head; white and maroon body; pink tail	65 x 95		considered	
Exotic Fish	Green head; white and maroon body; yellow tail	65 x 95		rare	
Exotic Fish	Grey head; white and pink body; green tail	65 x 95			
Exotic Fish	Pink head; white and yellow body; green tail	65 x 95			

Seagull, 1960

This model of a flying seagull was produced as a bathroom wall decoration.

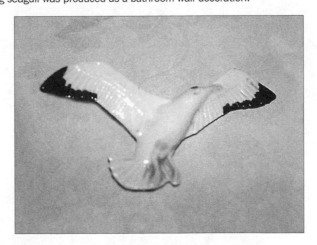

Backstamp: Unmarked

Name	Colourways	Size	U.S. $	Can. $	U.K. £
Seagull	White; black wing tips; yellow beak and feet	225 x 80	90.00	100.00	45.00

Teenage Pottery Cameo Plaques, 1960

First issued in 1960, the original price was 12/6d.

Backstamp: Embossed "Wade Porcelain Made in England"

Name	Colourways	Size	U.S. $	Can. $	U.K. £
Cliff Richard	Marron; gold edge, multicoloured print	95 x 70	150.00	175.00	80.00
Marty Wilde	Maroon; gold edge, multicoloured print	95 x 70	150.00	175.00	80.00

Wee Willie Winkie, 1959-1960

These four nursery wall plaques were only produced for a short time. They depict scenes from the children's nursery rhyme, "Wee Willie Winkie," on the recessed face. Each plaque has a different illustration and two lines from the rhyme. There is a recessed hole in the back for hanging on a wall. They were originally sold with black and gold "Genuine Wade Porcelain" labels on the backs. These plaques are extremely hard to find.

Backstamp: Black transfer print "Wade England"

Name	Colourways	Size	U.S. $	Can. $	U.K. £
Wee Willie Winkie runs through the town	White; multicoloured print	133	200.00	225.00	100.00
Upstairs and downstairs in his nightgown	White; multicoloured print	133	200.00	225.00	100.00
Tapping at the window, peeping through the lock	White; multicoloured print	133	200.00	225.00	100.00
Are the children in their beds, its past 8 o'clock	White; multicoloured print	133	200.00	225.00	100.00

Wild Fowl, 1960

This set includes four duck wall plaques in natural colours. A loop is provided for hanging.

Mallard drake

Shoveller drake

Pintail

Shoveller, female

Backstamp: **A.** Black transfer print "Wildfowl by Wade of England" and model name
 B. Black transfer print "Wildfowl by Wade of England" model name and signature of Peter Scott
 C. Unmarked

Name	Colourways	Size	U.S. $	Can. $	U.K. £
Mallard drake	Grey; green head; brown neck; white/beige wings; orange feet	230 x 245	250.00	275.00	120.00
Pintail	Green and black head; beige, grey and white wings; grey feet	240 x 205	250.00	275.00	120.00
Shoveller drake	White/black body; black/green head; beige/white wings	190 x 220	250.00	275.00	120.00
Shoveller female	Grey and brown body; green head	175 x 200	250.00	275.00	120.00

Yachts, 1960

These brightly coloured yachts, designed for decoration in a bathroom, have a number on their sails. A set has been seen which has a print of a sailor on the sail but have no backstamp; it is believed these may have been a prototype design. At some time in late 1960, the production of these plaques was moved to Wade Ireland. The original price was 9/11d.

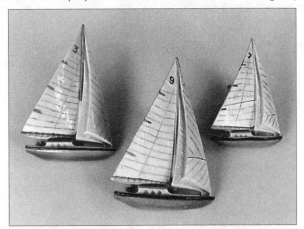

Backstamp: **A.** Embossed "Wade England" in recess
B. Embossed "Wade Ireland" in recess

Name	Colourways	Size	U.S. $	Can. $	U.K. £
Yacht, no. 7	Blue hull; brown roof; white/grey striped sails	Small/85 x 20	70.00	80.00	35.00
Yacht, no. 7	Dark green hull; dark blue roof; pink sails	Small/85 x 20	70.00	80.00	35.00
Yacht, no. 7	Green hull; blue roof; beige/mauve sails	Small/85 x 20	70.00	80.00	35.00
Yacht, no. 3	Blue hull; brown roof; white/grey striped sails	Medium/110 x 26	70.00	80.00	35.00
Yacht, no. 3	Blue hull; dark green roof; pale green sails	Medium/110 x 26	70.00	80.00	35.00
Yacht, no. 3	Dark blue hull; dark green roof; pale green sails	Medium/110 x 26	70.00	80.00	35.00
Yacht, no. 9	Blue hull; brown roof; white/grey striped sails	Large/115 x 30	70.00	80.00	35.00
Yacht, no. 9	Red hull; yellow roof; blue sails	Large/115 x 30	70.00	80.00	35.00
Yacht, no. 9	Red hull; brown roof; dark blue saile	Large/115 x 30	70.00	80.00	35.00
Set of three	(small, medium and large)		150.00	175.00	75.00

WALL POCKETS

KNOWN SHAPE NUMBERS

Wall pockets are flat-backed vases that have a hole in the back top edge so they can be hung on a wall. They are glazed inside to hold water.

Shape 159, Gothic Ware, 1940, 1946-1953

These triangular-shaped wall pockets are decorated with an embossed design of swirling leaves and tulips characteristic of Gothic Ware.

Backstamp: **A.** Black ink stamp "Gothic Wade Heath England" and impressed "159"

            B. Gold transfer print "Wade made in England - hand painted - Gothic" and impressed "159"

Colourways	Colourways	Size	U.S. $	Can. $	U.K. £
Gothic	Cream; lilac and pink flowers; green and gold leaves	165 x 165	80.00	90.00	40.00
Gothic	Creamy orange; pale pink flower; pale green leaves	165 x 165	80.00	90.00	40.00
Gothic	Pale yellow	165 x 165	80.00	90.00	40.00

Shape 223, Leaves and FLowers, 1935-c.1940

These wall pockets have a panelled front with an embossed design of flowers and leaves.

Backstamp: **A.** Black ink stamp "Flaxman Wade Heath England made in England"
            B. Black ink stamp "Flaxman Hand Made Pottery by Wade Heath England"

Colourways	Colourways	Size	U.S. $	Can. $	U.K. £
Flowers and leaves	Mottled green	175	60.00	70.00	30.00
Flowers and leaves	Mottled yellow	175	60.00	70.00	30.00

Shape 224, Round Top, 1935-c.1940

These wall pockets have an embossed design of flowers around the top.

Backstamp: Black ink stamp "Wadeheath Ware England"

Colourways	Colourways	Size	U.S. $	Can. $	U.K. £
Round top	Mottled blue and orange	180 x 153	60.00	70.00	30.00
Round top	Mottled orange, yellow and brown; blue, orange and pink flowers	180 x 153	60.00	70.00	30.00
Round top	Mottled white, blue and yellow	180 x 153	60.00	70.00	30.00

Shape 225, Fleur-De-Lis, 1935-c.1940

Backstamp: Black ink stamp "Flaxman Wade Heath England," with impressed "225"

Name	Colourways	Size	U.S. $	Can. $	U.K. £
Fleur-de-lis	Pale yellow	220 x 118	60.00	70.00	30.00

Shape 226, Fan, 1935-c.1940

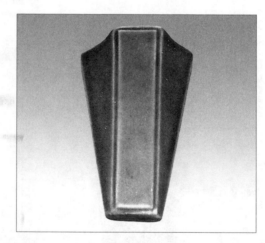

Backstamp: Black ink stamp "Wadeheath Ware England," with impressed "225"

Name	Colourways	Size	U.S. $	Can. $	U.K. £
Fan	Cream; violet and blue flowers; green leaves	Medium/145 x 90	40.00	45.00	20.00
Fan	Mottled blue and orange	Medium/145 x 90	40.00	45.00	20.00
Fan	Mottled orange and grey	Medium/145 x 90	40.00	45.00	20.00
Fan	Mottled green and orange	Medium/145 x 90	40.00	45.00	20.00
Fan	White; turquoise criss-cross stripes	Large/150 x 150	40.00	45.00	20.00

Shape 228, Blocks, 1935-c.1940

These wall pockets resemble a tower of building blocks when viewed upside down.

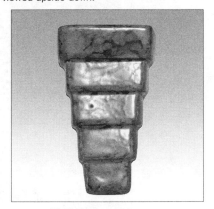

Flowers

Mottled brown and orange

Backstamp: Black ink stamp "Flaxman Wade Heath England," with impressed "228"

Colourways	Colourways	Size	U.S. $	Can. $	U.K. £
Flowers	Cream, yellow, blue, pink and green	138	75.00	85.00	40.00
Mottled	Mottled brown and orange	138	50.00	60.00	25.00
Mottled	Mottled turquoise and brown	138	50.00	60.00	25.00

Shape 229, Tulip, 1935-c.1940

Red and yellow tulip with green leaves

Yellow tulip with green leaves

Backstamp: Black ink stamp "Wadeheath Ware England" with impressed number "229"

Colourways	Colourways	Size	U.S. $	Can. $	U.K. £
Tulip	Red and yellow tulip; green leaves	155 x 95	125.00	150.00	65.00
Tulip	Yellow tulip; green leaves	165 x 95	125.00	150.00	65.00

Shape 249, Basket Ware, 1935-c.1940

Backstamp: Black ink stamp "Wade Heath England," with impressed shape number "249"

Colourways	Colourways	Size	U.S. $	Can. $	U.K. £
Basket ware	Cream; grey, pink and yellow flowers; green leaves	145 x 185	70.00	80.00	35.00

Shape 281, Rose, 1935-c.1940

*Photograph not available
at press time*

Backstamp: Black ink stamp "Wade Heath England," with impressed shape number "281"

Colourways	Colourways	Size	U.S. $	Can. $	U.K. £
Rose	Yellow; pink roses; green leaves	205 x 100	125.00	150.00	65.00

UNKNOWN SHAPE NUMBERS

Japanese Garden, 1998-2000

Backstamp: Printed "The Gallery Collection Japanese Garden inspired by original 1930's Wade Heath Designs Wade Made in England 31"

Colourways	Colourways	Size	U.S. $	Can. $	U.K. £
Japanese Garden	Mottled yellow, green and lilac	205	20.00	25.00	10.00

Round Top, 1935-c.1940

Backstamp: Black ink stamp "Flaxman Ware hand made Pottery by Wade Heath England"

Colourways	Colourways	Size	U.S. $	Can. $	U.K. £
Round top	Mottled yellow, green and lilac	140 x 88	40.00	45.00	20.00

Scrolls, 1935-c.1940

Backstamp: Black ink stamp "Wade Heath England"

Colourways	Colourways	Size	U.S. $	Can. $	U.K. £
Scrolls	Mottled green and grey	180 x 153	60.00	70.00	30.00

Sombrero, 1935-c.1940

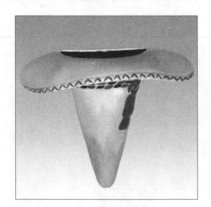

Backstamp: Black ink stamp "Wade Heath England"

Colourways	Colourways	Size	U.S. $	Can. $	U.K. £
Sombrero	Yellow; orange and black stitching, tassel	165	90.00	100.00	45.00

INDEX

A

B

M

If you want to know what is going on in the world of Wade then you must join the

Official International
Wade Collectors Club

The Official International WADE Collectors Club

Felix THE CAT

Membership offers, besides the pleasure of sharing the hobby, such intangibles as greater appreciation of Wade collectables through initiation into techniques of designing, modelling and production. You can find out about new products - designed to charm and capture the heart. The 2007 membership picece is Felix the Cat.

ANNUAL MEMBERSHIP BENIFITS

Membership figurine:	exclusive to club members only.
Membership Pin:	designed to compliment the membership figurine
Membership Certificate:	personalised, complete with date of membership
Membership Card:	entitles you to 10% discount at fairs and at the Wade shop on selected items.
Quarterly Magazine:	full of news on limited editions, club news, fairs and events, articles on old Wade, and sales and wants. PLUS the opportunity to purchase member only limited editions.
Members only offer:	exclusive to club members for 2007 a limited edition set of whimsies

MEMBERSHIP APPLICATION FORM

Simply photocopy this form and send it to: The Offical International Wade Collectors Club, Westport Road, Burslem, Stoke-on-Trent, ST6 4AG, England
Tel: +44 (0)1782 255255; E-mail: club@wadecollectorsclub.co.uk; www.wadecollectorsclub.co.uk

Please enrol me as new a member

❑ Annual Membership (12 mos. from receipt) £ 30.00 ; US$ 52.00
❑ Two Year Membership (24mos. from receipt) £ 54.00 ; US$ 98.00
❑ Family Membership (12 mos. from receipt - 4 family members) £ 100.00 ; US$ 185.00

❑ My cheque for............£ payable to Wade Collectors Club is enclosed or debit my credit/charge card

Title.............First Name.......................................
Last Name...
Address...
....
....
Post/Zip Code...
Tel. No...

❑ Visa   ❑ Mastercard   ❑ Switch

card no [ ][ ][ ][ ][ ][ ][ ][ ][ ][ ][ ][ ][ ][ ][ ][ ][ ][ ]

The sum of...
Card expires on month [ ][ ] year [ ][ ] security no [ ][ ]
Issue number (switch only)................................
Signature...

❑ Please tick the box if you would like us to automatically renew your membership using your nominated card.
Please allow 28 days for processing your membership.   Membership prices are correct at time of printing, Jan 2007.